WEB SEARCH
STRATEGIES

BRYAN PFAFFENBERGER

MIS:
PRESS

A Subsidiary of
Henry Holt and Co., Inc.

Trademarks

Throughout this book, trademarked names are used. Rather than put a trademark symbol after every occurrence of a trademarked name, we used the names in an editorial fashion only, and to the benefit of the trademark owner, with no intention of infringement of the trademark. Where such designations appear in this book, they have been printed with initial caps.

ASSOCIATE PUBLISHER: Paul Farrell
MANAGING EDITOR: Cary Sullivan
EDITOR: Debra Williams Cauley
COPY EDIT MANAGER: Shari Chappell
PRODUCTION EDITOR: Joe McPartland
TECHNICAL EDITOR: Carole Leita
COPY EDITOR: Annette Devlin

For Suzanne, always

ACKNOWLEDGMENTS

Creating a book like this one isn't a solitary job, and I'd like to convey my thanks to all the people who helped me in so many ways.

Since I'm not a librarian, I knew I'd need expert guidance, and I found it in Carole Leita (http://www.ci.berkeley.ca.us/bpl/leita/), reference librarian (and, more recently, Internet Librarian) at the Berkeley Public Library in Berkeley, California. Carole provided an expert technical edit of this entire book, and did far more than find the usual technical gaffes: She contributed an expert librarian's perspective to this book's philosophy of Web searching, and I'm very much in her debt. Incidentally, if you're wondering how I found Carole, the answer's within these pages—through a search of the Web! I searched for librarians who were taking the lead in mapping the Web for their patrons, and was really impressed with Carole's Internet trailblazer page (http://www.ci.berkeley.ca.us/bpl/bkmk/). After a flurry of email exchanges, Carole was on board, and this book is much the better for it.

Sally Elliot, of the Internet Business Connection, graciously permitted us to include a copy of The Internet Sleuth on the disk packaged with this book. The Sleuth is a top-notch Web site, accessible by means of your browser's File Open command, that contains links and search text boxes for more than 750 of the Web's top search sites. It's an incredible resource, as you'll surely agree after giving it a try. Thanks, too, to SeaChange Corporation, which permitted us to include an evaluation copy of BookWhere, a Z39.50 browser that enables you to access library databases containing citations to millions of books. David Wall, a freelance writer based in Charlottesville, Virginia, helped me make this book's arduous schedule by drafting several of the chapters that follow—thanks, Dave. When the manuscript reached New York, MIS's seasoned publishing professionals went to work. Special thanks go to this book's production editor Joe McPartland, who shepherded the manuscript through its various hurdles and is responsible for this book's readable, open design. Editorial details were tackled by Annette Sroka Devlin.

Most of all, I'd like to thank Debra Williams Cauley, acquisitions editor, whose unflagging enthusiasm, hard work, and good cheer proved indispensable in getting this book through a tight production schedule. Authors are sensitive creatures, and it helps enormously to work with somebody who really believes in a project, as Debra believed in this one.

Contacting the Author

I'd love to hear from you regarding your suggestions for the next edition of Web Search Strategies. Have you found some fantastic search services and sites that aren't discussed in this book? An indispensable trailblazer page? Let me know (bp@virginia.edu), and I'll add a link, review, and credit to Search ME!, this book's Web site (http://watt.seas.virginia.edu/~bp/searchme/welcome.html). If you'd like to know more about me, check out my home page at http://bpmac.seas.virginia.edu/default.html).

CONTENTS

STEP TWO: FINDING SOMETHING THAT'S RELEVANT

CHAPTER 4: LOCATING INFORMATION:
THE QUICK, PINPOINTED SEARCH 81

CHAPTER 5: BROWSING FOR INFORMATION:
SUBJECT TREES 93

CHAPTER 6: BROWSING FOR INFORMATION: TRAILBLAZER PAGES 113

STEP THREE: LEARN THE TECHNIQUES OF DEEP SEARCHING

STEP FOUR: PERFORM A DEEP SEARCH

CHAPTER 10: SEARCHING LYCOS 165

CHAPTER 14: SEARCHING WEBCRAWLER 203

STEP FIVE: EXPLORE SPECIALIZED SEARCH RESOURCES

CHAPTER 15: FINDING GENERAL-INTEREST
REFERENCE INFORMATION 207

CHAPTER 16: FINDING SPECIAL-INTEREST REFERENCE INFORMATION 233

CHAPTER 17: FINDING CURRENT NEWS AND WEATHER 257

CHAPTER 18: FINDING GOVERNMENT INFORMATION 275

CHAPTER 19: FINDING STOCK MARKET
AND INVESTMENT INFORMATION 291

CHAPTER 25: SEARCHING USENET, GOPHER, TELNET, AND WAIS... 383

STEP SIX: KEEP UP WITH WHAT'S NEW

CHAPTER 26: WHAT'S NEW RESOURCES........................... 393

CHAPTER 27: SEARCHING FOR WHAT'S NEW.................... 403

STEP SEVEN: GIVE SOMETHING BACK

INTRODUCTION

By now, millions of people have surfed the World Wide Web—and they're starting to realize something. While the Web's entertaining and packed with useful information, it's *very* difficult to find what you're looking for.

Too many people try a little Web surfing but then give up on the Web as a serious information resource because it's too hard to find the information they want. But they're making a serious mistake. It *is* possible to find information on the Web—you just need to know what you're doing.

My most recent reminder: Yesterday, I ducked into a colleague's office, where he sat at the keyboard, fuming, "I found this UNBELIEV-ABLY USEFUL Web site two weeks ago, and I forgot to save it as a bookmark." (In Netscape, his favorite Web browser, you can save the location of favorite Web sites as a *bookmark* so that they're easy to visit again.)

"I've been searching for two hours now," he said. "It's gone." He looked as though he was about ready to put his fist through the monitor.

"No it isn't," I said. "You just don't know how to find it." I sat down at his PC and performed a quick search, using a couple of the tricks I've learned. A couple minutes later, there it was, on-screen. "How did you do that?" he demanded.

This book is the answer. It presents a sure-fire, seven-step strategy for finding information on the World Wide Web (and through the Web, the wider Internet). I can guarantee you this: If it's out there, you'll be able to find it after reading this book.

No matter what profession or career you're pursuing, the skills this book teaches are worth knowing. Why? It's a done deal: The Web is emerging as the *de facto* computer information system for the 21st century. It is already in daily use by millions of people, and the number of *Web sites*—computers running Web *server* software—is doubling every 53 days, according to one recent estimate. It won't be long before mastery of the Web will be *de rigueur* for professionals in just about any line of work, not to mention consumers.

Knowing how to use the Web intelligently means knowing how to locate useful information on the Web, and this book shows you how.

C'MON. THERE REALLY ISN'T ANY *Useful* INFORMATION ON THE WEB—IS THERE?

You've probably heard that the World Wide Web has no established on-line payment mechanism (though it's coming). For this reason, people who publish information on the Web don't receive any quick cash for their efforts. And too many people conclude, "If it's free, it must be worth the price."

That's dead wrong. To be sure, there's a lot of junk on the Web, most of it produced by college students with too much time on their hands. (An example: A student's list of all the T-shirts in his drawers and closet.) But many people and organizations are making valuable information available for a variety of reasons. Some are doing it as a public service. Others are selling advertising space on their sites. And still others make rich information resources available in the hope that they can sell you additional information or services, for a fee.

SEARCH TIP

Is it junk or a jewel? Here's how to find out: In just about every large corporation, you'll find information specialists. Their job? To seek out new, on-line sources of information and figure out whether they're worth the pixels they're printed on. They're highly trained, and they can do this at a snap ("That one? It's junk!"). Want to know how they do it? Take a look at the following Web document: "How to Critically Analyze Information Sources" (http://urislib.library.cornell.edu/skill26.htm), written by an expert team of Cornell University reference librarians.

Make no mistake about it. The Web is already the richest computer-accessible information storehouse, by a wide margin. In the years to come, it will become indispensable for just about everyone—professionals, students, consumers, businesspeople, librarians, you name it.

This Web site says the U.S. captured an alien spacecraft in 1947! Wow!

A word of advice: Don't believe everything you read on the Web. In academic circles, information doesn't get published unless researchers in the area judge the document to be worthwhile (this is called peer review). But there's no review of any kind, peer or otherwise, for most Web documents. For this reason, *caveat emptor*—let the buyer beware (I mean, let the browser beware)—is the watchword of the day when you're searching the Web.

Still, this fact alone doesn't mean that the information on the Web is worthless, only that you've got to be on your guard. John F. Kennedy once said that the most fundamental belief underlying democracy was that ordinary people possess common sense and good will—and for the most part, that's true, at least judging from the better efforts of people publishing on the Web. Sure, some of the information you'll find has been gathered and collated by amateurs, but this fact alone doesn't mean that it's unreliable.

Just remember that you're on your own. When you access a Web document, try to determine who wrote it, and where it's coming from. Does the author have any credentials in the area?

continued...

continued...

Often, people include links to their home pages, and home pages often contain links to resumes. You may find out that the page was created by a 19-year-old college student with too much free time—or by one of the leading experts in this field of knowledge. In addition, check out the trailblazer pages created by experts in an area (see Chapter 6). A trailblazer page is a page containing one person's collection of high-quality links in a specific field of knowledge. The fact that they've recommended a site amounts to a form of peer review, unless there's a specific disclaimer that the sites mentioned haven't really been scrutinized for quality.

A final point: Don't make crucial decisions based on a Web document—such as whether to invest in a certain stock, to sell your house for a certain price, or to seek one kind of medical treatment over another—without getting a second opinion from somebody who knows what they're talking about.

An Example: Just How Safe Is This Car?

I wouldn't consider doing anything of importance, whether in my personal or professional life, without turning to the Web for information and guidance. Here's a story that tells why.

My wife recently returned from a car-hunting expedition with glossy brochures describing an expensive European automobile. "I'm really sold on this car," she said. "It's the safest car on the road." As I listened, I remembered a newspaper article that I saw somewhere, concerning safety crash statistics for a variety of new cars, and it seemed to me that the dealer's claim might have been a little, well, exaggerated.

In the past, digging up this newspaper article would have meant a trip to the library. Instead, I fired up Netscape, and within a couple of minutes I handed her a printout listing the latest crash test statistics.

And what did we find? The car she was looking at was certainly one of the safer cars on the road—but it was not the safest, according to these statistics. The list showed that there were several other vehicles, some significantly less expensive, that she should consider if safety and price are her top criteria. (The funniest thing was that my much-loved but seemingly-not-so-safe Ford Probe GT, a sports coupe, turned out to offer just as much head-on crash protection as the pricey European sedan.)

Digging Deeper

Of course, there's more to judging a car's safety than head-on crash results, so we went back to the Web—and after another half hour, we knew which cars currently meet the 1997 mandates for side door reinforcement, which cars performed best on the new oblique collision tests, and much more.

The best thing we found was a truly frightening exposé of dealer showroom tactics. We were shocked to learn how automobile dealers prey on your gullibility, guilt feelings, and desire to please others. We learned how to defend ourselves against these disgusting tactics—and what's more, we learned of a service that, for $20, can assure you a quote ranging from 2% to 6% over the dealer invoice. You can buy the car directly from this service, or you can take the quote to your local dealer and use it as the baseline for negotiation.

Who makes all this information available? Much of it is from Edmund Publications Corporation, publishers of the respected *Edmund Automobile Buyer's Decision Guides*, which I'm sure you've seen at local bookstores and supermarkets. At its Gopher site, there's a wealth of valuable information about new and used car prices, safety statistics, tips on handling dealers, and much more.

What's in it for Edmund Publications? They want you to know about some of the cool, new, Net-savvy marketing they're doing, including a great service that enables its readers to contribute to a dealer database. The top marks go to dealers willing to negotiate *up* from the dealer invoice rather than *down* from the list price.

But Edmund Publications' site is just the tip of the iceberg. Take a look at the sidebar, "Web Resources for New Car Shoppers." You'll see what came out of a *deep search*—a search conducted according to this book's principles. There are a host of individuals and organizations making information available on the Web.

WEB RESOURCES FOR NEW CAR SHOPPERS

Car Smart. Part of *Popular Mechanics* magazine's excellent Web site, this page—updated weekly—lists the incentive programs currently offered by the major car manufacturers, such as rebates and discounted financing.

Credit Check. Find out what the three major credit service bureaus are saying about you for less than $50 (http://www.deal-ernet.com/cgi-bin/texdnv?file=/reynolds/credit/ccredit.htm).

Insurance Institute for Highway Safety 1995 Crash Test Reports. The surprising results from an attempt to replicate "real-world" crash conditions—running a car at 40 mph at an angle into a deformable barrier. The biggest surprise? Chevrolet's Lumina and Ford's Taurus are just as safe as the expensive Volvo 850.

Insurance Theft Reports. Did you know that a Mitsubishi Montero sport utility vehicle is 18 times more likely to be stolen than the average car or that a Saturn is 10 times less likely to be stolen? All the data's here, thanks to the Insurance News Network (http://www.insure.com/auto/thefts/index.html).

***Popular Mechanics*' Owners Reports.** Thousands of *Popular Mechanics* readers sound off about specific makes and models.

State Farm Insurance Ratings for New Cars. Here's the data your insurance agent will use to determine how much to charge you for insuring a given car. The data is based on how often the cars are in accidents, the severity of the accidents, the costs of repairs, and how often the cars are stolen (http://www.insure.com/auto/models/index.html).

Technical Service Bulletins and Recall Data. What's gone wrong with the car you're thinking about buying? Find out here: http://www.alldata.tsb.com/. For another list of current recalls, see http://www.cyberauto.com/catalogs/auto_info/repairs/recalls.html.

continued...

continued...

Top-Scoring Vehicles. Robert Bowden's The Car Place has lots of useful information, including reviews and a summary of J.D. Power and other evaluations of today's top automobiles: http://www.cftnet.com/members/rcbowden/lists.htm.

Web Sites Dedicated to Specific Makes/Models. Get more information about the car you're thinking about buying. Many of these sites are maintained by owner/enthusiasts, rather than automobile manufacturers, so expect to find very interesting information that includes criticism (http://www.w3.org/hypertext/DataSources/bySubject/Automotive/automakers.html).

But Couldn't You do This with a Simple Search?

You've probably heard about *search engines* such as InfoSeek and Lycos, which maintain searchable databases of Web documents. By now, you've probably tried an InfoSeek search from a Web browser, and you may have gotten some interesting results. Using what you already know, you can locate a few interesting documents. You can perform a rough 'n ready superficial search. Perhaps that's enough, if you're the Web equivalent of a Sunday driver.

But I don't think that's enough for you. I'm assuming that readers of this book have more serious goals: They're determined to make the Web an indispensable component of their information-seeking strategy.

That's why this book teaches a comprehensive approach to Web information retrieval. You'll learn how to use all of the Web's information-locating tools, and what's more, you'll learn how to use them in the correct order. After reading this book, you'll be able to locate virtually *every* document on the Web that contains information on topics of interest to you—and what's more, you'll know how to locate important new documents that appear after your first deep search is completed.

SEARCH TIP

There's still a role for the good ol' library: The Web's an indispensable component for anyone's information strategy. But that doesn't mean that libraries should be boarded up—far from it. Although the Web's loaded with information, there's a lot of proprietary, fork-over-your-money information that's never going to appear on the Web. A case in point for our automobile example: *Consumer Reports'* frequency-of-repair averages. Librarians are also getting into the Web, and they are doing some impressive things; in the future, you'll be able to get help searching the Web by stopping by your local library's reference desk. And while you're there, you can get expert help in finding information from non-Net sources.

OK, I'M SOLD. WHAT ARE THE SEVEN STEPS?

Here's a quick overview:

Step One: Know What You're Up Against. The Web was never intended to serve as a mass information-retrieval system, and it has serious deficiencies in this respect. If you want to retrieve information efficiently and accurately from the Web, you need to understand the Web's limitations, understand the range of search tools that are available, and learn how to prepare your browser for a thorough Web search. From Step One, you'll know why you must master the techniques of *free-text searching*—with one or more key words—if you want to harvest the Web's information resources.

Step Two: Find Something that's Relevant. With your list of key words, you'll next perform a quick initial search using InfoSeek, my favorite of the Web's many search services. You'll learn how to use InfoSeek search tools that are ignored by 99.8% of the people who use the service—and once you do, you'll never search without them again. From Step Two, you'll find out whether there's a document somewhere on the Web that's dead-center on your search topic.

Step Three: Learn the techniques of deep searching. You can use the Web's search tools without knowing much about search techniques, such as the use of *Boolean operators* and *truncation*. From long experience, search engine designers know that most people just don't take the time to learn about such mysterious things. Without this knowledge, though, they won't be able to perform a *deep search* of theWeb—a search that turns up all or most of the relevant information that's out there.

If you really want to get the maximum from the Web, though, you'll want to learn deep searchning techniques. It's not hard, and Web Search Strategies makes the learning easy by providing simple, clear explanations. From Step Three, you'll possess the knowledge you need to perform a deep search of the Web.

Step Four: Perform a Deep Search. Here's where you pull out the stops and ransack the Web, performing deep searches on all of the Web's search engines. A *deep search* involves far more than typing one or two key words and clicking the **Submit** button. You'll learn how to use poorly document and undocumented search tools that can greatly enhance the accuracy of your search. You'll also learn the differences among the various search engines, which have their own strengths and weaknesses. From Step Four, you'll have a list of just about everything on the Web that's relevant to your search topic.

Step Five: Explore Specialized Search Resources. There's more to the Internet than the World Wide Web. Here, you learn how to use special search tools for locating Gopher documents, Telnet-based resources, WAIS databases, Usenet postings, and software located in FTP archives. You'll also learn how to locate people and jobs and how to use an on-line version of the library's reference desk. From Step Five, you'll have many additions to your growing list of useful Internet resources.

Step Six: Keep Up with What's New. Every day, thousands of new documents appear on the Web—and one or more of them might be dead-center on your interests. Here, you'll learn how to scan the new documents quickly so that your list is kept up-to-date. From Step Six, you'll develop an update strategy that you can use periodically—say, once a week or month—to make sure you're tracking the newest documents on your subject.

Step Seven: Give Something Back. The Web isn't optimized for information retrieval—but it has lots of helpful people, who willingly share their hotlists and trailblazer pages. That's the Internet spirit, and it's helping to overcome the Web's information-retrieval deficiencies. In this spirit, Step Seven invites you to contribute *your* Web discoveries by publishing your hotlist. If you don't have access to a Web server, you can send it to me by following the instructions you'll find inChapter 28. From Step Seven, you'll learn how to share your discoveries with others—and make yourself thes center of an information-gathering community.

WHAT DO I NEED?

To search the Web, you need just the basic Web-browsing equipment:

- A personal computer (a Macintosh or Windows system)
- A Web connection
- A browser (I recommend Netscape Navigator, but you can use this book with any graphical browser)

I'm assuming that you're already connected to the Web and that you've learned how to use your browser program. If not, may I suggest you take a look at this book's companion volume, *World Wide Web Bible*.

ABOUT THE DISK PACKAGED WITH THIS BOOK

Designed for Windows systems, the disk includes the following search tools:

- Search ME! Keyed to this book's discussion of Web search tools, these Web pages provide links to all the search services discussed in *Web Search Strategies*. To access Search ME!, use your browser's File Open command to open the file named **welcome.htm** (it's located in the SEARCHME folder). You don't need to be online to open this file, but you'll need an Internet connection to access the Web hyperlinks contained in Search ME! (If you're using a Mac that's equipped to access Windows disks, you can read these files.)

- Internet Sleuth. Here's a very useful compendium of more than 750 searchable databases that can be accessed via the Web—and what's more, the Sleuth pages include text boxes so that you can initiate the search right from your computer. To access the Sleuth, use your browser's File Open command to open the file named **index.htm** (it's located in the Sleuth folder). If you find this resource as valuable as I do, you will want to go directly to the Internet Sleuth site online to take advantage of the latest updates. (Note: These files are also accessible to users of suitably equipped Macs.)

- BookWhere! This Windows-compatible program enables you to search for books and other resources in huge library databases, including the biggest of them all: The Library of Congress's computerized catalog. This program requires Microsoft Windows 3.1 or Microsoft Windows 95.

Also included on the disk are links to the home page of Webodex, a hotlist organizer that's highly recommended for organizing all the useful sites you're about to discover.

A WORD FROM THE AUTHOR

You're about to begin a journey of personal enrichment! I know that you wouldn't have purchased this book if you didn't have serious information acquisition goals. Perhaps you want to find out which classroom activities work best with gifted children, how to take a vacation that will teach you compelling lessons about the natural environment, or where—and when—to invest wisely in real estate. If it's on the Web, you'll find it, with this book's help.

I'd like to hear from you, too, concerning your suggestions for improving this book for the next edition. My email address is bp@virginia.edu. I'd especially like to hear about hotlists or trailblazer pages that this book's readers have developed, since I'd love to feature a list of them in the next edition.

FROM HERE

To get started with this book's seven-step strategy, flip to Chapter 1. You'll learn why a smart, tactical search strategy is needed to make sure you access all the information you need!

CHAPTER 1

WHY IT'S SO HARD TO FIND INFORMATION ON THE WEB

Let's start with the basic point: The Web was never designed to serve as a global information system. Fortunately or unfortunately, that's what it's become. Anyone hoping to utilize the Web's amazing information resources needs a strategy to overcome its many information-retrieval deficiencies.

This chapter surveys these deficiencies, and explains the basic challenge of Web information retrieval. After you've read it, you'll know the truth about why the Web comes up short as an information retrieval system—and you'll also have a significant advantage when it comes to planning an intelligent Web information retrieval strategy.

HYPERTEXT: COOL AND CONFUSING

The World Wide Web is based on the principles of *hypertext*, a nonsequential method of viewing textual information. The nonsequential part refers to the fact that readers can pick their own way through the material by clicking *hyperlinks* (underlined or distinctively colored words or phrases). Usually there are two or more hyperlinks on a given page, so you can choose your own way through the material. When you click a hyper-link, you see the document that's connected to that link.

This section introduces hypertext, and it's worth reading even if you already know what hypertext is. You'll learn what study after study has concluded: Hypertext systems may be easy to use, but they make it very difficult to find the information you're looking for.

KEY TERM

hypertext

A nonlinear method of viewing textual information. In a hypertext document, readers choose their own paths through the material by clicking hyperlinks.

KEY TERM

hyperlink

In a hypertext document, an underlined or distinctively colored word or phrase that, when clicked with the mouse, displays another document (or a different portion of the same document) on-screen.

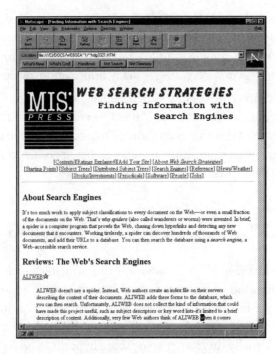

Figure 1.1 Web document with hyperlinks.

Understanding Hypertext

It's hard to convey the hypertext concept in a book, but here's an attempt. Suppose you're reading a hypertext document on your computer screen:

> North Carolina's Outer Banks, one of the state's premier tourist destinations, are **barrier islands.** Measuring only 7 to 12 feet above sea level, the islands are sometimes overwashed during violent storms, such as the **Halloween Storm** of 1991. In calmer weather, visitors flock to the Outer Banks to take advantage of its many **recreational opportunities.**

If you click **barrier islands,** here's what you see:

> A **barrier island** is a land form made up entirely of sand, without any underlying anchor of rock. Lacking such an anchor, barrier islands are subject to change by the forces of wind and sea. North America's most striking barrier islands are found in North Carolina's **Outer Banks.**

Clicking **Outer Banks** returns you to the original document. If you then click **recreational opportunities,** you see the following:

> Vacationers love the Outer Banks for its fine **beaches,** excellent seafood **dining,** rich **history,** abundant **wildlife,** and quaint little **towns** with great **shopping.**

If you wished to continue exploring, you could click **Halloween Storm** to learn more about this destructive 1991 storm and its effect on the Outer Banks—or you could click any of the other links to find out about all the fun things you can do there!

See what they mean by nonsequential? You can pick your own way through the material. That's what's so cool about hypertext, and that's what distinguishes hypertext from other forms of writing, as the following section explains.

Multiple Pathways

In comparison to traditional media, the key point about hypertext is that it provides multiple pathways through the material, as shown in Figure 1.2.

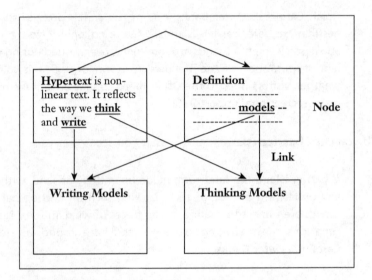

Figure 1.2 Nodes and links in a web (from V. Balasubramaniam, "State of the Art Review on Hypermedia Issues and Applications," http://www.isg.sfu.ca/~duchier/misc/hypertext_review/index.html).

If you click **Hypertext** in Figure 1.2, you see the Definitions page. On that page, you can choose **writing models** or **thinking models**—but you can also get to these pages by clicking **think** or **write** on the first page.

A well-designed hypertext breaks information down into page-sized chunks, as the following section explains, and enables you to navigate through the chunks any way you please.

The Art of Chunking

To take full advantage of hypertext, a hypertext author must approach the task of writing in a very different way. Specifically, a hypertext author *chunks* the information to be contained in the hypertext—that is, breaks it down into parts (of approximately one or two pages) that can be displayed independently.

If I were writing a book about the Outer Banks, I'd begin with the geology. I know, it's boring, but I really do want you to understand why it is that a big wave might just roll over the whole island. You really ought to know this if you're thinking about buying beachfront property or visiting in the early fall, when hurricanes develop. Then I'd discuss other topics, in some sort of logical sequence.

In a hypertext, though, I'd chunk down all the text into a series of one-pagers, giving each a title such as the following:

Ecology

Lighthouses

Barrier reefs

Hurricanes and Nor'easters

Vacation rental properties

Investment in vacation rental properties

Beaches

Shopping

Shipwrecks

Windsurfing

Restaurants

The Nature Conservancy

Kayaking

[Etc.]

After the chunks are written, a hypertext author links them so that it's possible (ideally) to go from any one page to any other page. The result is a *semantic net*, in which all concepts are interlinked in every way possible (Figure 1.3).

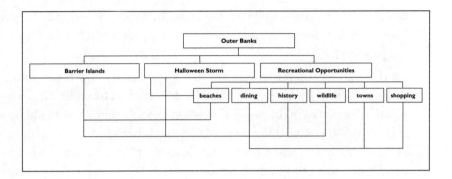

Figure 1.3 Semantic net.

SEARCH TIP

Think synonyms! As you'll learn later in this book, you'll maximize your chances of retrieving relevant documents if you can think of—and list—just about every word that's closely related to your subject. For the Outer Banks example, good search synonyms include the major towns on the Banks (Kitty Hawk, Duck, Corolla, Avon, Ocrococke), the recreational activities available there (windsurfing, kayaking, fishing), and the names of attractions (Wright Brothers, shipwrecks, lighthouses). Whenever you're preparing to search, get started by making a lengthy list of words that might help to uniquely identify the document you're looking for.

KEY TERM

semantic net
In a hypertext, the web or matrix formed by linking every concept with every other related concept.

Once these pages have been chunked and linked as a semantic net, you can work through them in any way you want. You can ignore my geology lecture and go straight to the topic that interests you—say, Restaurants. From there, you can go to Kayaking—or anywhere else for that matter. If you prefer to stick your head in the sand and ignore the pages concerning storms, so be it. It's your decision.

Hypertext frees the reader from the constraints imposed by authors, who would love to drag you through a sequence of ideas. That's why so many readers react instinctively to hypertext by saying, "This is cool." You can think of hypertext as a sort of Readers' Lib.

Hypertext doesn't work equally well for all kinds of documents, as you might imagine. It's best for written material that doesn't need a sequence. Algebra textbooks and novels aren't good candidates for hypertext, obviously, but catalogs are ideal.

BROWSE YOUR WAY TO DISORIENTATION

How do you locate information in a hypertext? By *browsing*, a method of information access in which you click hyperlinks to explore the material that's available. In a well-planned hypertext of limited size, a thoughtful author provides internal navigation aids, which should include the following features:

- **A welcome page.** This is the page that's normally displayed when you first access the hypertext. It explains the hypertext's purpose and provides some good starting points. Figure 1.4 shows a well-conceived welcome page.

- **A home button.** When clicked, this button redisplays the welcome page.

- **An index.** This page lists all the pages in the hypertext, enabling you to jump to any of them.

- **Other internal navigation aids.** In a well-conceived hypertext, authors provide navigation aids—typically, a row of buttons—that enable you to figure out how to find your way. Minimally, these include buttons that access the welcome page and the index, but thoughtful authors include additional buttons. Figure 1.5 shows well-designed navigation aids; it's apparent what they do, thanks to the text explanations (which also function as buttons for people using text-only browsers). In Figure 1.6, you see an unfortunate but all-too-common penchant of graphics-savvy Web authors: Creating navigation aids that look very nice on-screen but do not have any identifiable function.

browsing
In a hypertext, a method of information access in which you explore what's available by clicking hyperlinks that look interesting or useful.

KEY TERM

Figure 1.4 A well-conceived welcome page.

Figure 1.5 Well-conceived navigation aids.

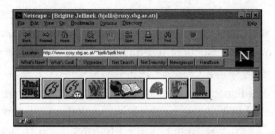

Figure 1.6 Incomprehensible navigation aids.

The big drawback of hypertext is disorientation, that "lost in hyperspace" feeling. You click away at hyperlink after hyperlink, and sooner or later you just don't know how you wound up where you are, or how you'll get back. A thoughtful hypertext author provides navigation aids that prevent you from getting lost or disoriented. But such aids work only for a closed hypertext system, in which a single author or team of authors prepares and integrates all of the material. What happens when a hypertext system becomes global in scope?

THE LITTLE WEB THAT GREW

The World Wide Web started as a small-scale experiment in document exchange—and very quickly grew beyond its creators' wildest expectations. Had they known how large the Web would become, they almost certainly would have designed it very differently.

The World Wide Web got its start as a small-scale experiment in Internet-based document exchange. From the beginning, it was intended only to provide a reasonably user-friendly interface to a varied collection of documents within a relatively limited area of knowledge. Searchers were assumed to be knowledgeable about the subject matter and would not need very much help navigating the system or judging the quality of the documents' contents. As will be seen, these characteristics were fine for the Web's initial usage base, but they impose grave restrictions on document retrievability now that the Web has been scaled up to global proportions.

The Web's birthplace is the European Laboratory for Particle Physics, which is known by the acronym of its French name (Conseil Europeen pour la Recherche Nucleaire). CERN is the center of a world-wide network of high-energy physics researchers.

Like academic think tanks elsewhere, CERN has some permanent researchers, but most of its scientists visit there on one- or two-year fellowships. These researchers, called fellows, need to keep in contact with local researchers during their visit, as well as with colleagues posted at universities and research centers worldwide. And after the fellows leave, they need to keep in contact with CERN so that they can keep abreast of fast-breaking developments there.

Understanding their fellows' need for local and long-distance collaboration, the CERN computer services staff saw computer networks as a communication medium as well as a means of sharing programs and data. In the early 1980s, CERN experimented with a variety of computer networks, both local area networks (LAN) and wide area networks (WAN). When CERN staff learned of the Internet, they knew almost immediately that it held the answer to their fellows' collaboration difficulties. By 1988, CERN had established a link to the Internet and, by 1990, had become the largest Internet site in Europe.

CERN's early experience with the Internet provided fertile soil for the birth of the Web. Recalls Ben Segal, who was responsible for the introduction of the Internet into CERN, an "entire culture of distributed computing" had been created at CERN; everyone was thinking about ways of spreading computer resources around and creating new, computer-based means for scientific collaboration. By providing electronic mail, mailing lists, and newsgroups, the Internet came with many useful tools. What it lacked was a user-friendly way of allowing scientists to exchange documents with each other. That's why the Web was created.

By the late 1980s, Tim Berners-Lee, a computer specialist who fully understood the Internet, conceived of a hypertext system that would integrate the various high-energy physics sites, using the Internet as a medium. From the beginning, the Web was designed to offer easy point-and-click access to a wide variety of document types, including notes, reports, drafts of papers, databases, computer documentation, and on-line help.

Berners-Lee's innovations include the following key elements of Web technology:

- **The Hypertext Markup Language (HTML).** This language enables a Web author to identify the parts of a document using plain ASCII text rather than complicated formatting commands. The formatting is left to a browser program, such as NCSA Mosaic or Netscape. HTML also enables Web authors to create hyperlinks and embed them in their documents.

- **The Hypertext Transport Protocol (HTTP).** This is the standard that enables Web documents to be exchanged via the Internet.

HTML and HTTP have made an enormous contribution to the Internet's popularity and usability. However, they are international standards, and to the extent that existing programs and practices embody these standards, we're all stuck with their limitations. The biggest problem with HTML is that the language currently provides no widely used means for categorizing documents. In the next section, you'll see why this is a serious drawback for information retrieval purposes.

Looking at an HTML Document

To prepare a Web document, a Web author uses a word processing program or an HTML editor to prepare a plain text file. Within this file, the author places HTML tags, most of which come in pairs: a beginning tag (such as <H1>) and an ending tag (</H1>). In this way, the author marks the text so that browsers will recognize the marked portions as a certain part of the document (such as the title or a first-level heading). The following shows an example of a simple HTML document; Figure 1.7 shows what this document looks like when displayed by a browser. Note that the title doesn't even appear in the document: You only see it on the title bar of the browser.

```
<HTML>
<HEAD>
<TITLE>This is the document's title</TITLE>
</HEAD>
<BODY>
<H1>This is the first-level heading</H1>
<P>This is a paragraph of text. The text must
be demarcated by tags. </P>
<BLOCKQUOTE>This is an extended quotation.
It is formatted with the BLOCKQUOTE tag.
</BLOCKQUOTE>
<ADDRESS>This format is used for the author's
email address and the date of last
modification </ADDRESS>
</BODY>
</HTML>
```

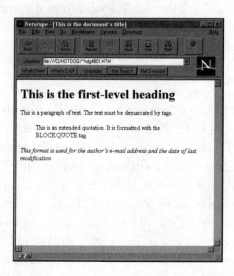

Figure 1.7 An HTML document on-screen.

The most important thing to note about this HTML example isn't so much what's there; it's what's *not* there. Decades of experience with information retrieval in database systems shows that efficient information retrieval requires that authors include information *about* the document that enables searchers to narrow the focus of their search. Such information should include the following:

- **Document Type.** What kind of document is this? Is it a research paper, a memo intended for limited distribution, an advertisement, or a college student's list of the types of socks he has in his drawer?
- **Key Words.** What words best describe the overall subject of this document? And what words would best differentiate it from other documents in the same category?
- **Subject Classification.** How would this document best be categorized according to some established system of subject classifications, such as the Library of Congress subject catalog headings?
- **Abstract.** What are the main points that this document covers? What are its main conclusions?

Information about document type, lists of key words, a subject classification, and an abstract are key components of documents that have been optimized for efficient retrieval. But you can scan the HTML that underlies Web documents all day and you won't find this information in any of them.

As you'll see below, proposed extensions to HTML call for the inclusion of such information using the <META> tag, but most browsers don't implement this tag and it requires programming before the information becomes useful. For now, you can count on the following fact: Very few Web authors give the slightest thought to information retrieval when they're creating their documents. All too often, they don't even bother to choose descriptive titles. That's one of the things—among several—that makes the Web an information retrieval nightmare.

LOST IN HYPERSPACE

Summing up the points this chapter has made thus far, the picture isn't pretty:

- Hypertext systems are known to have one fatal flaw: Browsing isn't an efficient method for information retrieval. In a relatively small hypertext, authors can circumvent this by providing internal navigation aids and indexes. When a hypertext grows beyond the ability of a single individual or team to provide such aids or indexes, it becomes increasingly difficult to retrieve information and users experience severe disorientation. The result is that the system appears to be almost infinitely rich in information—but you can't get to the information, and you become disoriented and frustrated when you try.

- The World Wide Web had its origins in a small, homogenous community of high-energy physics researchers. It was intended to provide a user-friendly means for accessing a variety of documents. No provisions were made for categorizing documents because the members of this community already knew what they were, or could guess. Today, the Web has grown far beyond its original homogenous roots. It contains all kinds of documents, from trash to treasure, and there's no way to predict what you're going to get—all the documents are thrown together into one teeming cauldron. Worse, Web authors typically create and publish their documents without giving a thought to how their documents could be more efficiently retrieved.

- Now that the Web has been scaled up beyond its modest, socially homogenous origins, its twin defects—disorientation and Web authors' inattention to the problems of information retrieval—are amply evident.

In the next chapter, you'll learn about the various tools that Web developers have devised in order to combat the Web's deficiencies as a system for information retrieval. As you'll see, the tools aren't perfect, largely because they have to deal with the built-in inadequacies of HTML. And that's all the more reason that you need a carefully planned search strategy.

THE <META> TAG—AND WHY IT WON'T SOLVE THE PROBLEM ANYTIME SOON

This section is a bit technical, so you can skip to the next section if you're not familiar with HTML and would just as soon take my word for it. It's about the <META> tag, an HTML tag that's supposed to solve the information retrieval problem on the Web—but as I'm going to argue, it's not very likely to succeed.

Recognizing the problems of Web information retrieval, the authors of the HTML 2.0 specification called for the use of the <META> tag. "Meta" means "information about information." This sounds like just the thing to cure the Web's information retrieval problems, doesn't it? After all, what's wrong with most HTML documents is that they don't include information *about* the document, such as an indication of the document type, key words, subject classifications, and an abstract. As you'll see, the <META> tag isn't likely to solve the problem anytime soon. The tag is a classic case of technical overreach. It's technically sweet, but its designers didn't think through the practicalities—as a result, very few people use it.

The <META> tag has two *attributes*, which are used to include specific information about the document:

NAME. This identifies the type of information.

CONTENT. This identifies the meta-information that you want to include.

You use the tag in the following way:

```
<META NAME="name of information type" CONTENT="the
information you want to give">
```

Here's an example of a properly written META tag for a document containing information about the Outer Banks:

```
<META name="document_type" content="Travel Guide">

<META name="destination" content="Outer Banks">

<META name="keywords" content="North Carolina, Duck, Kitty
Hawk, Corolla, Avon, vacation property, hurricanes, kayak-
ing, wind surfing">

<META name="distribution" content="local">

<META name="abstract" content="This document contains
information about the history, geography, and vacation pos-
sibilities of North Carolina's Outer Banks, one of the East
Coast's premier vacation destinations.">
```

Sounds great, huh? Well, it's not. You can place this information into all the HTML documents you want, but browsers will simply ignore it. Why?

The <META> tag was designed from the beginning not as an aid for general information retrieval on the Web, but as a resource programmers could use to create powerful, server-based information retrieval systems. In other words, the server program—the program that makes Web documents available—must be programmed by a professional programmer to recognize the specific NAMEs that you've used and to compile this information into a user-accessible database of some sort. Very few Web servers have been configured to do this, for the simple reasons that it's expensive and time-consuming—and what's more, Web authors *still* don't care to take the time to enhance the retrievability of their documents. Worse, there's no standard, agreed-upon system for NAME nomenclature.

The next chapter discusses search engines, which are based on programs that rove the Web gathering information about documents. These programs *could* be configured to read <META> information and compile it for retrieval purposes. You could inform such a search engine something like the following: "I'm interested in the Outer Banks, but I only want to see travel guides."

But this nice little plan has one huge drawback: Web authors would have to agree on something like a systematic NAME nomenclature. This might happen, but it runs against human nature, at least insofar as Web authors are concerned. Web authors simply don't understand the problems of information retrieval on the Web and don't care about them. They're much more interested in how their pages look than in how their pages can be found. On the Web, the dominant metaphor is publishing, not information retrieval.

TOWARD A WEB SEARCH STRATEGY

Given the Web's flawed structure, you're going to need all the help you can get to retrieve the information you're looking for.

First, you'll need to become an expert in *free-text searching*. Since there's no (practical) way that Web authors can identify key words or subject classifications for their documents, you must fall back on search techniques that index some or all of the words appearing in a document. Free-text searching has some notorious drawbacks. The worst, as you'll see, is that free-text searches produce a high number of totally irrelevant documents. (You'll see why in the next chapter.) But you can overcome this and other deficiencies by learning some advanced search techniques.

Second, you'll need a healthy dose of skepticism about the quality of the information you're going to retrieve. Because there's no mechanism to identify and select specific types of documents, a Web search is going to throw all kinds of documents at you—and many of them aren't worth the bytes they're printed on.

Third, you'll need to take full advantage of the efforts made to categorize documents on the Web. As you've learned in this chapter, HTML provides no practical means to do this, so it must be done by others. Most of the people who do it are volunteers, and in consequence the coverage is poor. But you should still take advantage of their efforts.

KEY TERM

free-text searching
A method of accessing information by searching a database that consists of all or most of the words occurring in a collection of documents. You type the key word or words, and the search engine displays a list of the documents containing these words.

FROM HERE

The next chapter surveys the various tools that people have devised in an effort to overcome the Web's drawbacks as an information retrieval mechanism. As you'll see, they're clever—sometimes devilishly clever—but they're patchwork solutions, grafted onto the Web's flawed structure.

If you're already familiar with Web search tools, you might want to skip to Chapter 3, which provides practical information for formulating your search strategy.

CHAPTER 2

A QUICK SURVEY OF WEB SEARCH TOOLS

Now that you know what you're up against when you try to find information on the Web, you'll surely agree that you'll need all the help you can get. Happily, innovators worldwide have been hard at work trying to solve the information retrieval shortcomings of the Web. Although they haven't come up with a single "killer" application that can retrieve information flawlessly, they have created an impressive suite of tools. By using them in a logical way—and most importantly, in the right *sequence*—you can find the information you're looking for.

This chapter introduces the information-discovery tools you'll use when searching the Web. Here's a quick overview, beginning with the one you've probably already tried—surfing. As you'll find, there are much more powerful tools available than surfing—and once you understand their strengths and limitations, you'll better understand how to make them work together effectively.

SURFING

When the Web was first conceived, the only information-retrieval mechanism thought necessary was browsing (navigating among documents by clicking hyperlinks). Today, browsing is better known as *surfing*, a document discovery technique that all too often adds up to just so much wasted time. Surfing might have been sufficient if the Web had never grown beyond its origins—in the late 1980s, as you learned in Chapter 1, the Web initially linked just a few hundred researchers in high-energy physics.

surfing
Exploring the Web by clicking hyperlink after hyperlink; a serendipitous technique for discovering new sites.

KEY TERM

With a Web containing millions of documents, surfing has become a mind-boggling exercise in disorientation and serendipitous discovery, a favorite pastime of late-night hyperlink addicts. As an information retrieval method, surfing won't cut it. You'll seldom come away from a surfing session without discovering *something* fascinating, but don't count on finding anything relevant to your research goals. All too often, your surf session turns out to be nothing more than so much *thrashing*, thoroughly useless even though you spent hours doing it and consumed more computer power than was used to develop the hydrogen bomb.

thrashing
In Web surfing, to surf frenetically but unprofitably, without any clear goal in mind and without finding anything useful.

KEY TERM

What's wrong with surfing as an information-retrieval technique? You're dependent on the trails that others have blazed. To surf your way to relevant documents, some kindly Web author somewhere had to place a relevant hyperlink in a Web document. No hyperlink, no surfing. In any given area, however, there are many relevant documents that aren't referenced by hyperlinks; most Web authors don't have the time to keep their link lists up-to-date and complete, preferring to throw in a few juicy ones and leave the rest up to you.

Don't dismiss surfing entirely, though. It's like browsing the stacks in a good library: You may come across a jewel of a site quite by accident. In addition, it's a great idea to surf away from a page that's loaded with relevant links. And if you aren't really serious about your search project, it's a wonderful way to waste time. In the chapters to follow, I'll advise you to surf a bit whenever you've found a site that lists lots of hyperlinks in your area of interest.

STARTING POINTS PAGES

To help Web users find their way in a more orderly fashion, several organizations have made *starting points pages* available. Among these organizations are research institutes (such as the National Center for Supercomputing Applications [NCSA], the birthplace of NCSA Mosaic), Internet service providers, browser vendors, and a number of Web-savvy individuals, whose efforts put many of the commercial products to shame.

Why Use a Starting Points Page?

A starting points page provides a number of interesting and useful URLs to explore, ranging from the utilitarian to the ultra-cool. Among the organizations making such pages available are official Internet organizations, such as the Network Information Center (NIC); vendors of Web browsing software, such as Netscape, Air Mosaic, and NCSA Mosaic; and private individuals.

Starting points pages provide a good way to get acquainted with the Web, but it isn't likely that they'll contain the information you're looking for. The best starting points pages include links to the Web's search tools, enabling you to use the page as a springboard to daily information-gathering activities.

KEY TERM

starting points page
A page, often provided by a vendor of browser software or an on-line service, that includes a number of useful and cool hyperlinks. A starting points page benefits first-time Web surfers by providing examples of the Web's riches, but does not aim for comprehensive coverage.

Why aren't starting points pages useful for search purposes? In a word, scope. To be sure, many starting points pages are actually mini-subject trees, with headings that group hyperlinks by subject (such as "Business Sites," "Weather," "Arts and Humanities," and more). A subject tree, introduced below, tries to provide a subject catalog of thousands of Web sites. But a starting points page doesn't try to list many available resources on a subject, as a subject tree does. It provides a few entry points for the beginning of your Web adventure. But they're still worth looking at—particularly if the page groups links to the Web's best subject trees and search engines.

The Starting Point

A very nice starting points page is called, appropriately enough, Starting Point (Figure 2.1). It's made available by Superhighway Consulting, Inc. You'll find links to news, weather, sports, entertainment, business, investing, professional, reference, shopping, travel, magazine, and education sites. For more starting points page suggestions, see the sidebar, "Starting Points Pages Rated."

SEARCH TIP

Like the Starting Point? Why not make this page the *default start page*, so it displays every time you start your browser? To do so, check your browser's documentation to find out how to change the default start page. With Netscape, first select the Starting Point URL with the mouse and copy the URL to the Clipboard. Then open the Options menu and choose **Preferences**. Click the **Styles** tab. In the Start With area, click **Home Page Location**, and click the cursor within the text box. Press **Ctrl + V** to paste the URL into the text box, and click **OK** to confirm.

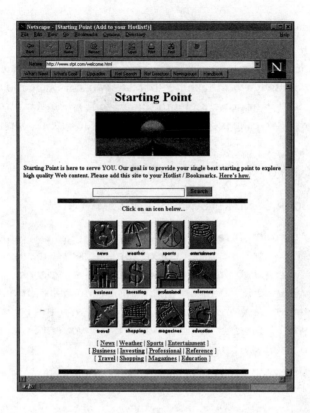

Figure 2.1 Starting Point (http://www.stpt.com/welcome.html).

KEY TERM

default start page
The page that your browser automatically displays every time you start the program. Normally this is the browser publisher's home page, but you can usually change this to any page on the Web.

STARTING POINTS PAGES RATED

The following lists some of the Web's more popular starting points pages and includes ratings using a star system. A rating of

continued...

continued…

four stars is excellent; this is a very good candidate for anyone's default start page. A three-star rating indicates that the page is definitely worth taking a look at. Two stars suggests that the service might prove useful to some, while a one-star rating indicates that the page is somewhat overrated (despite its popularity).

Starting Points Pages

JOHN S. MAKULOWICH'S AWESOME LIST ★

An Internet trainer, John Makulowich has assembled a list of "the glory and grandeur of the Internet, the sine qua non of Cyberspace, the main characters in the evolving drama…," with special focus on the needs of journalists, trainers, and first-time Web users. The problem is that the list isn't very well organized. Worth a look, but I wouldn't use it for my default start page.

URL: http://www.clark.net/pub/journalism/awesome.html

INTERNET SERVICES LIST ★ ★

Scott Yanoff's highly regarded starting points page contains an excellent selection of high-quality Web sites, organized by subject. But it's a bit out of date.

URL: http://www.uwm.edu/Mirror/inet.services.html

NERD WORLD MEDIA ★ ★ ★

A fun starting point that divides more than 8000 sites into two major categories, Leisure and Knowledge; these categories are further broken down into a variety of subject headings. Not at all academic, Nerd World Media is an excellent starting point for consumers, Web enthusiasts, and computer users.

URL: http://www.nerdworld.com/users/dstein/index.html

continued…

continued...

PC/COMPUTING'S WEB MAP ★ ★ ★

Organized as a clickable imagemap, this starting points page provides a graphical entry point for popular sites in areas of interest to personal computer users, consumers, computer hobbyists, and parents.

URL: http://www.ziff.com/~pccomp/webmap/

POINT ★ ★ ★

Point is famous for its "top 5% of the Web" awards, which purport to identify the cream of the Web crop. A subject-oriented starting points page containing high-quality Web sites, Point indexes sites in the following subject areas: education, business/finance, entertainment, news/info, leisure activities, government and politics, science/technology, computers/Internet, shopping, arts/humanities, health/medicine, global village, kids, and "the road less traveled."

URL: http://www.pointcom.com/

TREASURES ON THE INTERNET ★ ★ ★

Educator Craig Fifer has put together a very nice starting points page, which should prove especially interesting to educators.

URL: http://pen.k12.va.us/~cfifer/treasures.shtml

WHOLE INTERNET CATALOG ★ ★ ★

A part of the Global Network Navigator (GNN) service, the Whole Internet Catalog (WIC) lists 1200 of the best sites on the Web. Organized like a subject tree, but with far fewer entries, WIC groups sites according to the following subject

continued...

continued...

categories: arts/entertainment, business/finance, daily news, education, government/politics, health/medicine, humanities/social sciences, Internet, life/culture, recreation/sports/hobbies, science/technology, and travel.

URL: http://gnn.digital.com/gnn/wic/index.html

SUBJECT TREES

Remember your school library? You probably used the subject catalog to search the library's resources by subject. A dictionary of computing, for example, would be filed under the heading, "Computers—Dictionaries." A subject catalog is a great place to start if you don't have a particular author or title in mind.

Who makes subject catalogs? People—ideally, trained people. Librarians spend a long time in library school learning how to classify materials by subject, and they use well-established subject classification schemes to do so. In the United States, the Library of Congress subject classifications are widely used in academic libraries, while the Dewey Decimal System is widely found in public and school libraries.

The Web's Subject Catalogs

Is there anything like a subject catalog for the Web? Yes, but don't expect anything as well-organized as the subject headings in your local library. You'll find a number of *subject trees* on the Web, including the famed Yahoo, but they're unlike subject catalogs in the following ways:

- **Coverage.** The Web's subject trees are mainly volunteer efforts. Even if they're commercial, they're not staffed adequately to provide full coverage of the Web. You'll find a few thousand documents in subject trees, leaving millions of documents unindexed. Still, they aim for comprehensiveness, even if they're so far short of the goal that the result is almost laughable.

- **Quality.** The Web's subject trees weren't designed or created by professionally trained librarians—in consequence, their subject classifications don't conform to any of the established library systems. Some of them could use some good old-fashioned editing, too: the McKinley Internet Directory, for example, contains misspellings and duplicate entries that cause retrieval problems.

- **Accessibility.** Here's one way in which Web subject trees are superior to library card catalogs: They contain active links to the documents they index. Once you've found a document that looks interesting, just click the hyperlink to see the document on-screen. You can then return to the subject tree, if you wish, to browse for more documents.

- **Search Capabilities.** Unlike a library's card catalog, searched manually, most Web subject trees enable you to perform key word searches of the documents they index. The search engines vary in power and capabilities. They're discussed in detail in Chapters 9 through 14.

The Web's subject trees are far from perfect, but they're an indispensable component of a Web search strategy.

KEY TERM

subject tree
A Web site that attempts to categorize Web documents using subject classifications. Resembling the subject catalog in a library, subject trees contain active links to the documents they index. Unlike starting points pages, subject trees try to be comprehensive, although even the biggest of them indexes only a small fraction of the documents available on the Web.

Navigating a Subject Tree

Why is it called a "subject tree"? The term "tree" connotes the index's hierarchical organization. When you access a subject tree, you see an initial screen with subject headings, such as those shown in Figure 2.2. This is the "trunk" of the tree. When you click one of the subject headings (such as "Arts"), you go to one of the "branches" (see Figure 2.3). Eventually, you go far enough out on the branches to run into the names of specific documents (see Figure 2.4). You can see one of the documents just by clicking its hyperlink.

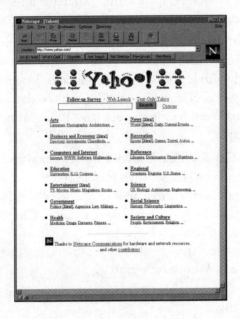

Figure 2.2 Yahoo (top level).

You'll learn more about how to use Yahoo in subsequent chapters.

Is it such a bad thing that most of the Web's subject trees use ad hoc subject classifications? Not necessarily. Rather than imposing an academic classification scheme on the Web's profusion of document types, the creators of subject trees have tried to classify the documents actually appearing on the Web. For example, Table 2.1 lists the subject classifications used in GNN's Whole Internet Catalog (WIC), a starting points page that lists some 1200 of the best Internet sites. Although WIC is essentially a starting points page that doesn't aim for comprehensiveness, its well-chosen subject classifications nicely illustrate the subject strengths of the Web.

Figure 2.3 Yahoo subject tree (Arts).

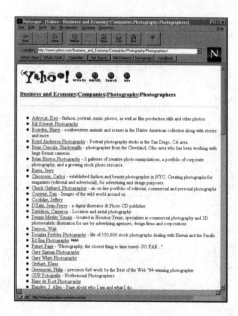

Figure 2.4 Yahoo subject tree (Photographers).

Table 2.1 Whole Internet Catalog Subject Classifications

Arts & Entertainment

Architecture	Movies (Previews and Fan Pages)	Science Fiction
Art Exhibits		Sound Files
Comics	Movies (Reviews and Indexes)	Stars & Famous People
Dance	Music (Bands & Styles)	Television (Networks & Channels)
Digital Images		
E-Zines	Music (News & Reference)	Television (Shows & Fan Pages)
Fashion	Photography	
Humor	Radio	Theater
Magazines		

Business & Finance

Agriculture	Management	Taxes
Career & Employment	Marketing	Yellow Pages (Telephone)
Government Information	Nonprofits	
	Personal Finance Real Estate	Yellow Pages (WWW: General)
Internet Commerce-Investment	Small Business	Yellow Pages (WWW: Industry)

Computers

Computer & Video Games	Languages & Programming	Publishing & Multimedia
Dictionaries	Macintosh	Software & Shareware
General Indexes	Magazines	
Graphics	Microsoft Windows	Unix
Hardware Manufacturers	OS/2	Virtual Reality

Daily News

News Sources (U.S.)

News Sources (International)

News Audio

Business News

Stock Quotes

Weather Report

Sports News

Entertainment News

Daily Diversions

Columnists

Sites of the Day

What's New on the Web

Personals

Education

Dictionaries & Reference Guides

Educational Technology

Financial Aid

Higher Education

K-12 Education

Libraries

Parenting

Sites for Kids

Government & Politics

International Government

Governments Worldwide

Law

Crime & Criminal Justice

War & Peace

U.S. Politics

Election '96

Indexes to U.S. Government Resources

Executive Branch

Judicial Branch

Legislative Branch

Agencies

Intelligence Agencies

Department of Defense

U.S. State & Local Government

Health & Medicine

Alternative Medicine

Disability

Diseases and Conditions

General Health

Mental Health

Nutrition

Professional Medicine

Safer Sex

Substance Abuse

U.S. and International Health Organizations

Veterinary Medicine

Humanities & Social Sciences

Anthropology

Archaeology

Black & African
    Studies

Classics

Economics

History

Languages

Literary Journals

Literature

Online Book
    Collections

Philosophy

Poetry

Psychology

Women's Studies

Writing &
    Journalism

Internet

Browsers

Chat

Community
    Networks

Cool Hotlists

HTML (Basic)

HTML (Advanced)

HTML (Icons &
    Graphics)

Indexes (WWW)

Indexes (General)

Indexes (Personal
    Home Pages)

Internet User

Guides

Search the Internet

Security

Standards

Usenet

White Pages

Life & Culture

Activism

The African-
    American
    Experience

Gay, Lesbian,
    Bisexual, and
    Transsexual
    Resources

Latino Culture

Men's Resources

Mysticism & Occult

Native Cultures

Religion &
    Spirituality

Sexuality

65+

Support Groups

Women's Resources

Recreation, Sports, & Hobbies

Baseball

Cars, Motorcycles & Motor Sports

Cooking

Crafts

Food & Drink

Football

Games

Gardening

Genealogy

Hobbies

Hockey

Holidays & Special Occasions

Outdoor Recreation

Pets & Assorted Animals

Spectator Sports (General)

Sports & Fitness

Water Sports

Science & Technology

Artificial Intelligence

Astronomy

Aviation and Aeronautics

Biology

Chemistry

Engineering

Environmental Studies

Geography

Geology

Mathematics

NASA & Space Exploration

Oceanography

Paleontology

Physics

Weather & Meteorology

Travel

Destinations

Food & Lodging

Guidebooks & Tips

Magazines

Reference

Transportation

Travel & Health

Travel Narratives

Work & Study Abroad

SEARCH TIP

Most subject trees include search capabilities that enable you to search the subject tree as if it were a database. This isn't the same thing as a search engine, discussed later in this chapter—you're not searching the entire Web, only the documents contained in the subject tree. Still, searching a subject tree is a very good place to start, since a subject tree search is more likely to retrieve a relevant document (one that actually pertains to your interests). For more information on searching subject trees, see Chapter 5.

RATING SUBJECT TREES

Looking for a good subject tree? Here's a list of the Web's current subject tree offerings, using the four-star rating system introduced in the previous section. Four stars are used to flag indispensable subject trees; the three-star services are very good, but have some flaws; two-star services are worth a look. One-star services are for the insatiably curious only. You'll find full coverage of the four- and three-star services in Chapter 5 of this book.

Subject Trees

BUBL ★ ★

An outgrowth of the British Bulletin Board for Librarians, BUBL grew into a database of Gopher resources, and it's well on its way to becoming a subject tree of Web resources. Given that most of the librarians involved are academic reference librarians, the focus here is strictly academic, but it's a treasure trove of high-quality sources. If you're partial to formal systems of subject classification, you'll appreciate that BUBL is organized according to the Uniform Decimal Classification (UDC) scheme, which assigns decimal values to subjects. If you don't like the UDC classifications, you can switch to an alphabetical tree

continued...

continued...

(http://www.bubl.bath.ac.uk/BUBL/Treealphabet.html).

URL: http://www.bubl.bath.ac.uk/BUBL/Tree.html

GALAXY ★ ★ ★

Maintained by TradeWave Corporation, Galaxy is one of the few Web search tools created with the assistance of people trained in librarianship. It contains an unusual and intelligent feature: Documents are categorized by type (something that ought to be supplied automatically by HTML authors, as noted in the previous chapter). A typical section includes a list of "collections" (trailblazer pages), periodicals, directories, nonprofit organizations, corporate home pages, and more, enabling you to quickly identify the type of information you're after. Subject headings include: business/commerce, community (including charitable organizations, consumer issues, safety, and veterans affairs), engineering and technology, government, humanities, law, leisure/recreation, medicine, reference/interdisciplinary information, science, and social science. The Galaxy catalogs more than 20,000 Web sites, 1500 Telnet sites, 4.6 million Gopher titles, and 290,000 searchable Web titles.

URL: http://imc.einet.net/galaxy.html

MCKINLEY INTERNET DIRECTORY ★ ★ ★

This subject tree, produced by The McKinley Group, differs from its competitors by including ratings of the Web sites it indexes (currently some 20,000 sites). You can also search Magellan, a database currently containing 80,000 unrated sites. McKinley's top-level index includes the following subject headings: arts and music, business and economics, communications, computing and mathematics, education, engineering/technology, government/politics, health/medicine,

continued...

continued...

humanities/social sciences, the Internet (naturally), law/criminal justice, popular culture, philosophy, science, and sports/recreation.

URL: http://www.mckinley.com/

MOTHER-OF-ALL BBS ★

And now, as they used to say on Monty Python, for something completely different: The Mother-of-All BBS. Mother, as I'll abbreviate it, goes all the way down the road to user extensibility that's only hinted at by the send-in-your-own URL features of other subject trees. In fact, everything on Mother has been contributed by users. Your contributions can consist of a URL, or you can create a new subject category—or, in Mother's terminology, a bulletin board. This is it, folks—the peoples' subject guide. What's out there, like it or not, is what you get. Unfortunately, that includes a fair number of pranks and cheesy commercial schemes as well as some very interesting documents.

URL:
http://www.cs.colorado.edu/homes/mcbryan/public_html/bb/summary.html

YAHOO ★ ★ ★ ★

Decidedly hipper than the subject trees discussed thus far, Yahoo—short for Yet Another Hierarchically Odiferous Oracle—is the work of David Filo and Jerry Chih-Yuan Yang of Stanford University. Subject categories such as "Body Art," "Indie/Alternative Music," and "Cybersex" testify that you're very far from the librarian mentality. Web enthusiasts themselves, Filo and Yang know how to get right to the point: Options at the top of the welcome page let you see what's

continued...

continued...

new, what's cool, and what's popular. Currently indexing more than 70,000 documents, Yahoo is one of the Web's treasures—and it's fully integrated with Open Text, one of the Web's best search engines (described later in this chapter).

URL: http://www.yahoo.com/

DISTRIBUTED SUBJECT TREES

A subject tree represents an attempt to create a more or less comprehensive subject index of Web documents. Unfortunately, the effort is doomed from the start. It's just too much work to stay on top of fast-breaking Web publishing developments in hundreds of subject areas. Even Yahoo, the best of them, indexes only 70,000 documents, and its coverage is spotty. To do a really good job of indexing the Web, Yahoo would have to grow into a very large company with dozens or even hundreds of employees—and it still wouldn't be able to cover everything on the Web.

But there's another way, and it's found by analogy to computer hardware. In computer networks, the answer to a bogged-down central server is a *distributed* system, in which the processing load is farmed out to workstations all over the network. Using this network design as an analogy, one can imagine a *distributed subject tree*, in which no attempt is made to create a single, central repository of subject-indexed documents. Instead, the responsibility for creating and maintaining each subject page is farmed out to individuals all over the Web whom I call *trailblazers*. These individuals specialize in just one subject area (such as Divorce/Separation or Italian Cooking), and they're the best people to do this job. They're in touch with on-line communities concerned with these subjects, they find out quickly when new Web sites appear, and they are the best judges of the quality of sites in their area of interest. Makes sense, doesn't it?

distributed subject tree
A subject tree that does *not* rely on a centralized system for discovering and classifying Web sites, but instead distributes this responsibility to dozens or hundreds of volunteers, each of whom is responsible for maintaining a page in his or her subject area of expertise.

KEY TERM

trailblazer
An individual, knowledgeable in a given subject area, who takes on the responsibility of maintaining a Web page focused on that subject area.

KEY TERM

You'll find two very impressive distributed subject trees on the Internet: the Clearinghouse for Subject-Oriented Resource Guides (http://www.lib .umich.edu/chhome.html), and the World Wide Web Organization's Virtual Library (http://www.w3.org/hypertext/DataSources/bySubject/Overview .html). In Figure 2.5, you see the opening page of the Clearinghouse's subject classifications.

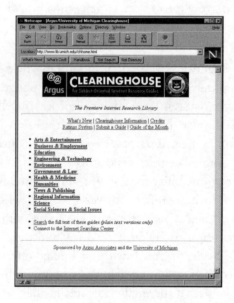

Figure 2.5 The Clearinghouse for Subject-Oriented Resource Guides.

Distributed subject trees provide an invaluable resource, given that they provide easy, subject-based access to trailblazer pages. But they index only a very small fraction of the total number of trailblazer pages on the Web. If you can't find a trailblazer page of interest to you in the Clearinghouse or the Virtual Library, you'll have to find one using a search engine.

DISTRIBUTED SUBJECT TREES

THE CLEARINGHOUSE FOR SUBJECT-ORIENTED RESOURCE GUIDES ★ ★ ★

An impressive project co-sponsored by Argus Associates and the University of Michigan, the Clearinghouse provides access to hundreds of trailblazer pages in a variety of subject areas, with an emphasis on business and academic subjects. But there's some fun, too, as you'll see in the Arts and Entertainment section. A plus: By January 1996, the Clearinghouse will have applied its top-notch rating system to each of the trailblazer pages in its collection.

URL: http://www.lib.umich.edu/chhome.html

THE VIRTUAL LIBRARY ★ ★ ★ ★

Organized by the World Wide Web Organization (W3O), the Virtual Library gathers trailblazer pages in a huge variety of subject areas, including the academic (with fields such as anthropology and applied linguistics) and the fanciful (there's a "roadkill" page, believe it or not). A plus for librarians: VL is experimenting with a Library of Congress classification system (see http://www.w3.org/hypertext/DataSources/bySubject/LibraryOfCongress.html).

URL: http://www.w3.org/hypertext/DataSources/bySubject/Overview.html

UNINDEXED TRAILBLAZER PAGES

Distributed subject trees provide organized access to hundreds of trailblazer pages, but there are thousands of trailblazer pages on the Web. In any given subject area, some of the best trailblazer pages aren't catalogued by the Clearinghouse or the Virtual Library (see the preceding section)—you'll have to discover them on your own.

Finding a good trailblazer page is often the key to unlocking the Web's information treasures. A case in point: Figure 2.6 shows The Computing Trailblazer, a production of the very knowledgeable folks at Ziff-Davis, publishers of *PC Magazine*, *PC Computing*, and *MacUser*. Loaded with useful information, the many pages include detailed, critical reviews of each site that's listed.

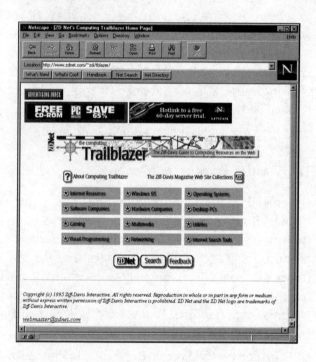

Figure 2.6 The Computing Trailblazer (http://www.zdnet.com/~zdi/tblazer/).

SPIDERS AND SEARCH ENGINES

It's too much work to apply subject classifications to every document on the Web—or even to a small fraction of the documents on the Web. That's why *spiders* (also called *wanderers* or *worms*) were invented. In brief, a spider is a computer program that prowls the Web, chasing down hyperlinks and detecting new documents. Working tirelessly, a spider can discover hundreds of thousands of Web documents and add their URLs to a database. You can then search the database using a *search engine*, a Web-accessible search service. This section introduces these powerful (if quirky) tools; Chapters 9 through 14 cover the best search engines in detail.

KEY TERM

spider
An automatic program that roves the Web, looking for new or updated documents to add to a search engine's database.

KEY TERM

search engine
A Web-accessible program that searches a database of Web documents, attempting to match key words you supply.

Using a Search Engine

To use a search engine, you access the search engine's site, type one or more key words, and click the **Submit** button (see Figure 2.7). If the search engine is able to locate any documents that match your search request, you see a list of the matches (Figure 2.8). The list includes hyperlinks that you can click to access the listed documents. Generally, the documents are listed using a scored *relevancy ranking*—the higher the number, the more relevant the document is likely to be to your search interests. Relevancy is computed by examining the frequency of your key words in the retrieved document.

relevancy ranking

KEY TERM

In a search engine, a method of ranking the retrieved documents by a numerical score. The higher the score, the more likely it is that the retrieved document is relevant to your search interests.

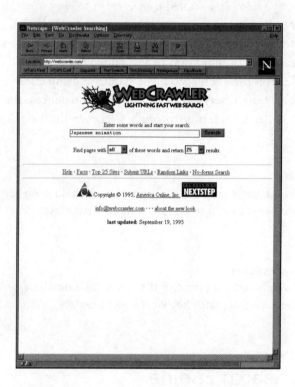

Figure 2.7 Using a search engine (WebCrawler).

Drawbacks of Search Engines

Search engines provide an indispensable resource for Web searching, but they have a number of serious drawbacks:

- **Poor precision.** You'll find that the list of retrieved documents contains a high percentage of irrelevant documents, called *false drops*. To put this point another way, most search engines have low *precision* (a precise search would produce a list of documents in which almost all of them would actually pertain to your search topic). The reason for this low precision is the inevitable ambiguities of language. Suppose you're looking for Web resources on backyard bird feeders. You type the key words "backyard," "bird," and "feeder," and launch your search—only to get a reference to a weird alternative music URL by the Backyard Birds, an unknown musical group, with a hyperlink to their MPEG audio file, "Bottom Feeder." Do these limitations mean that search engines are useless? No. If you understand their limitations and use this book's strategies for effective search engine use, you can vastly improve your potential to locate useful resources.

Figure 2.8 Viewing the list of retrieved documents (WebCrawler).

- **Poor recall.** Most of the Web's search engines consult databases of the most frequently used words in a document (such as the words drawn from the document's title and the first few sentences). They won't retrieve documents in which the key words for which you're searching are buried somewhere within the document. In other words, search engines may produce a list of documents that's low in *recall*, the degree to which a retrieval list includes all the documents that are actually relevant to your search topic.

- **Varied document quality.** A spider can't discriminate between a valuable document and a piece of Web flotsam; it just retrieves them all. In your list of retrieved documents, you'll find many that are completely useless for any purpose. For example, searches for just about any academic subject are likely to bring in lists of course offerings at colleges hither and yon—and all you'll see is the course title and number.

- **Varied indexing depth.** Some spiders retrieve only document titles; others retrieve the entire document text. Unless you understand how the spider works, you're not very likely to succeed with its search engines.

- **The need to use advanced search tools.** With most search engines, good results depend on your using advanced search tools, such as Boolean operators. However, many people do not know how to use these tools, and the sparse on-line help available with most search engines may not fully explain how and when to use them. You'll find a full explanation of these advanced search tools in Chapter 8, and Chapters 9 through 14 detail the specifics for each of the search engines this book covers.

- **Server overload.** With millions of people using the Web, search engines are taxed to the breaking point. Don't be surprised if you can't access InfoSeek or Lycos during peak usage hours.

Search engines are, at best, clumsy and inefficient tools for Web document discovery. Research on key-word searching has consistently shown that amateurs will be lucky to find 25% of the relevant information in a database. But you can get good results if you understand what you're up against and if you use the advanced search tools that most search engines provide.

KEY TERM

false drop
In a search engine's list of retrieved documents, a listed document that is not relevant to your search interests. All search engines produce false drops, some more than others.

KEY TERM

precision
In an information system, the ratio of relevant documents to false drops in a list of documents retrieved by a search. In a list with high precision, all or most of the documents pertain to your search subject. In a list with low precision, many or most of the documents are false drops.

KEY TERM

recall
In an information system, the ratio of the number of documents retrieved by a search to the number actually present in the database. In a search with high recall, the search retrieved most or all of the information actually available. In a search with low recall, the search failed to retrieve much of the relevant information.

RATINGS OF SEARCH ENGINES

The following lists and rates the Web's current search engine offerings, using the four-star system. Four-star services are indispensable. Three-star services are very useful, but have a prominent drawback. Two-star services might be worth a look if you haven't found anything using the others. One-star services aren't very useful but might be consulted if you're trying to find every last document on the Web in a particular area. You'll find full coverage of the four- and three-star search engines in Chapters 9 through 13 of this book.

continued...

continued...

Search Engines

ALIWEB ★

ALIWEB doesn't use a spider. Instead, Web authors create an index file on their servers describing the content of their documents. ALIWEB adds these forms to the database, which you can then search. Unfortunately, ALIWEB does not collect the kind of information that could have made this project useful, such as subject descriptors or key word lists—it's limited to a brief description of content. Additionally, very few Web authors think of ALIWEB when it comes time to publicize their site, so the database remains very small in comparison to Lycos or InfoSeek. ALIWEB is supported by NEXOR, a U.K. service provider. ALIWEB seems to represent a brilliant idea that didn't really come to fruit. A search for "Japanese animation" produced 45 hits, with poor precision.

URL: http://web.nexor.co.uk/public/aliweb/aliweb.html

CUI W3 CATALOG ★

The Centre Universitaire d'Informatique (CUI), housed in Geneva, Switzerland, maintains this catalog. One of the most popular search engines on the Web, it differs from other search engines in that it doesn't employ a spider. Instead, the search software consults a number of manually maintained lists, including NCSA's What's New, the Virtual Library, ALIWEB, the Internet Services List, and several others. Currently, the CUI W3 catalog contains 12,350 entries, which are generally of high quality but are hard to discover by searching methods. A search for "Japanese animation" produced no hits.

URL: http://cuiwww.unige.ch/

continued...

continued...

INFOSEEK ★ ★ ★ ★

By far the most precise search engine on the Web, this commercial service sets the standard. A Web-wandering spider is combined with manual document indexing, producing a very high quality database of 400,000 documents. (Note that recall may be higher with Open Text, thanks to its larger database.) Typically, an InfoSeek search generates a list of documents with far fewer false drops than competing search engines; included are two or three lines of sample text and a clickable URL. You can search for free, but full access to all of InfoSeek's data—including an index of computer publications and Usenet postings—requires payment of a monthly fee. A search for "Japanese animation" produced the maximum number of retrieved documents (100), with good precision.

URL: http://www2.infoseek.com/

INKTOMI ★ ★ ★

The newest search engine on the Web, Inktomi is the creation of University of California, Berkeley graduate student Paul Gauthier and Professor Eric Brewer. Inktomi is part of a Berkeley experiment to create scalable (expandable) computer systems using low-cost workstations and PCs; Inktomi's design enables the database to be expanded indefinitely without loss of retrieval speed. Currently indexing 1.3 million documents, Inktomi has the largest database of any of the Web's current services—and the search engine indexes the full text of each document. This translates into high-recall retrieval lists, but the service is somewhat handicapped by the simplicity of the search engine; many of the complex searches described in Chapter 8 aren't possible with Inktomi. The name? Inktomi is the name of a mythological spider

continued...

continued...

among the Plains Indians, a trickster figure who fights for the underdog and brings light to humanity. A search for "Japanese animation" produced 3514 hits—the best of any of the Web's search engines.

URL: http://inktomi.berkeley.edu/

JUMPSTATION ★

Maintained by Jonathan Fletcher, a systems programmer at Stirling University in Scotland, the JumpStation database is small by comparison to Lycos: just over 275,000 entries. Like WebCrawler, JumpStation's spider indexes all the words in the documents it finds, so it's a good choice if you're looking for words that might be buried deeply in a document (and not mentioned in the title or opening paragraph). A search for "Japanese animation" produced no hits.

URL: http://www.stir.ac.uk/jsbin/jsii/

LYCOS ★ ★ ★

Currently indexing more than five million unique URLs and approximately 1.8 million documents, Lycos has one of the Web's larger databases. Late at night, the Lycos search engine prowls the Web, hunting down new Web, FTP, and Gopher documents—at last count, about 5000 new documents per day, on average. Lycos is sometimes difficult to access during peak usage times. Lycos does not index the entire document text; instead, it indexes title words, the words found in the first few lines of text, and the most frequently occurring words in the rest of the document. Even so, Lycos searches are fairly low in precision, and may fail to retrieve relevant documents (low recall). The result of a Lycos search is a list of documents containing the key words,

continued...

continued...

ranked by relevance (1000 is the highest score, and indicates a likely "hit"). To help you judge the relevance of the retrieved documents, the list includes the first few lines of text from the document. A search for "Japanese animation" produced a list of 86 hits, with fair precision.

URL: http://www.lycos.com

NIKOS ★

Formerly known as Zorbamatic, Nikos—short for New Internet Knowledge System—indexes about 100,000 documents. Nikos is jointly funded by Rockwell Network Systems and California State Polytechnic University, San Luis Obispo. The result of a Nikos search is a list of hyperlinks sorted by relevance, with no additional information. In general, overall relevance and recall are poor. A search for "Japanese animation" produced 12 documents, with poor precision.

URL: http://www.rns.com/cgi-bin/nomad

OPEN TEXT ★ ★ ★ ★

Based on a spider, Open Text's search engine uses the very fast search engine developed by Open Text Corporation, a Canadian firm. Unlike most of the Web's search engines, Open Text indexes the entire text of the documents retrieved by its spiders, currently some 1 million in number. This ensures that your search will retrieve documents in which your key words aren't among the most frequently occurring words in the document, but it also means that the retrieval list will have low precision. The result of an Open Text search is a list of documents ranked numerically by relevance; you'll see the first few lines of text to help you judge the relevance for yourself. A unique feature: For each retrieved item, you

continued...

continued...

can choose to visit the page, see a list of the lines on the page containing matches to your key words, or search for similar pages. A search for "Japanese animation" produced an amazing 1045 hits (using the "All of these words" setting), amply testifying to this service's high recall capabilities.

URL: http://www.open text.com:8080

WANDEX ★

Wandex currently lists 29,000 Web documents from more than 12,000 sites and more than 6000 home pages. The database is too small to prove of much value, but you might want to try Wandex if you haven't found what you're looking for elsewhere. A search for "Japanese animation" produced only two hits.

URL: http://wandex.netgen.com/cgi/wandex

WEBCRAWLER ★ ★ ★

A Web search engine that got its start at the University of Washington, WebCrawler is currently managed by America Online. Unlike most Web search engines, WebCrawler's spider retrieves the entire text of the documents it finds—but this comes at a cost. To avoid consuming too many Internet resources, WebCrawler is programmed to crawl at a particularly slow pace. WebCrawler includes 1.8 million URLs in its database, but has only fully indexed about 190,000 documents. The result of a WebCrawler search is a list of URLs ranked by relevance (1,000 is the highest score, and indicates a likely "hit"). WebCrawler is fast, but you'll find that most of the retrieved documents are false drops. A search for "Japanese animation" produced 253 hits, with fair precision.

URL: http://webcrawler.com/

continued...

continued...

WORLD WIDE WEB WORM (WWWW) ★ ★

The creation of University of Colorado computer scientist Oliver McBryan, the World Wide Web Worm is another search engine with its own unique features. WWWW's spider roams the Web in search of new URLs, including graphics, video, and audio files. As of this writing, the spider had returned over 3,000,000 URLs. A drawback: WWWW searches only the text found in document titles and hyperlinks; precision and recall are both very poor. A search for "Japanese animation" produced 50 hits, with poor precision.

URL: http://www.cs.colorado.edu/home/mcbryan/WWWW.html

Unified Search Interfaces

Among the most popular search services on the Web are unified search interfaces, which provide access to several search engines at once. They do so in two different ways:

- Some unified search interfaces provide a list of search engines. They also provide text boxes that enable you to type key words, and initiate the search.

- Other unified search interfaces provide a single search box, and send the key words to several search engines at once.

These pages are among the most popular search services on the Web.

KEY TERM

unified search interface
A Web page that enables you to search more than one Web page at a time.

SEARCH TIP

Should you use a unified search interface? If you want to do a quick, approximate search, by all means give one of these services a try. To perform a high-quality deep search, however, you'll need to go to the search engines themselves. Most of the unified search interfaces do not permit you to take advantage of the advanced search features of the Web's search engines. You need these advanced features to perform a high-quality deep search.

RATINGS OF UNIFIED SEARCH INTERFACES

These services provide access to more than one search engine. You can try your search in several of them, increasing your chance of finding something useful.

ALL-IN-ONE SEARCH LIST ★ ★

This unified search engine interface provides access to dozens of search services in the following categories: World Wide Web, General Internet, Specialized Interest, Software, People, News/Weather, Publications/Literature, Technical Reports, Documentation, Desk Reference, Other Interesting Searches/Services. When you select one of these categories, you see a list of search services, with a text box and search button for each. Coverage is very comprehensive. Like other unified search engine interfaces, All-in-One doesn't enable you to take full advantage of the special search commands each service offers. The page is difficult to access uring peak usage hours

URL: http://www.albany.net/~wcross/all1srch.html

E-Z FIND ★ ★ ★

Another unified search interface that enables you to type key word just once. You search just one service at a time. A plus: You can choose between default OR or AND searching,

continued...

continued...

and you can switch case sensitivity on and off.

URL: http://www.theriver.com/TheRiver/Explore/ezfind.html

INTERNET SLEUTH ★ ★ ★ ★

Here's a unified search interface that's got it right. There are over 750 searchable databases included here; an awesome list. For each, there's a text box. The databases are organized by topic (such as Government and Reference), and there are links to popular search engines

URL: http://www.intbc.com/sleuth/

SAVVYSEARCH ★ ★ ★

Why not search all the Web's search engines with just one query? That's the idea behind SavvySearch. You type one or more key words in the search box, and select the categories you want to search (WWW Resources, Software, People, Reference, Commercial, Academic, Technical Reports, Images, News, and Entertainment. It's a great idea, but the implementation isn't so great–the service is frequently busy, and the search engine doesn't allow you to customize your search in any way. The results, presented as a list of URLs, show very poor recall

URL: http://www.theriver.com/TheRiver/Explore/ezfind.html

FIND-IT! ★

Here's a unified search service that, like the W3 Search Engines page, provides you with a list of search services, each with a search text box. The coverage isn't nearly as comprehensive as Internet Sleuth

URL: http://www.cam.org/~psarena/find-it.html

continued...

continued...

W3 SEARCH ENGINES ★ ★

This page doesn't provide a unified search interface; instead, you see a series of search boxes for a series of search engines and other search services. It's useful enough, but just bear in mind that you won't be able to take advantage of advanced search commands—and you'll probably be disappointed with both the precision and the recall of the retrieval lists

URL: http://cuiwww.unige.ch/meta-index.html

ADDITIONAL INFORMATION RETRIEVAL RESOURCES ON THE INTERNET

When you're searching for Web documents, you'll spend most of your time using the tools already surveyed in this chapter—starting points, subject trees, distributed subject trees, trailblazer pages, and search engines. But there are many additional tools you can use to retrieve information while using the Web. Here's a brief overview of the many search services that are covered in Chapters 15 through 24 of this book:

- **Reference.** Search dictionaries, an on-line thesaurus, geographic databases, zip code and area code databases, and much more. Reference services are discussed in Chapter 15 and 16.

- **Current News and Weather.** Search the full text of major newspapers and receive up-to-date weather maps. Current news and weather services are discussed in Chapter 17.

- **Government Information.** Search for legislative information, Congressional email addresses, government publications, and more. See Chapter 18.

- **Stocks and Investments.** Search for up-to-the-minute stock quotes, company information, business publications, and more. See Chapter 19.

- **Periodicals.** Search the full text of numerous published and online magazines, newspapers, electronic books, government publications, technical reports, and technical manuals. For more information, see Chapter 20.

- **Library Card Catalogs.** You can browse the on-line card catalogs of the world's finest research libraries. Find out how in Chapter 21.

- **Software.** Thousands of freeware, shareware, and commercial demo programs are available in public FTP file archives. These tools enable you to find and download them. Search services for software are covered in Chapter 22.

- **People.** Use these services to search for Net-connected individuals. Search services for locating people are discussed in Chapter 23.

- **Jobs.** Yes, there are plenty of employment opportunities on the Web. Find out more in Chapter 24.

FROM HERE

You're just about ready to try your first search. Before you do, though, take a few minutes to organize your browser so that you can store the documents you discover. You'll find complete information, including full coverage of Netscape's SmartMarks utility, in the following chapter.

C H A P T E R   3

PREPARING YOUR BROWSER

Chances are you really like your browser program, whether it's Netscape Navigator, NCSA Mosaic, Internet Explorer, or some other. Your browser opens the door to the Web. But did you know that almost all browsers fall down seriously in one area? Very few browsers provide the convenient tools you need to store and organize a *hotlist* of Web sites (also called "favorites" or "bookmarks"). To be sure, you've probably stored a few hotlist items, perhaps without difficulty. As a serious Web searcher, though, you're going to store and organize dozens or even hundreds of Web sites. Frankly, most browsers aren't up to the task.

Because most browsers can't handle lengthy, well-structured hotlists, at least not conveniently, several *hotlist managers* have appeared, including Netscape's SmartMarks program. For serious searching, you may wish to consider using one of these. Even if your browser offers good hotlist management, you may still want to obtain a hotlist manager to take full advantage of its advanced features, such as automatic updating of saved searches. (You'll learn more about this very nice feature later in this chapter.)

By introducing hotlist management tools, this chapter completes the presentation of Step One of your Web search strategy—understanding the tools you're using. In the previous chapter, you learned what's out there in terms of information-acquisition tools. In this chapter, you'll learn why good hotlist management is needed, and how to store and organize the information you retrieve. You'll also read about hotlist managers, enabling you to decide whether you should obtain one before you start searching. Once you've completed this chapter, it's time to start searching by using the quick, initial search technique presented in Chapter 4.

hotlist
In a Web browser, a list of favorite sites that you've stored so that you can return to them easily.
KEY TERM

hotlist manager
An add-on program that enhances your ability to store and organize hotlist items.
KEY TERM

WHAT TO LOOK FOR IN A HOTLIST MANAGER

Whether a hotlist manager is provided as part of a browser or as a stand-alone program, it should have the following features:

- **Organization by Submenu.** As you keep adding items to your hotlist, it grows unwieldy (see Figure 3.1). To combat this problem, you need to be able to define *submenus*—menus within menus. After you define submenus, your hotlist or bookmark menus contain *headers* instead of Web pages (see Figure 3.2); when you click one of the headers, you see the submenu. To get the most out of this feature, you need to devote some thought to organizing your submenus (see the sidebar).

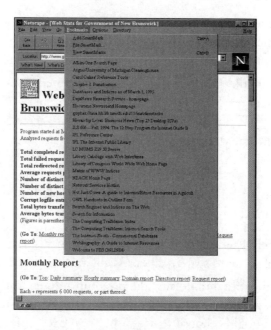

Figure 3.1 Hotlists quickly grow beyond their bounds on the hotlist (bookmark) menu.

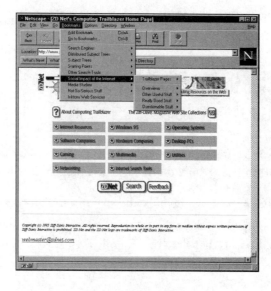

Figure 3.2 Submenus in a well-organized hotlist menu.

- **Automatic Sorting.** When you're looking at a lengthy list of Web document titles, you'll appreciate having them alphabetized. The better hotlist managers alphabetize your hotlist items automatically.

- **Searchable Hotlist.** By the time you've completed your first Deep Search (see Step Four), you'll have dozens—or maybe even hundreds—of hotlist items. You'll appreciate having a Search or Find command, which enables you to locate an item quickly within the hotlist.

A couple of advanced features, found currently only in Netscape's SmartMarks add-on, are:

- **Search Engine Interface.** This option displays a dialog box that enables you to search Yahoo, WebCrawler, Lycos, or InfoSeek.

- **Monitor.** In monitoring, the program automatically checks the site at intervals you specify. If the site has changed, you receive notification; you can also choose to view the new URLs, if any, that have been added to the page. Coupled with SmartMark's built-in search engine interface, the program's monitor can repeat a saved search and show you only the URLs that have appeared in the retrieval list since you last performed the search. A *very* nice feature!

RECOMMENDED SUBMENU ORGANIZATION

Here's a simple but effective plan for organizing the submenus in your hotlist or bookmarks menu. The plan has two objectives:

- Grouping search aids and making them accessible.
- Grouping the relevant Web sites you find and categorizing them so that they're available for use.

continued…

continued...

The following list recommends headers for the top-level of the menu, which you see when you first open the menu. The first five items provide access to the Web searching tools discussed in the previous chapter. When you click "Starting Points," for example, you see the starting points pages listed in Chapter 2. The headers "Subject Area #1" and "Subject Area #2" should be replaced by the topics you're researching, such as "Educational Administration" or "International Finance."

STARTING POINTS

SUBJECT TREES

DISTRIBUTED SUBJECT TREES

SEARCH ENGINES

OTHER SEARCH TOOLS

SUBJECT AREA #1

SUBJECT AREA #2

NOT-SO-SERIOUS STUFF

You can add more than one level of submenus. Within the first subject area, for example, you could add the following additional submenus:

SUBJECT AREA #1

Trailblazer Pages

Overviews

Really Good Stuff

Other Useful Stuff

Questionable Stuff

continued...

continued...

This organization helps you categorize retrieved Web sites by their value to your research. You could use a more substantive organization instead, such as the following:

SOUTH ASIA

Trailblazer Pages

Overviews

India

Pakistan

Sri Lanka

Bangladesh

Nepal

Bhutan

SEARCH TIP

Using Netscape? You can get a quick start on your hotlist by loading the one that's on the disk packaged with this book. On this disk, you'll find a Netscape-compatible bookmark file (called HOTLIST.HTM) that contains all the search aids discussed in the previous chapter. To open this file, insert this book's disk into your floppy disk drive. In Netscape, open the Bookmarks menu and choose **View Bookmarks**. From the File menu, choose **Import**. Use the dialog box to locate and highlight **HOTLIST.HTM**, and click **Open**.

At the low end of the spectrum, some browsers simply add your hotlist items to a hotlist menu. They provide no means to organize this list. What happens when you've added more than a dozen or two items? The menu becomes too long to be displayed, and you can't access them.

Other browsers provide the means to create submenus within the hotlist menu—and that's a good thing. As you'll learn in this chapter, you need to be able to categorize your hotlist items so that you can organize and retrieve them. If you've ever tried to use the submenu tools in Netscape Navigator 1.1, though, I'm sure you'll agree that they're less than convenient. Version 2.0's tools are improved, but you'll still appreciate using a tool such as SmartMarks.

USING SMARTMARKS

Netscape's SmartMarks add-on program greatly improves the bookmark-organizing capabilities of Netscape Navigator. But that's just the beginning. With SmartMarks, you can do the following:

- Organize your bookmarks into folders much more easily than with Netscape's default Bookmarks dialog box. You can title the folders as you please and can reorganize them using simple drag-and-drop techniques.

- Add annotations to your bookmarks.

- Set up automatic notification for changes to existing bookmarks, including changed or added links on a monitored page.

- Automatically receive bulletins regarding news or changes to a site from sites that support this feature.

- Search the Internet with the most popular search engines, using a single simple user interface.

- Save successful searches, and have them monitored so that you're automatically notified when new or changed links appear in the retrieval list.

Obtaining and Configuring SmartMarks

At this writing, SmartMarks was available as an add-on program for Netscape Navigator 1.2; future versions of Netscape may incorporate the utility. To obtain SmartMarks, check Netscape's home page at http://home.netscape.com/.

After you've installed SmartMarks, the program starts automatically when you start Netscape. You'll want to import your current bookmarks file. To do so, follow these instructions:

1. From the Tools menu, choose **Import**. You'll see the Select Import File dialog box.

2. Navigate to the location of your bookmark file (bookmark.htm). If you installed Netscape Navigator in its default location, the path will be **C:\NETSCAPE\BOOKMARK.HTM**.

3. Click **OK**. SmartMarks imports the existing bookmark file. Your bookmarks are named after you ("So-and-so's bookmarks").

Using the Enhanced Bookmarks Menu

After you install SmartMarks, the program replaces Netscape's Bookmarks menu with three SmartMarks options:

*   **Add SmartMarks.** Choose this command (or use the **Ctrl + A** shortcut) to create new bookmarks, just as you did prior to installing SmartMarks. You'll see your additions in the BookMarks menu. Later, you can store these bookmarks in folders.

*   **File SmartMarks.** Use this command to store bookmarks with optional information, such as comments. You can modify the bookmark name, enter a description, and add key words that make it easier to find the bookmark. You can also choose the folder to which you would like to add the bookmark.

*   **View SmartMarks.** This command displays the SmartMarks dialog box.

SEARCH TIP

When you're storing bookmarks with SmartMarks, your best bet is to choose the **File SmartMarks** option. You can give the bookmark a descriptive name, and you can also store the bookmark in the appropriate folder, saving you the trouble of doing this later.

Creating New Bookmark Folders

The first thing you'll need to do with SmartMarks is to create a new way of organizing your bookmark folders. As explained earlier in this chapter, you need to do this in order to store all the documents you'll discover while searching the Web. You'll create several new folders as you do this.

To create a new folder, click the **New Folder** tool on the toolbar. You'll see the Smart Folder Assistant (Figure 3.3). This assistant guides you through the process of creating your new folder. You give it a name, and optionally a description. You can then type key words, if you wish, that will enable you to find the folder you've just created.

Figure 3.3 Smart Folder Assistant.

Navigating the Folder Tree

The folder tree that you see in the SmartMarks dialog box (Figure 3.4) is identical to the folder trees you see in Windows Explorer. To view the bookmarks stored in a folder, just highlight the folder.

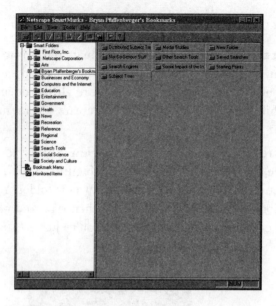

Figure 3.4 Add SmarkMarks dialog box.

A plus mark indicates that a folder has subfolders. To view the subfolder names, click the plus sign.

Using the Add SmartMarks Dialog Box

The best way to add new bookmarks to your SmartMarks menus is to use the **File SmartMarks** command, one of the three new commands you'll find on the SmartMarks menu. After choosing this command, you see the Add SmartMarks dialog box, shown in Figure 3.4.

In the Add SmartMarks dialog box, you have the following options:

- In the Document Title area, SmartMarks shows the document's current name. If this isn't descriptive of the document's title, change it.

- In the Description area, you can type descriptive text if you wish.

- In the File Into Folder area, you can select the folder into which you'd like to file your new bookmark.

- At the bottom of the dialog box, you see notification options. You can be notified when the page changes, and you can also choose to be notified if the page contains added or changed links.

Choosing Updating Options

One of the most innovative characteristics of SmartMarks is the program's ability to update sites. You'll receive notification if the site or its links change.

Notification isn't automatic—you have to choose it when you create the SmartMark, as described above. If you didn't choose notification when you created a bookmark, you can do so by highlighting the bookmark and clicking the **Monitor Changes** tool; you'll see the Monitor Page dialog box, which enables you to choose notification when the page changes (the default choice) and notification when links are changed or added. Click **OK** to confirm your notification choices.

Once you've selected some items for monitoring, you can choose how SmartMarks updates the monitored items. By default, the program updates manually—you must select the item and click the **Update** tool. If you wish, you can instruct SmartMarks to update the items at specified intervals. To change the updating method, choose **Preferences** from the Tools menu. When the Preferences dialog box appears, click the **Internet** tab. Choose a monitoring option in the Update Monitored Items area. You can choose to update the monitored sites at program start-up, at intervals you specify, or manually (the default). To update items manually, choose **Refresh** from the Tools menu.

SEARCH TIP

Unless you have a fast Internet connection, the manual updating method is best. Updating all your monitored links takes time with a slow 14.4 Kbps connection.

Searching the Web with SmartMarks

One of the best features of SmartMarks is the program's built-in search utility, which enables you to search the Web using Lycos, InfoSeek,

WebCrawler, and Yahoo. The use of this SmartMarks feature is discussed in Chapter 7.

FROM HERE

Once you've set up your browser, you're ready to try some searches. If you're looking for specific information, check out the next chapter, "Locating Information: The Quick, Pinpointed Search." You'll learn how to find what you're looking for with a simple search of the Web's most powerful search engines.

If you're looking for a few good sources in an area, check out Chapter 5, "Browsing for Information: Subject Trees."

USING WINDOWS 3.1? TRY WEBODEX ORGANIZER

Webodex Organizer is a hotlist manager marketed by Novaweb Inc. (http://novaweb.com/webodex/). Compatible with most current browsers, Webodex is preloaded with 150 "BEST SITES OF THE NET." The program enables you to store and organize your additional hotlist items with a easy-to-use Rolodex-like interface. If your running Windows 95, Netscape's SmartMarks utility provides the same functions. You can down SmartMarks for free from Netscape's home page.

CHAPTER 4

LOCATING INFORMATION: THE QUICK, PINPOINTED SEARCH

What are you looking for? For most people searching the Web, goals fall into three broad categories:

- **I'm after specific information—and that's all I'm interested in.** You don't want to build a huge bibliography. You just want to find something out. The *locating strategy* is for you. What's NASA's current plan for a manned Mars expedition? Where's the text of the Clinton administration's proposed changes to U.S. copyright law? How can I tell if my house is equipped with polybutylene pipes? Your best bet is to try a quick, pinpointed search, as described in this chapter.

- **I'd like to see some good stuff in a subject area.** You don't necessarily want to build a huge bibliography, but you'd like to see some good, useful documents in a given subject area. You're interested in the *sampling strategy*. What does the Web have to offer somebody who's interested in classical music? Home automation? Physical therapy? Your best bet is to browse a subject tree, as described in Chapter 5.

- **I want to find *everything* on the Web in my subject area.** This is serious stuff—you're a professional or an educator who focuses on a given subject, and you'd like to construct a first-class *collecting strategy*. You also want to keep it current. To accomplish these tasks, you'll need to harvest the full potential of the Web's search engines. You'll need to learn the secrets of *deep searching*. Get started in Chapter 7.

the locating strategy
In Web searching, a search strategy that places emphasis on finding a specific, useful piece of information. For this strategy, you need a quick, pinpointed search using a high-recall search engine.

KEY TERM

the sampling strategy
A search strategy that places emphasis on collecting a few sources of high quality. For this strategy, browse a subject tree and find a trailblazer page.

KEY TERM

the collecting strategy
A search strategy that seeks to discover and catalog every available Web document pertinent to a subject of professional interest. For this strategy, you'll need to master deep searching (see Chapter 7 and 8).

KEY TERM

deep searching
Performing a search using the tools of information retrieval professionals, such as Boolean operators, truncation, proximity operators, and more. These are described in Chapters 7 and 8.

KEY TERM

USING A SEARCH ENGINE: THE BASICS

No matter which search engine you choose, the overall process is the same. Here's an overview:

- **Understand the search engine's limitations.** Does it include Gopher, FTP, and Archie information, or just Web (http) documents?

Does it index document content, or just document titles and URL text? Understanding what's in the database will help you devise more effective search terms. For example, if you know that the database contains text from URLs, you can find sounds, graphics, and other multimedia resources by typing file extensions (such as AU, JPG, and MPEG).

- **Access the search engine.** Don't try to search during peak usage hours (12 to 3 PM Eastern time) unless you're patient enough to endure long waits.

- **Type one or more search words in the text box.** To avoid over-loading the search engine, start with a fairly specific list. Type the most important word first (some search engines give greater weight to the first word in the query). To look for documents discussing the red wines of Oregon, for example, type **wine oregon red**.

- **Choose search options, if any are available.** Some search engines let you search different parts of Web documents, such as titles, document content, or hyperlink text.

- **Click the "Start Search" or "Submit" button.** Clicking this button initiates the search.

- **View the list of retrieved documents.** Most search engines rank the search results numerically, with the first document having the highest score (1,000 with most search engines, although some use 100 and others use higher scores). If you find a document that looks like it's relevant, just click the cited hyperlink.

- **Refine and repeat the search, if necessary.** Common problems include too many documents or too few. See "Search Engine Tips and Hints," later in this chapter, for guidelines.

FINDING THE RIGHT KEY WORDS

To search effectively, you need one or more search words, called *key words*. Choosing the right key word or words helps to assure good results. So what's a good key word?

key word

KEY TERM   A word that describes the search subject in which you're interested. The search engine searches its database, retrieving only those documents that contain the key word you supplied.

Tips for finding the right key words for a focused search:

- **If possible, use a phrase.** If you can think of a phrase that describes your search topic, such as "landscape photography," "space shuttle," "Ford Contour," or "product liability," then begin your search by typing this phrase. Restrict the search so that the search engine retrieves only those documents that contain this phrase *as a phrase*, that is, with the two words next to each other. With most search engines, you must enclose the phrase in quotation marks so that the search engine retrieves only those records in which the words occur as a phrase.

- **Think of one to three words that *unambiguously* describe the subject.** Suppose you're interested in the outstanding white wines of southern Australia—the Coonawarra district in particular. Try searching with "Coonawarra wine white." If this search doesn't retrieve anything, you can try using slightly more general words (such as "Australia wine white").

- **Don't forget to try searching with synonyms.** Many documents of interest might be retrieved by using alternate key words. In addition to "white wine Coonawarra," try searching with "south Australia chardonnay."

SEARCH ENGINE TIPS AND HINTS

No matter which search engine you're using, you'll find the following tips will help you search more effectively:

- **Check your spelling.** Before pressing **Enter** or clicking the **Start Search** button (or its equivalent), make sure you have typed the search terms correctly. If you find a spelling mistake, correct it before initiating the search.

- **Don't use commonly occurring articles or Web terms.** Most search engines have a *kill list* that automatically deletes words such as "and," "the," and "http," but including such words could generate an error message, forcing you to repeat the search.

- **Don't type plurals.** Some search engines automatically include the plural form in your search, while others search with truncation—which means that they'll find the plural forms automatically. Type the singular form of all search words.

SEARCHING OPEN TEXT

For a quick, pinpointed search, you need a search engine with the following characteristics:

- **A large database.** You're shooting for high recall. Use a search engine with a database of at least one million Web documents.

- **Full-text indexing.** The information you want might be buried somewhere in the midst of a document—or at the end. Some search engines index only the first few lines of text. Open Text and WebCrawler index the full text of the document.

The search engine that best combines these two characteristics, at least at this writing, is Open Text—and that's where you should start your quick, pinpointed search.

Accessing Open Text

To access Open Text, use the following URL:

```
http://www.opentext.com:8080/omw/f-omw.html
```

You'll see Open Text's Simple Search page, shown in Figure 4.1.

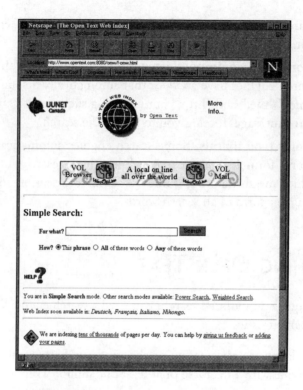

Figure 4.1 Open Text's Simple Search page
(http:\\www.opentext.com:8080\omw\f-omw.html).

SEARCH TIP

You'll learn more about Open Text's many search options in Chapter 9, but for now there's something important to notice: the three options below the search box. You can search for **This phrase**, **All of these words**, or **Any of these words**. Which is the best one to choose?

- This phrase. If you're searching for words that always or almost always occur in a phrase, such as "Sri Lanka," "home theater," or "hot tub," use this option. You'll get a focused list of retrieved documents with high precision.

- All of these words. If you're searching for two or more key words and they don't occur in a phrase, click this option. For example, suppose you're interested in California landscape photography. If you type these three words and select this option, Open Text won't retrieve the document unless the document contains all of these words. Note: If the key words you're using are not a phrase, be sure to click this option.

- Any of these words. This isn't a very good choice unless you retrieved hardly anything with the first two settings. This search greatly increases the number of documents you retrieve. It does so because it lists any document that contains any of the key words. For example, consider a search for "California or landscape or photography." This search will retrieve any document that mentions "California," "landscape," or "photography." Most of the documents will be wildly irrelevant.

Typing the Key Words

With Open Text's Simple Search page on-screen, you're ready to type your search words. Just which options you choose depends on which key words you've chosen.

- **Did you type a phrase?** If so, you can search with the default option—**This phrase**. Open Text will retrieve only those documents in which your key words occur as a phrase.

- Did you type two or more key words that aren't a phrase? If so, be sure to click the All of these words option. If you click **Any of these words**, you'll get a lot of false drops.

Suppose you're interested in purchasing a home theater, but you don't know the first thing about it. You're looking for a good introduction to the subject. Try searching for "home theater," which is a phrase.

To initiate your search, click the **Search** button. Open Text searches its database and displays the first 10 results in a new Web page (Figure 4.2).

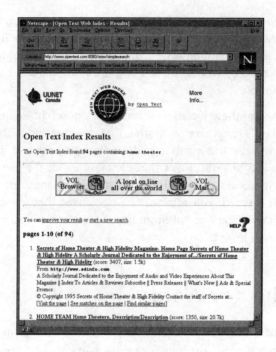

Figure 4.2 Results of an Open Text search.

Scanning the Retrieved Documents

Did your search work? Here's how to tell:

- **How many documents were retrieved?** A well-focused search produces a retrieval set that's small enough for you to scan comfortably. Most people have the patience to look at five or ten documents; very few have the patience to look at one hundred. In general, if your search retrieved about 20 documents or fewer, you're doing pretty well. If the search retrieved more or many more, you may wish to try a more focused search, as described in the next section. But scan the first few documents first.

- **Is there anything pertinent to your search subject?** Most search engines place the documents most pertinent to your key words near the top of the list, so take a look at the first few documents. In this search, there are several excellent introductions to home theater systems listed. Take a look—if one of them's OK, your search is done (even though the search retrieved too many documents). If your search retrieved nothing of interest, see "What To Do If the Search Turned Up Nothing," later in this chapter.

WHAT TO DO IF THE SEARCH TURNED UP TOO MANY DOCUMENTS

With most searches, you'll find that the search retrieves more documents than you've time to review. The Open Text search for "home theater," for example, retrieved 94 documents—too many to download and read. To find something useful, you'll need to refine and focus your search. I'd like to obtain an overview document (see Chapter 3) that describes and introduces home theater systems. So let's try focusing the search so that it retrieves an overview document.

Open Text provides an easy way to narrow the scope of your search. On the Open Text Index Results page (see Figure 4.2), click **improve your result**. You'll see the Refine your result page (Figure 4.3), which enables you to type an additional key word. If you type **description** in the second Search For box and click **Search**, you'll see the retrieval list shown in Figure 4.4. Right at the top is a *hit*. It's a nontechnical, plain-English description of a home theater system—a great place to start.

hit
A document that is relevant to your search interests.

KEY TERM

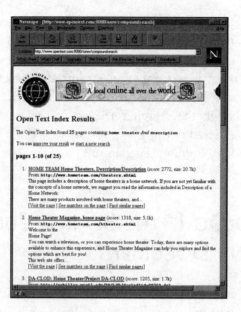

Figure 4.3 Open Text Index Results page.

Figure 4.4 Focused retrieval list

The method just described is only one of several ways you can narrow a search. You'll learn about more of them in Chapter 6.

WHAT TO DO IF THE SEARCH TURNED UP NOTHING

The usual problem with searches these days is too many documents. After all, the Web now contains some 7 million documents! Still, you may find that your search retrieves no documents at all, or a few documents that turn out to be irrelevant.

If your search turned up nothing useful, consider the following:

- **Check your spelling.** You may have typed one or more words incorrectly. To see what you typed in the search text box, click the **Back** button on your browser.

- **Try alternative key words.** If you search for "social *impact* of the Internet," you'll find some great documents—but you can find more by searching for the "social *implications* of the Internet." You'll find even more if you substitute "Web" for "Internet."

- **If your key words aren't a phrase, don't use the phrase search setting.** In Open Text, the phrase setting is the default. But a search for "California landscape photography" produces zero hits (at this writing). However, a search using the **All of these words** option found 202 documents—and there are several dead-on hits (including an on-line exhibition of Ansel Adam's prints).

- **Try searching again with fewer search terms.** A search for "black and white laser printer" may produce poor results, since very few authors use the term "black and white" when referring to a laser printer's monochrome output. Try searching for "laser printer" instead.

PERFORMING QUICK INITIAL SEARCHES WITH OTHER SEARCH ENGINES

Open Text is a great place to start your quick initial search. But you should try other search engines, too. Each has its own strengths and weaknesses, and each has a chance of delivering just what you're looking for.

With each of these search engines, you can perform a simple, quick search just by typing the key words in the text box and clicking **Search**. To perform a phrase search in these search engines, do the following:

- **InfoSeek.** Type double quotation marks around your search phrase (**"home theater"**).

- **Lycos.** Phrase searches aren't currently possible with Lycos. However, Lycos gives a higher rank to documents in which your key words occur close together.

FROM HERE

Many people search the Web to get information fast, and this chapter has described the best technique for doing so. If you'd like to compile a list of good sources in an area in which you're interested, your best bet is to try a subject tree, as described in the following chapter, and trailblazer pages, as described in Chapter 6. And if you're bent on producing a *webliography*—a comprehensive bibliography of all the available sources on the Web in your area of interest—you'll need to learn the principles of deep searching, as explained in Chapters 7 and 8.

C H A P T E R 5

BROWSING FOR INFORMATION: SUBJECT TREES

Looking for a few good documents pertaining to your subject of interest? If so, your strategy is the *sampling strategy* introduced in the previous chapter—a strategy in which you hope to come up with a half dozen or so high-quality documents. To get started, you should focus on two resources:

- **Subject Trees**, which aim for comprehensiveness and cover a wide range of subject areas. In this chapter, you'll learn how to browse for useful Web sites using the three best subject trees: Yahoo, Magellan, and TradeWave Galaxy.

- **Trailblazer Pages**, which gather useful hyperlinks in a well-focused subject area. Often the individuals who create trailblazer pages are extremely knowledgeable in the subject, and they may have done an outstanding job of selecting the best available resources. You'll learn how to find trailblazer pages in the next chapter.

The Web's subject trees catalog only a small proportion of the Web's millions of documents. Still, you're in luck if the subject tree contains documents in the subject of your interest. Subject trees are selective, so you're assured that the documents you're accessing are among the most popular, well-developed, and stable in their respective areas. A new trend: Magellan includes ratings, using a four-star system similar to that used to rate movies in newspapers and magazines.

This chapter begins by describing the general process of using subject trees; it continues by examining Yahoo, Magellan, and TradeWave Galaxy in more detail.

USING A SUBJECT TREE

To use any of the subject trees discussed in this chapter, follow these steps:

1. Access the subject tree by typing its URL. You'll see the subject tree's welcome page, which includes its *top-level directory*. This directory lists the subject tree's main subject headings. Figure 5.1 shows the top-level directory of Yahoo.

top-level directory
In a subject tree, the page that lists the service's main subject headings.

KEY TERM

2. Click the subject heading that best describes your area of interest. You will probably see a page containing more subject headings. If so, keep clicking the heading that best describes your area of interest. Eventually you'll reach a page that lists Web documents (see Figure 5.2).

3. If you find a hyperlink to an interesting Web document, just click it and have a look. To return to the subject tree, use your browser's **Back** button.

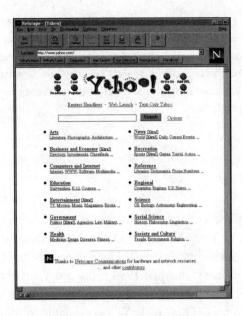

Figure 5.1 Top-level directory (Yahoo).

Figure 5.2 Subject tree page containing links to Web documents (Yahoo).

Can't find anything by browsing in the subject tree? Try the subject tree's search engine. Most subject trees enable you to search their catalogs by means of a key word search, similar to the key word searches you perform when you access a search engine (see Chapter 4). For more information on searching the subject trees discussed in this chapter, see the sections to follow.

SEARCH TIP

YAHOO

The Web can be a dangerous thing to play with when you're trying to get a doctorate, as Jerry Yang and David Filo would surely agree. You just might find yourself getting pulled away from the books and into full-time, big-league business. In April 1994, Filo and Yang, then Ph.D. candidates in Stanford's engineering school, developed Yahoo as a way of storing their favorite sites. They made Yahoo available to others simply as a courtesy. But Yahoo began to grow, both in size and popularity.

Yahoo's offbeat name, coupled with Filo and Yang's excellent sense of what's hot (and what's not), made it a hit among burgeoning numbers of Web users. Soon, Stanford's computers began to groan under the load. Netscape Communications Corp. gave Stanford a respite by providing a home for Yahoo, but Filo and Yang still faced the dilemma of updating Yahoo—a task that had grown beyond the capabilities of two people. So they started Yahoo, Inc., opened an office in Mountain View, and got some help. They're all working hard—on a typical weekday, they add as many as 850 sites.

Instead of charging for Yahoo access, Filo and Yang decided to seek advertisers—and as a glance at Yahoo reveals, the strategy's working. For now, Yahoo is thriving and growing. Currently listing more than 40,000 documents, Yahoo is accessed by an estimated 300,000 individuals daily. And what about those doctorates? The Ph.D.s are on hold for now; both Filo and Yang have taken leaves of absence from their doctoral studies at Stanford.

Right now, Yahoo is the best subject tree on the Web: It's easy to use and it's packed with the information that Web users want. The future? Filo and Yang want Yahoo to remain the premier subject tree on the Web, and they're working hard to make sure that it does (in his brief on-screen bio, Filo says that he sleeps "every third night").

Since Yahoo's incorporation, users have seen a steady stream of innovations, beginning with Yahoo's cool new look. The big news at this book's writing is the integration of the OpenText search engine into Yahoo.

Accessing Yahoo

To access Yahoo, use the following URL:

```
http://www.yahoo.com
```

You'll see Yahoo's top-level directory (see Figure 5.1). Note that a few subject subheadings are listed under each of the top-level directories; if you wish, you can access one of these by clicking it.

YAHOO FEATURES

[Xtra!]	Click here to see Reuters news pertinent to this subject category.
Sunglasses	This symbol flags entries that Yahoo's authors judge to be among the best in the current subject category. Check here first!
New!	The entry was added within the last three days. If this tag appears next to a directory title, the directory contains items that were added within the last three days.
@	This heading appears more than once in the subject tree. If you click on this heading, Yahoo will display the primary category under which this heading is filed.
(6639)	A number such as this one represents the number of entries categorized beneath this subject heading.

It's easy to navigate within Yahoo. At the top of each Yahoo screen, you'll see a row of buttons (Write Us, Add URL, Search, and Info). To return to the top-level directory, just click **Yahoo**!

Cool Yahoo Features

On Yahoo's top-level page, you'll see a number of buttons that access nifty Yahoo features:

- **New.** Click here to see "What's New on Yahoo."
- **Cool.** Click here to go directly to the Entertainment: Cool Links page.
- **Headlines.** The latest Reuters news stories (Top Stories, Business, International, Sports, Entertainment, and Politics), updated several times per day.
- **Popular.** The most popular subject categories in Yahoo.

Navigating Yahoo

As you move your way down into a directory, keep your eye on the pages' titles. For example, click **Entertainment**. You'll see the Entertainment page, and the page's title says—you guessed it:

`Entertainment`

Now select **Comics**. The next page's title says:

`Entertainment: Comics`

Note that the previous page, "Entertainment," is now a hyperlink. You can click this word to go back up in the subject tree.

If you click **Cartoonists** on the Comics page, you see the Cartoonists page, which has the following title (see Figure 5.3):

`Entertainment:Comics:Cartoonists`

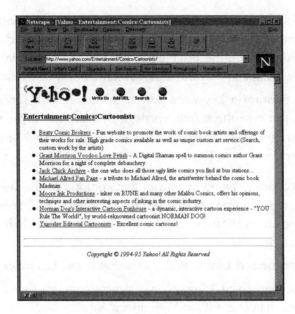

Figure 5.3 Cartoonists page (Yahoo).

Note that both "Entertainment" and "Comics" are hyperlinks now. You can go back up one level or two levels in the subject tree, if you wish.

Searching Yahoo

Among Yahoo's many excellent features is a search engine that enables you to perform key-word searches on Yahoo's entries. Open Text, the company that makes the Open Text search engine available (see Chapter 9), provides the search software—and it's excellent. In fact, Open Text searching is so beautifully integrated with Yahoo that this site may provide all the search support you'll ever need—an excellent subject tree that's intelligently integrated with an equally excellent search engine.

SEARCH TIP

Looking for a way to carry out a unified search, one that covers both a search engine's indexed sites and more than a million unindexed Web documents? Just perform a search with Yahoo. The Open Text search engine searches the Open Text database of more than one million Web sites as well as sites that have been indexed in Yahoo.

NOTE: The description of Yahoo's search engine that follows is based on the demo version of the Open Text/Yahoo integrated service (http://demo.yahoo.com); the production version had not been released at this book's writing and may differ somewhat from what's described here.

To perform a key-word search in Yahoo with Open Text's search engine, just type the search words in the text box at the top of the category list, and click **Search**. You'll see a page sorted into the following three sections:

- **Categories.** Yahoo categories that conform to the key word or words you typed. For example, if you type "sailing," you'll see a list containing "Recreation:Sports:Sailing," "Regional:Countries:Italy:Sports:Sailing," and more.

- **Categorized Links.** Web pages that have been indexed in Yahoo.

- **Uncategorized Links.** Links drawn from an Open Text search of more than one million Web documents.

To perform an advanced search, click the **Options** button that you'll find next to the search text box. Chapters 7 and 8 discuss advanced search options in more detail; for now, here's a list of these options:

- **Case matching.** to perform a case-sensitive search, click the check box next to "Capital letters in your words must be matched exactly."

- **Field matching.** "By default, the Open Text search engine matches words in the Title and Comments sections of Yahoo records. You can also match words in the URL.

- **Boolean operators.** You can choose a default OR operator ("at least one of the words"), a default AND operator ("all words"), or a phrase search ("all words as a single phrase").

- **Truncation.** You can perform a substring match ("words can be found within other words or as complete words") or an exact match ("words can be found ONLY as complete words").

Table 5.1 Yahoo Subject Classifications

Arts
Literature, Photography, Architecture

Business and Economy [Xtra!]
Directory, Investments, Classifieds

Computers and Internet
Internet, WWW, Software, Multimedia

Education
Universities, K-12, Courses

Entertainment [Xtra!]
TV, Movies, Music, Magazines, Books

Government
Politics [Xtra!], Agencies, Law Military

Health
Medicine, Drugs, Diseases, Fitness

News [Xtra!]
World [Xtra!], Daily, Current Events

Recreation
Sports [Xtra!], Games, Travel, Autos

Reference
Libraries, Dictionaries, Phone Numbers

Regional
Countries, Regions, U.S. States

Science
CS, Biology, Astronomy, Engineering

Social Science
History, Philosophy, Linguistics

Society and Culture
People, Environment, Religion

MAGELLAN

Magellan—is a subject tree with a difference. Approximately 30,000 sites are rated using a four-star system (see Figure 5.4); an additional 500,000 sites can be searched but are not yet rated. Included are Gopher, Telnet, and FTP sites as well as Web pages. When you click one of the reviewed items, you see a page containing more information about the site, including names, addresses, and telephone numbers (Figure 5.5). Nicely integrated with a powerful search engine, Magellan is a good choice if you're looking for a few high-quality sites.

Figure 5.4 Magellan ratings.

The Magellan subject tree differs from other subject trees in one other respect. Instead of listing hyperlinks using many levels of nested subdirectories, the way Yahoo does, Magellan is fully integrated with a search engine—the lists of sites you see are the results of searches. For the

McKinley group who publishes Magellan, the advantage here is less work: There are no subdirectory pages to maintain.

Figure 5.5 Information page for a rated site.

Browsing Magellan

To access Magellan, use the following URL:

```
http://mckinley.netcom.com/
```

You'll see the top-level Magellan page, shown in Figure 5.6.

As you can see, Magellan's default interface is a search engine, which is covered later in this section. To browse Magellan's subject tree, click **Browse Catagories**. You'll see the categories page, shown in Figure 5.7.

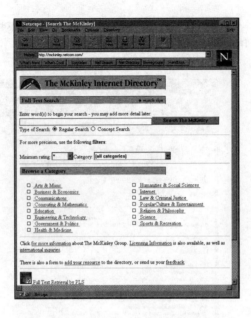

Figure 5.6 Top-level Magellan page.

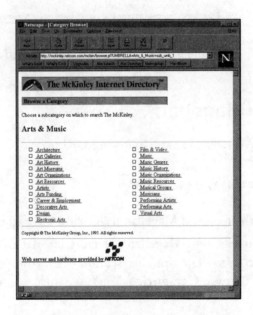

Figure 5.7 Magellan Categories page.

To browse for sites of interest within Magellan, click one of the top-level subject headings (Table 5.2). You'll see a subcategory page such as the one shown in Figure 5.8. These names aren't the titles of subdirectories. On the contrary, they're key words; clicking one of them initiates a key word search of Magellan's reviewed sites.

Figure 5.8 Subcategory page (Magellan).

Table 5.2 Magellan Subject Headings

Arts & Music

Business & Economics

Communications

Computing & Mathematics

Education

Engineering & Technology

continued...

continued...

Government & Politics

Health & Medicine

Humanities & Social Sciences

Internet

Law & Criminal Justice

Popular Culture & Entertainment

Religion & Philosophy

Science

Sports & Recreation

Focusing Your Search

There's only one problem with Magellan's obligatory searches: They may return more site reviews than you've time to scan. If so, you'll need to focus your search by using additional key words. To do so, simply scroll to the top of the list of Web sites and type one or more additional words in the text box. Click **Focus Search** to narrow the retrieval list down to just those documents containing the word(s) you specify.

Searching Magellan's Unrated Sites

If you couldn't find anything of interest among the rated sites, you can try searching Magellan's huge database of unrated sites. Currently indexing some 500,000 sites, Magellan is searched using the same procedures you'd use with a Web search engine such as OpenText or Lycos.

Since all the results you get from Magellan are the result of searches, you can view Magellan as a search engine rather than a subject tree—and you might as well. The top-level Magellan page includes a text box for searching. To access Magellan's, advanced search capabilities click the **Advanced Search** button. You'll learn more about advanced search techniques in Chapters 7 and 8 but for now, here are a couple of tips:

- **Searching for a phrase.** As noted in Chapter 4, you should perform a phrase search if your search topic is well described by a two-word phrase, such as "classic cars" or "country music." To search for a phrase with Magellan, you need to use the ADJ operator. This word instructs the search engine to retrieve only those documents in which the linked words appear next to each other. To search for "classic cars," type **classic ADJ cars**.

- **Using two or more key words.** If you're searching for two or more words that don't appear in a phrase, you need to use the AND operator (for example, "California AND wineries"). If you don't use the AND operator, Magellan will retrieve documents that contain one term but not the other, and you'll probably find that the retrieval list is too lengthy. You can use the AND article by typing two or more words seperated by AND, or you can just click the **AND** button.

- **Restricting the search by rating.** If you're looking for the best sites, select a minimum star rating in the Minimum rating box. Magellan will not retrieve sites ranked lower than the minimum rating you choose.

- **Restricting the search by subject.** To restrict the search to one of Magellan's top-level subject headings, choose a subject from this list box.

To initiate the search, click **Search the Magellan.**

TRADEWAVE GALAXY

Formerly known as EINet Galaxy, this subject tree has resurfaced with a new name—but the old qualities are still there. It's an extensive subject tree, indexing over 290,000 documents, and it's well integrated with a serviceable search engine. TradeWave Corporation, Galaxy's sponsor, devises custom Internet solutions (called Virtual Private Internets) for corporate customers; Galaxy is intended to serve as a demonstration of the company's net-building prowess. Pretty good demonstration, I'd say.

To access TradeWave Galaxy, use the following URL:

```
http://www.einet.net/
```

A unique feature of Galaxy is that Web sites are categorized by document type (Figure 5.9). This enables you to differentiate between "meaty" pages—Web documents that actually contain useful information—and the thousands of "fluff" pages, which contain little more than announcements or passing references to your topic of interest.

Figure 5.9 Retrieved links sorted by document type (Galaxy).

Under the subject heading "Information Retrieval," for example, you find items indexed under "Documents," "Articles," "Books," "Guides," "Announcements," "Product Descriptions," "Collections," "Discussion Groups," "Directories," and "Organizations." These classifications help you to find the type of material you're seeking. This is a feature that other Web subject trees would do well to emulate.

Browsing Galaxy

To browse the Galaxy subject tree, just click one of the top- or second-level categories, both of which are visible on Galaxy's welcome page

(Figure 5.10). You can go back to previous levels of the subject tree by clicking the subject name hyperlink at the top of the page. To return to the top of the tree, click the **Galaxy** hyperlink in the menu bar at the top of the page.

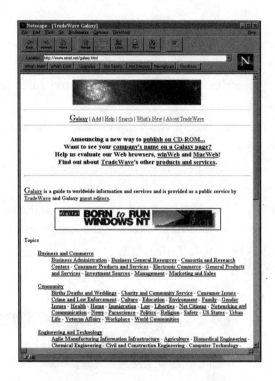

Figure 5.10 Galaxy's top-level page.

SEARCH TIP

Not sure where to find the page you're looking for? Click the **Search** button. When the Search page appears, click the **Galaxy Pages** option and type the word or words you're searching for. This option restricts the search to the titles of Galaxy pages. Click **Search** to initiate the search; you'll see a list of Galaxy pages that contain the words you've typed.

Searching Galaxy

You can also find information in TradeWave Galaxy by searching—and it's worth a look. To search Galaxy, click the **Search** button in Galaxy's menu bar. You'll see the search page shown in Figure 5.11. You can choose to search the following:

- **Galaxy Pages.** This button restricts the search to the titles of Galaxy pages.

- **Galaxy Entries.** Click here to search the titles of Galaxy indexed pages.

- **Gopher.** Click here if you would like to include the titles of Gopher Jewels documents in the retrieval list.

- **Hytelnet.** Click here if you would like to include HyTelnet documents in the retrieval list.

- **World Wide Web Text.** Click here to search the full text of Web listings in Galaxy (not the full text of the documents themselves).

- **World Wide Web Titles.** Click here to search the titles of Galaxy indexed pages (nearly 300,000).

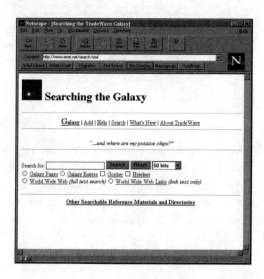

Figure 5.11 Searching Galaxy.

Using more than one key word? By default, Galaxy retrieves documents that contain any of the words you type—and that's not good for a focused retrieval list. To focus the search, use the AND operator (for example, "Japanese AND animation"). This operator restricts the search to documents that contain *all* of the words you typed. Note: You can't do a phrase search in Galaxy.

FROM HERE

If you're sampling the Web for a few good documents in your area of interest, you're not quite done: You should try to find a trailblazer page. For the lowdown, see the next chapter.

CHAPTER 6

BROWSING FOR INFORMATION: TRAILBLAZER PAGES

The Web is so huge that it's very difficult for anyone to keep up with the deluge of new documents. That's why subject trees such as Yahoo can't hope to fully index the Internet, unless their operating budgets suddenly ascend to Department of Defense levels. That's unlikely, so you can count on fractional coverage for the time being.

But there's hope. Recognizing the paucity of the Web's subject trees, hundreds of individuals are devoting their time to creating trailblazer pages in a variety of subject areas. So why not create a *distributed subject tree*? In a distributed subject tree, the subject tree's maintainers make no attempt to try to categorize the entire Web by themselves. Instead, they provide links to trailblazer pages, leaving the task of gathering and categorizing Web documents to the experts in specialized subject areas.

Sounds like a great idea, right? Unfortunately, it hasn't yet borne fruit in a big way. To be sure, there are a couple of distributed subject trees available right now, and they're covered in this chapter. But each of them lists only a small fraction of the total number of trailblazer pages on the Web. If you can use one of these services to discover a trailblazer page, you're in luck—but you may have to search for a page in your subject area.

WHAT'S SO GREAT ABOUT TRAILBLAZER PAGES?

A good trailblazer page provides useful information about a subject and collates the best of the Web's hyperlinks so that they're readily available for your use. If you find a really good trailblazer page your work is over, since the page will have gathered all the links that you'd otherwise have to discover for yourself.

A very good example: Dean Hughson's Divorce Page (http://www .primenet.com/~dean/; see Figure 6.1), which recently won the Point Survey's Top 5% of the Net award (and deservedly so). In this page, Dean summarizes a wealth of Web-based information of interest to anyone contemplating or going through a divorce—or trying to cope with the aftermath. Among the strengths of the site is a list of approximately 100 links related to divorce. Maybe you could assemble a better webliography of divorce-related information, but you'd be working for a long time.

USING INDEXED TRAILBLAZER PAGES

As mentioned previously, there's no single comprehensive database of all the Web's trailblazer pages. In fact, there's no single agreed-upon nomenclature for these pages: some people call them meta-pages, while others call them indices. I like to call them trailblazer pages, but don't bet that you'll run across that term elsewhere.

So how do you find trailblazer pages? You could use using a search engine such as Lycos or Open Text—and you may have to. But there's potentially an easier way: There are lists of trailblazer pages in four locations on the Web, including the Web's distributed subject trees:

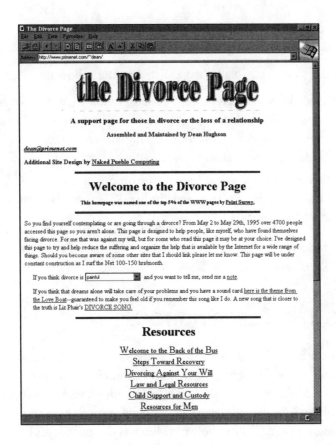

Figure 6.1 Divorce page.

Clearinghouse for Subject-Oriented Resource Guides (http://www.lib.umich.edu/chhome.html). This University of Michigan project seeks to establish guidelines for high-quality trailblazer pages, and currently indexes dozens of them. The emphasis is on academic subjects.

Virtual Library (http://www.w3.org/hypertext/DataSources/bySubject/Overview.html). A project of the World Wide Web Organization (W3O), the Virtual Library charted the way for distributed subject trees—but it's a bit long in the tooth. Although some new pages have been added in the past couple of years, the site is still very far short of its potential as a Grand Central Station for trailblazer pages. The emphasis is academic, with some notable exceptions—such as the Roadkill page.

You'll also find trailblazer pages listed in the following subject trees:

TradeWave Galaxy. Galaxy used to solicit what it calls "guest editors" to assemble trailblazer pages in a number of areas, and managed to get a couple of dozen takers. Although these pages are still available, TradeWave is currently not accepting anymore guest editors.

Yahoo (http://www.yahoo.com). You can also find trailblazer pages in Yahoo, where they're called "indices", and can be found at the top of most Yahoo pages.

The following sections discuss the use of each of these resources to find trailblazer pages.

USING THE CLEARINGHOUSE

A project affiliated with the University of Michigan Library, the Clearinghouse for Subject-Oriented Resource Guides (Figure 6.2) seeks to provide a central access point for "value-added topical resource guides"— in other words, trailblazer pages. Anyone can submit a trailblazer page for inclusion in the Clearinghouse, as long as the page is an HTML page and collages Internet resources in a well-defined subject area.

To access the Clearinghouse, use the following URL: http://www.lib.umich.edu/chhome.html

The Clearinghouse Ratings System

A unique aspect of the Clearinghouse is the use of a rating system, which covers four aspects of trailblazer pages:

- **Level of Resource Description.** Does the trailblazer page describe the links it contains and provide helpful information?

- **Level of Resource Evaluation.** Does the trailblazer page include judgments regarding the quality of the provided links, including an assessment of both usability and authority (author's qualifications)?

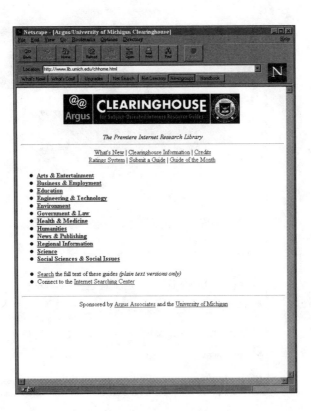

Figure 6.2 Clearinghouse for Subject-Oriented Resource Guides.

- **Organization** Is the trailblazer page well organized?
- **Level of Meta-information** Does the trailblazer page include information about why it was created, how it was researched, how often it's maintained, and who the author is?

At this writing, the ratings had not yet been applied to the trailblazer pages listed in the Clearinghouse, but they're promised for January, 1996.

To get an idea of how a top-rated trailblazer page looks, check out the Guide of the Month, accessible by means of a link that appears on every page of the Clearinghouse. The Guide of the Month at this book's writing was the X Guide to Japan (Figure 6.3), a project affiliated with Stanford University (no, the "X" does not refer to adult films!).

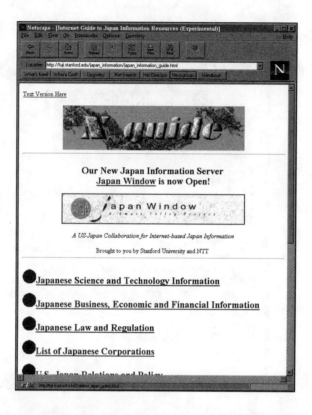

Figure 6.3 A well-organized trailblazer page (X Guide to Japan).

CLEARINGHOUSE TRAILBLAZER JEWELS

Computer-Mediated Communication (http://www.rpi.edu/Internet/Guides/decemj/icmc/top.html). John December's celebrated collection of CMC-related links.

FeMiNa (http://www.femina.com/). Aliza Sherman has created what she calls the first comprehensive Internet-based catalog of online resources for women and girls. Although the site was new at this writing, she's well on the way. A wonderful contribution to the Web.

continued…

continued...

Railroads   (http://www-cse.ucsd.edu/users/bowdidge/railroad/ rail-home.html). Railfans, look no further. Robert Bowdidge has assembled an impressive collection of Web links concerning railroads of all kinds, including model railroads.

Browsing the Clearinghouse

You can browse the Clearinghouse just as you would any subject tree. The initial page lists the Clearinghouse's subject headings; click one of these to see a list of the trailblazer pages filed under that subject. To access one of the pages, just click its hyperlink.

Searching the Clearinghouse

A unique feature of the Clearinghouse—and one that's poorly implemented, unfortunately—is the Search link, which enables you to search the full text of some of the listed trailblazer pages for text you specify. This feature is worth a try, but it has many limitations, all of which stem from the fact that the search engine is a Gopher server which can't cope with HTML documents. As a result, you can search only the plain text guides, not the HTML versions. You can't use advanced search techniques (such as Boolean operators), and the result of the search is a humdrum Gopher page, organized in no particular order.

Whither the Clearinghouse?

If you're looking for a trailblazer page, the Clearinghouse is worth a look—but don't expect it to become the Web's Grand Central Station for trailblazer pages. The Clearinghouse lists several dozen of them, to be sure, but I would estimate that several thousand trailblazer pages exist on the Web, and more are created each day. Part of the problem lies in the Clearinghouse's reliance on author submissions. I'd guess that fewer than one in 100 trailblazer authors knows of the Clearinghouse's existence, and of these, only a small proportion would bother to submit their pages to the Clearinghouse for inclusion; there's a long form to fill out, and people just don't have enough time.

THE VIRTUAL LIBRARY

A project of the World Wide Web Organization (W3O), the Virtual Library was the Web's first distributed subject catalog. Although VL contains a number of useful trailblazer resources, it hasn't kept pace with the rapid expansion of the Web and many of its pages are woefully out of date.

To access the Virtual Library, use the following URL:

```
http://www.w3.org/hypertext/DataSources/bySubject/
Overview.html
```

Browsing the Virtual Library

You can view the Virtual Library in two ways:

- **Alphabetical organization**. All the available trailblazer pages are listed in alphabetical order (Figure 6.4).

- **Library of Congress Subject Classification**. This is an experimental organization, but it appears to be working at this writing (Figure 6.5). In this view, VL becomes a subject tree organized according to the Library of Congress subject classification scheme. To access the Autos page, for instance, you click **Technology**, then **Transportation**, and then **Autos**.

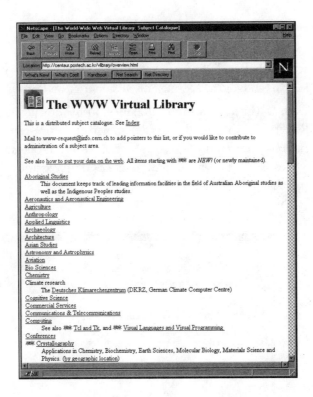

Figure 6.4 Virtual Library alphabetical listing of trailblazer pages.

VIRTUAL LIBRARY TRAILBLAZER JEWELS

African Studies (http://www.w3.org/hypertext/DataSources/bySubject/AfricanStudies/africanWWW.html) The Schomburg Center for Research in Black Culture shows how it's done—a fantastic trailblazer page, nicely organized and featuring dozens of useful links.

History of Science, Technology, and Medicine (http://www.asap.unimelb.edu.au/hstm/hstm_ove.htm) Tim Sherrat's well-organized web page—there's an overview and many subordinate pages—

continued...

continued...

assembles many resources in these fields, including biographies of active scholars, links to active university programs, specialized collections and journals, e-mail discussion lists, and much more.

Games (http://www1.cis.ufl.edu/~thoth/library/recreation.html) Robert H. Forsman, Jr., has assembled an impressive collection of games-related links, covering board games, models, role-playing games, and recreation, as well as computer games. Lots of fun, and don't miss Robert's home page.

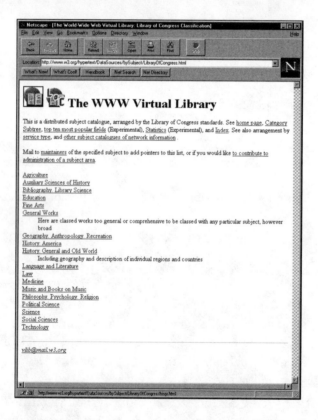

Figure 6.5 Virtual Library's Library of Congress subject organization

Searching the Virtual Library

The Virtual Library has no search facilities, but you can search the CUI W3 Catalog (Figure 6.6). This isn't a spider-based search engine; its database is composed of listings from a variety of manually updated sources, including the Virtual Library's alphabetical list of subjects.

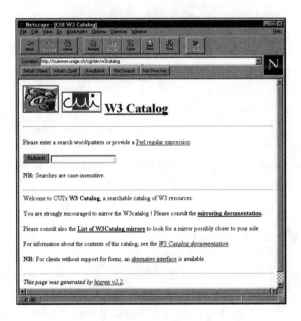

Figure 6.6 CUI W3 Catalog.

To access the CUI W3 Catalog, use the following URL:

```
http://cuiwww.unige.ch/w3catalog
```

If this site is busy or slow, try the North American mirror site:

```
http://www.winc.com/W3Catalog.html
```

To look for a Virtual Library subject in the CUI W3 catalog, type one or more search terms and click the **Submit** button. You'll see a lot of extraneous information in the list, but browse down to see if you can find the distinctive VL icon (an open book).

Evaluating the Virtual Library

The Virtual Library was conceived back in the days when the Web was small and documents were few. Unfortunately, VL hasn't kept pace with the times. During a period in which the number of documents on the Web has exploded by several orders of magnitude, VL has added a few additional pages—but just a few. Obviously, there's something wrong with the approach taken by both the Clearinghouse and the Virtual Library, which rely on author submissions. To create a Grand Central Station of trailblazer pages on the Web, somebody's going to have to hunt them down—and there's still no Web service that's really doing this job.

TradeWave Galaxy

TradeWave Galaxy, one of the Web's better subject trees (see Chapter 5), initiated a Guest Editors program in which experts in selected subject fields were invited to create trailblazer pages. Unfortunately, it has been suspended, and it's doubtful that the program will return. Still, you can access the few guest pages created before the program's suspension, and they're well worth a look.

To access the guest editors' pages in TradeWave Galaxy, use the following URL:

```
http://www.einet.net/editors.html
```

You'll see the Galaxy Guest Editors page, shown in Figure 6.7. This page lists the guest editors' trailblazing efforts.

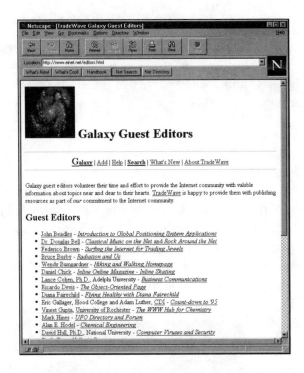

Figure 6.7 Galaxy Guest Editors page.

TRADEWAVE GALAXY TRAILBLAZER JEWELS

Wendy Bumgartner's Hiking and Walking Home Page (http://www.teleport.com/~walking/hiking.html). Frequently updated and well organized.

David B. Hull's Computer Virus and Security Page (http://www.einet.net/galaxy/Engineering-and-Technology/Computer-Technology/Security/david-hull/galaxy.htm). This page provides an excellent introduction to the subject, but doesn't aim for comprehensiveness. A good place to start for anyone concerned about computer viruses.

continued...

> *continued...*
>
> **Joseph E. Schmalhofer III's Entry-Level Jobseeker Home Page**
> (http://www.einet.net/galaxy/Community/Workplace/joseph-schmal-
> hofer/jobs.html). A fantastic resource for anyone seeking the first full-
> time position in virtually any field. Great advice and tons of links.

YAHOO

The best of the Web's subject trees, Yahoo also provides a growing repository of trailblazer pages, called *indices* in Yahoo's nomenclature. You'll
find the indices at the end of the second-level subject categories—and
these pages are gold mines. Figure 6.8 shows Yahoo's collection of trailblazer pages in the arts. It's an impressive collection.

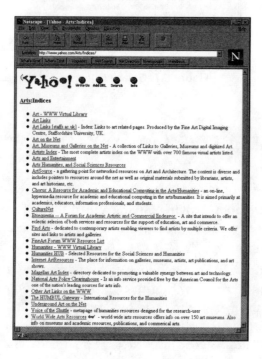

Figure 6.8 A Yahoo Trailblazer Page for Art.

SEARCHING FOR TRAILBLAZER PAGES

If you can't find a trailblazer page in the subject trees already discussed, you'll have to search using one of the Web's search engines. Can you search for "trailblazer" followed by one or more key words in your subject of interest? Unfortunately, you can't. There's no agreed-upon nomenclature for these pages. I've seen all of the following terms used to describe the thing we're talking about here—namely, a collection of Web and Internet links in a well-defined subject area. Each is listed with the current number of Lycos-indexed documents that contain this word:

collection (40907)

compendium (2445)

guide (287)

home page (2477)

homepage (30902)

hub (4638)

index (7806)

indices (5706)

meta-page (651)

subject guide (344)

subject index (838)

I suppose I've just made matters worse by introducing my own term, "trailblazer page," but I do think it's more descriptive than any of these.

The trouble is, it's almost impossible to search effectively for trailblazer pages—unless, that is, you're patient enough to repeat the search several times, looking for the most commonly used terms ("home page," "index," "indices," and "meta-page"). Still, it's worth doing. A search for "Anthropology home page" netted the very nice trailblazer shown in Figure 6.9.

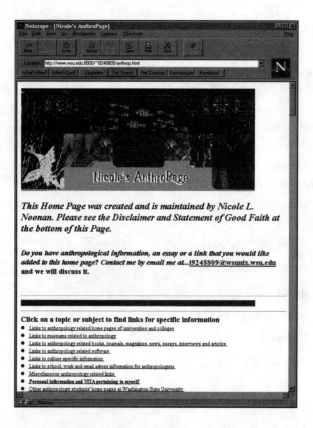

Figure 6.9 Nicole's AnthroPage.

LIBRARY TRAILBLAZERS

Maybe the best place to look for trailblazer pages is where you would have looked before the Internet came along—your local library. Everywhere, librarians are getting into the Web, and they're doing far more than browsing: They're creating trailblazer pages to help library patrons find information on the World Wide Web. For example, check out the Berkeley Public Library's trailblazer pages (Figure 6.10), which are nicely designed to meet patrons' needs (http://www.ci.berkeley.ca.us/bpl/bkmk/index.html). I wouldn't call this a Web starting points page; it's based on long and careful reflection concerning the reference and research needs and interests of Berkeley Library's patrons.

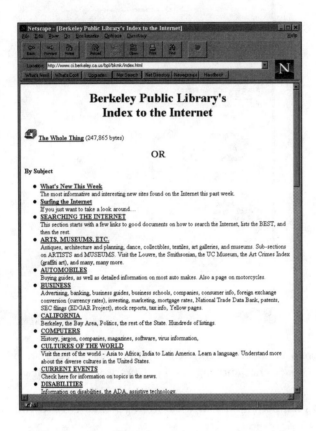

Figure 6.10 Berkeley Public Library trailblazer pages.

In colleges and universities, librarians are devising pages that meet the searching needs of undergraduate and graduate students, as illustrated by the excellent trailblazer pages created by librarians at the University of Virginia's Science and Engineering Library, a pioneer in this area. (Figure 6.11 shows the electrical engineering resources accessible from the Library's home page at http://www.lib.virginia.edu/science/SELhome.html.)

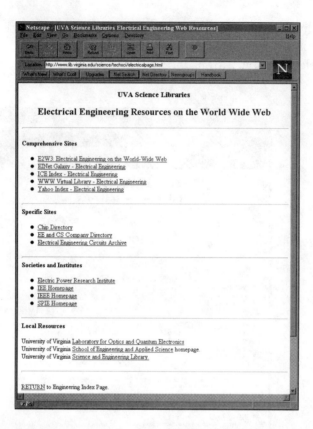

Figure 6.11 Electrical Engineering trailblazer page created by staff at the Science and Engineering Library, University of Virginia.

What's happening at *your* local library? Chances are you can log on and find out right now.

FROM HERE

This chapter concludes Step 2, "Find Something That's Relevant." Next, you'll learn how to perform a deep search using search tools and tricks that aren't at all obvious from the search pages of the Web's search engines. You'll learn how to hone and tailor your searches so that they retrieve just the information you want.

CHAPTER 7

CONSTRUCTING A DEEP SEARCH: BOOLEAN OPERATORS

You're serious about this. You want more than a few good citations. You want to perform a deep search and find just about everything on the Web that's relevant to your subject. If so, you'll need *Boolean operators*.

What are Boolean operators? In brief, they're connecting words—specifically, AND, OR, and NOT—that you can use to indicate the relationship among key words in your search question. For example, suppose you're searching for "azalea and rhododendron." The AND operator tells the search engine, in effect, "Show me only those documents that contain *both* of these words." Using Boolean operators, you can construct search questions that produce much better results than the default searches in most of the Web's search engines.

Is this Boolean stuff worth learning? You bet. Once you've learned how to use Boolean operators, you can hone your research question so that it produces a top-notch retrieval list. You can cut down the number of documents retrieved—or expand the number. You can even exclude pesky, unwanted documents that pertain to an irrelevant topic. For example, suppose you're searching for works on "azalea and rhododendron," but you're retrieving lots and lots of documents from some darned Azalea Corporation, which makes some kind of veeblefitzer for high-pressure toilets. To keep them out of your retrieval list, you can search for "azalea AND rhododendron NOT toilet."

Boolean operators
In a search question, the words AND, OR, and NOT, which are used to indicate the relationship among the key words you've typed.

KEY TERM

WHO WAS THIS BOOLE GUY?

George Boole (1815–1864) was an English schoolteacher, little known in his day. To amuse himself, Boole invented what he called an "algebra" of concepts—a way of writing down concepts in a formal language and then solving them as one would solve an algebraic equation. For Boole, concepts could be viewed as sets—groups of ideas or objects. For example, among flowers, red flowers are a set. A set is a group of objects or concepts that share one or more common elements.

Boole identified three ways to describe the contents of a set. Speaking of the things that one might find in the garden, one can identify the following:

- **red flowers.** In this set, one finds only those flowers that are red. The red garden trowel isn't included because it isn't a flower.

- **red objects or flowers.** This set includes the red trowel as well as the red flowers. Anything that's red gets included.

- **flowers, not red.** This set includes flowers of any color, as long as they're *not* red.

continued...

continued...

Boole hoped that his logical algebra would help people think through difficult conceptual problems, but his work wasn't widely known outside mathematical circles.

Boolean algebra might have remained a curiosity were it not for a remarkable 1937 discovery. Another English logician, named Alan Turing, proved that any mathematical problem could be solved by a machine capable of mimicking the simple operations of Boolean logic. Around the world, mathematicians and computer designers knew instantly that the computer age was coming—and that Boolean algebra held the key to computer circuit design. Today, Boolean algebra is used to design microprocessors, which solve problems just as Boole foresaw—by carrying out logical operations.

For computer users, Boole's legacy pops up in database searching, where Boolean operators—AND, OR, and NOT—provide the means to describe search concepts.

NARROWING THE SEARCH: THE AND OPERATOR

What's the most common problem with search engines? Your search retrieves too many documents. If that's your problem, the solution may lie in the use of the AND operator. The AND operator narrows the scope of your search. For example, suppose you search for "chardonnay AND sauvignon blanc." The AND operator tells the search engine, in effect, "Retrieve *only* those documents that contain *both* of these terms.

The following diagram (Figure 7.1) illustrates how the AND operator works. One circle corresponds to the document set containing "chardonnay," while the second corresponds to the document set containing "sauvignon blanc." Where the two circles intersect, you find documents containing both concepts. The only documents retrieved by an AND search are those that lie in the darkened area at the intersection of the circles.

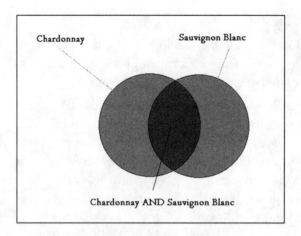

Figure 7.1 Searching with the AND Operator.

A search for "Chardonnay AND Sauvignon AND Blanc" in Open Text netted a total of 68 documents, with very high precision.

BROADENING THE SEARCH: THE OR OPERATOR

Sometimes, you'll find that a Web search retrieves too few documents. If so, you can broaden the search using the OR operator. When you link two or more terms using the OR operator, you tell the search engine, in effect, "Show me the documents that contain *any* of the key words I've typed." For example, suppose you search for "astrophysics OR astronomy." You'll get lots of documents, including those that mention astrophysics and astronomy, astrophysics but not astronomy, and astronomy but not astrophysics. In the following diagram (Figure 7.2), the darkened area represents the documents that will be retrieved by an OR search for "astronomy OR astrophysics."

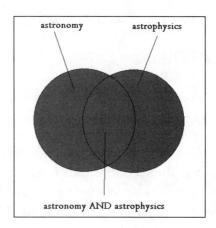

Figure 7.2 Searching with the OR Operator.

Obviously, some of these documents will prove to be irrelevant to your research focus—and there might be too many documents to review. In Open Text, a search for "astronomy OR astrophysics" netted a bewildering 16,150 documents.

Still, an OR search provides a great way to cast your net wide if you're shooting for a *high recall* search. (A high recall search is one in which you aim to retrieve all or most of the relevant documents that are actually out there on the Web. The opposite of a high recall search is a high precision search, in which you seek a retrieval list consisting mostly of relevant documents.)

Once you've retrieved a lengthy list of documents from an OR search, you can scroll through it looking for "hits." (You'll find lots of false drops, too.) Once you've found a hit, you can examine it and determine how to define your search question more precisely.

SEARCH TIP

Looking to find just about everything on the Web that's relevant to your search interests? Try an OR search in which you list all the synonyms you can think of, connecting all the words with the OR operator. Suppose, for example, that you want to find everything on the Net that's relevant to bowling. Phrase your search question with every bowling synonym you can think of, including *tenpin, duckpin, lawn, boccie, candlepin, fivepin, ninepin.* (*Boccie*, in case you're curious, is an Italian form of lawn bowling.)

EXCLUDING UNWANTED DOCUMENTS: THE NOT OPERATOR

As you scan your retrieval list, you'll sometimes notice that many or most of the false drops stem from another meaning of your search word. For example, suppose you're interested in rockets—the kind that shoot up in the sky. When you search for "rockets," you'll find plenty of pages devoted to the Houston Rockets basketball team. To refine your search to exclude the Houston Rockets, you can use the NOT operator. Sometimes this operator is spelled BUT_NOT, which helps to clarify its meaning.

The NOT operator provides a way to exclude unwanted documents from the retrieval list. When you use the NOT operator in a search question, such as "rockets NOT Houston," you tell the search engine, in effect, "Show me all the documents that contain 'rockets' EXCEPT the ones that also mention 'Houston.'" A search for "rockets" in Open Text netted 1807 documents, with low precision; a search for "rockets NOT Houston" narrowed the list down to 1315 documents.

The following diagram (Figure 7.3) shows the effect of a NOT search. The only documents retrieved are those in the darkened area.

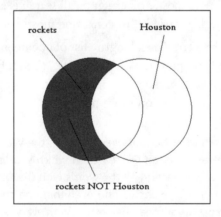

Figure 7.3 Searching with the NOT Operator.

SEARCH TIP

The more you scan your retrieval list, the more ways you'll find to exclude documents. In the search for "rockets NOT Houston," for instance, you'll find that some Houston Rockets pages don't mention "Houston," so they're not excluded; you should add "NBA" to the NOT list. In addition, there's a very popular comic book series called *Love and Rockets*, which could be excluded by NOT-ting "love." There's also an on-line kids' comic called "Rocketship Ginger," which you'll probably want to exclude, too. An Open Text search for "rockets NOT Houston NOT NBA NOT love NOT Ginger" netted a very much more focused, high precision list of 888 documents.

CONSTRUCTING A BOOLEAN SEARCH WITH SMARTMARKS

Chapter 3 introduced Netscape's SmartMarks utility, which helps you organize and store your bookmarks. SmartMarks also includes an easy-to-use Find tool, which enables you to construct Boolean searches of Yahoo, Lycos, WebCrawler, and InfoSeek. A unique feature of this program is the capability to save well-formulated searches, which you can repeat later or run at regular intervals.

Creating a Search with the Find Tool

To start the Find tool, choose **Find** from the Tool menu. You'll see the Find dialog box, shown in Figure 7.4. In the Search box, choose the search service you prefer. Try InfoSeek to see how this tool works.

Figure 7.4 Smart Finder dialog box (SmartMarks).

After you choose InfoSeek, type your first search word in the blank box, and click the **More** button. The dialog box expands, adding an additional row, as shown in Figure 7.5.

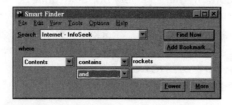

Figure 7.5 Smart Finder dialog box after clicking the **More** button.

By default, the Find tool uses an AND search with InfoSeek. If you wish to change the Boolean operator, drop down the list box and make another choice (you can choose AND, OR, or BUT_NOT). To add more conditions to the search question, just keep clicking the **More** button. (You can add up to four conditions to the original search question.) For an illustration, see Figure 7.6.

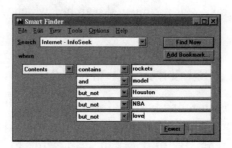

Figure 7.6 Adding more conditions.

When you're finished adding conditions, click the **Search** button. SmartMarks contacts the search service, and you'll see the results in the Netscape window (Figure 7.7).

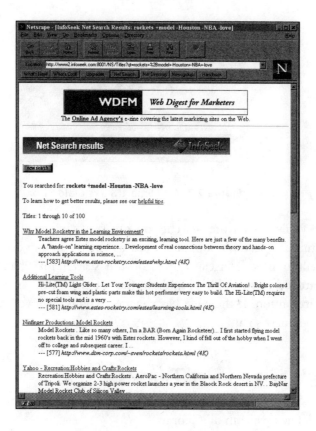

Figure 7.7 Results of SmartMarks search.

Saving a Search

Once you've crafted a good search question, you can save it—and after you do, you can tell SmartMarks to notify you if the retrieval list changes or contains new or changed links.

To save your search, click the **Add Bookmark** button. You'll see the Add SmartMarks dialog box, shown in Figure 7.8. In the File Into Folder area, click the folder in which you'd like to store the search. In the Description box, type a brief description of the search. If you'd like notification of changes, click one or both of the check boxes at the bottom of the dialog box. When you're finished, click **OK**.

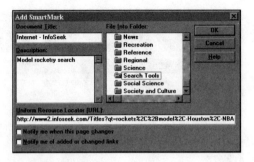

Figure 7.8 Add SmartMarks dialog box.

Once you've saved the search, you can run it manually at any time by selecting the search's bookmark, just as you'd run any bookmark. If you elected to have Netscape monitor the search for changes, click the **Monitored Items** folder, highlight the search you've saved, and click the **Update** button. If the page has changed, you'll see a vertical bar next to the bookmark's name.

BOOLE'S TIPS AND TRICKS

Take a few tips from ol' George:

- **Synonyms**. Use the OR operator to make sure that you've searched for all the possible variations—including common misspellings—of your key words. Examples: "cd-rom OR cdrom," "butterflies OR butterflys," "Sarajevo OR Sarayevo."

- **Order of Execution**. Most Web search engines evaluate Boolean expressions from left to right, and give the first term the greatest weight in assessing relevancy—so begin with the most important term. If you're searching for "Amtrak" and "federal subsidies," but you're more interested in "federal subsidies," put the latter term first.

- **Try a *Really* Focused Search**. Doing a focused, pinpointed search? Try stacking up a bunch of AND operators ("chardonnay AND willamette AND valley AND oregon AND bargain"). If you get zero documents retrieved, subtract one term at a time and try again until you start getting hits.

FROM HERE

There's more to learn about deep searching. The next chapter completes the knowledge you'll need to perform a deep search of the Web, covering search fields, truncation, and additional concepts that you'll need to understand to search effectively. Once you've read Chapter 8, you'll be ready to perform a deep search using the Web's most powerful search engines, which are discussed individually in Chapters 9 through 14.

Chapter 8

More Secrets of the Information Retrieval Masters

Once you've learned the techniques of Boolean searching, you're well on your way to a successful deep search of the Web. But there are a few more search concepts to learn, and they're covered in this chapter. In many cases, they hold the key to searching successfully.

Like Chapter 7, this chapter covers the general concepts of deep searching. You'll find specific information about each of the Web's best search engines—Open Text, Lycos, InfoSeek, Inktomi, excite NetSearch, and WebCrawler—in Chapters 9 through 14.

WHAT PORTIONS OF WEB DOCUMENTS ARE INDEXED?

Search engines vary. Some search engines index only the words appearing in the title and URL of the documents indexed in their databases. Other search engines index every conceivable component of a Web document and let you choose which parts of the document to search. Here's a list of these components:

- **URL**. The document's URL may contain one or more words that match your search key words, but don't count on it.

- **Title**. This is the text that appears within the <TITLE>...</TITLE> tags in an HTML document. Normally, this text is displayed on the browser's title bar. Don't count on the title containing useful or even accurate information. Web authors are notoriously lax about using descriptive and identifying titles, and some omit titles entirely, thinking that the Heading 1 (<H1>) text is really the document's title—it isn't.

- **First Heading**. This is the text that appears within the <H1> ... </H1> tags, which many Web authors mistakenly believe to be the title of their document.

- **Content**. Some search engines index all of the document's text. You'll get the best results from searches of a document's content, although you can count on a lot of false drops, too.

- **Excerpt**. Some search engines do not index all of the document's text, preferring to index just the first few lines (which ought, after all, to contain the most important text in the document). However, an excerpt search will not retrieve documents that discuss material of interest to you in the middle or end of the document.

- **Links**. Words appearing within hyperlinks contained in the document may also be added to the database.

Figure 8.1 displays a typical Web document and points out these components.

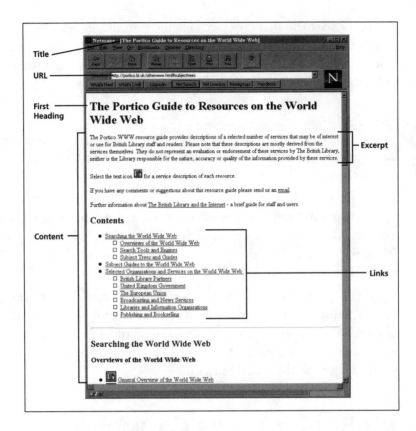

Figure 8.1 Components of a typical Web document.

FOR A PINPOINTED SEARCH, TRY RESTRICTING THE SEARCH TO SPECIFIC FIELDS

In the previous section, you learned that search engines vary in the type of information they collect from the Web documents they index. For example, some index the URL, the title, and the document content, while others index only the URL and title.

In the database that the search engine consults, each of these distinct types of information is called a *field*. Each field corresponds to a certain component of a typical Web document, such as the title, the first heading, the URL, or hyperlinks within a document.

field

In a search engine's database, a named storage area set aside for storing a certain type of information, such as the title or first heading of a Web document.

KEY TERM

With some search engines, you can restrict the search to a single field. For example, Open Text enables you to search any of several fields separately. If you wish, you can restrict the search to the first heading, or the title, or the URL.

If you're using a search engine that enables you to restrict the search, try restricting the scope of your search to the document's title or the first heading. Maybe, just maybe, there's a thoughtful Web author out there who actually chose a descriptive title. If so, you'll retrieve the document within a short, well-focused retrieval list.

DON'T BOTHER TYPING COMMONLY USED WORDS

To cut down on processing time, most search engines work with an *exclusion list*, a list of commonly occurring words that the search engine ignores. Included on such lists are commonly used articles (such as "the, a, an"), common prepositions ("in, on, around, to"), common verbs ("be, is, are"), and words that occur in almost all Web documents (such as "html").

If you used a word that's on the exclusion list, you'll see a message at the top of the retrieval list informing you which words were not used in the search.

IMPROVE RECALL BY USING TRUNCATION

Another important way in which search engines differ concerns the treatment of *substrings*, that is, portions of a word. In searching, the most common use of substrings lies in *truncation*, in which you type just the first part of a word (such as "butterfl"). This is done to match documents containing variations on the word (including "butterfly" and "butterflies"). Often, truncation is needed to make sure that you retrieve all the documents containing variations on a word you've typed.

On the Web, some search engines (such as Lycos) are set up to interpret what you type as a truncation, whether you intended this or not; this is termed **automatic truncation.** For example, a Lycos search for "rock" will retrieve documents containing "rocky," "Rockies," "rocket," "rockets," "rocketry," and more than 90 additional terms. Truncation is very useful for improving recall, but it's murder on precision.

SEARCH TIP

If you don't need truncation, turn it off to improve the precision of your retrieval list. If you're searching for "rock" (the music), find out how to disable truncation so you don't get thousands of documents pertaining to basketball teams, mountain ranges, and missiles.

KEY TERM

substring
A portion of a word.

KEY TERM

truncation
A search technique that involves cutting off the last few letters of a word so that the search will retrieve plurals and other variations (for example, searching for "butterfl" retrieves documents containing "butterfly" or "butterflies").

automatic truncation
In a search engine, a default setting in which searches automatically employ truncation (so that "butterfl" matches "butterfly" and "butter-flies").

KEY TERM

Some search engines, such as InfoSeek, perform *exact word matches* by default. In an exact word match, the search engine does not assume that you've typed a truncation. Instead, it matches only the characters you've typed. If you type "butterfl," for example, the retrieval list will include only those documents—if any—in which the characters "butterfl" occur as a separate word. Other search engines, such as Lycos, enable you to use a special exact-match operator to disable truncation.

exact word match
In a search, a setting that requires the search engine to retrieve only those documents in which the key word occurs as a separate word, with exactly the spelling you typed. Truncation is disabled.

KEY TERM

Still other search engines, such as WebCrawler, stem the key words you type. In stemming, the search software attempts to determine the root of the key word you've supplied, and searches with the root instead of the exact characters you've typed. The simplest form of stemming is to remove common endings, such as -ing, -s, and -es. More sophisticated stemming transforms "imagination" into "imagine," and "rocketry" into "rocket."

stemming
In a search engine, an automatic operation that reduces key words to their roots; the search proceeds using the root form of the word.

KEY TERM

WATCH OUT FOR CASE SENSITIVITY

Most of the search engines you'll encounter on the Web perform *case-insensitive searches* by default. In a case-insensitive search, the search engine ignores capitalization patterns and retrieves any document containing the search word (in any combination of lowercase and uppercase letters). An exception: InfoSeek takes case into account if you type any capital letters in your key words. For more information, see Chapter 11.

case-insensitive search

A search that ignores capital letters. In a case-insensitive search, "keystone" retrieves Keystone, keystone, or KEYSTONE.

KEY TERM

case-sensitive search

A search that takes capital letters into account. In a case-sensitive search, the search word "keystone" retrieves only those documents matching this precise pattern of capitalization (Keystone and KEYSTONE are not retrieved).

KEY TERM

TO IMPROVE PRECISION, TRY USING PROXIMITY OPERATORS

In Chapter 4, you learned that phrase searches are among the most accurate and useful searches you can try. In a phrase search, the search engine retrieves only those documents in which two or more words occur next to each other, and in the sequence you typed them. For example, suppose you type the phrase "virtual reality." In a phrase search, the search engine will retrieve only those documents that contain the phrase "virtual reality." A document in which these two words occur, but separated by one or more words, will not be retrieved.

The advantage of phrase searching is that it increases the precision of your retrieval list. A document that contains the phrase "virtual reality" is likely to have something to say about that subject; a document that discusses "virtual operating systems" and "the reality of installation headaches" may not, even though both words are present.

With some search engines, you can use *proximity operators* to create variations on the phrase-searching theme. Some search engines offer no proximity operators, while others offer several. Here are the adjacency operators offered by InfoSeek:

- **Near each other, in any order**. To be retrieved, the document must contain the key words you typed, and they must appear within several lines of each other. It doesn't matter which one comes first. In a search for "virtual reality," for example, this option would retrieve a document that mentioned "reality" followed by "virtual" several lines later.

- **Very close to each other**. To be retrieved, the document must contain the key words you typed, and they must occur within one line of each other. They must also occur in the order you typed. In the "virtual reality" search, this option would retrieve a document containing the sentence, "When one speaks of 'virtual,' what comes to mind is something very different from 'reality.'"

- **Within one word of each other**. To be retrieved, the document must contain the key words you typed, and they must occur within one word of each other. They must also occur in the order you typed. In the "virtual reality" search, this option would retrieve a document that mentioned "virtual (simulated) reality."

- **Next to each other (phrase searching)**. To be retrieved, the document must contain the key words you typed, and they must occur in the exact order you typed them, with no other words intervening. In the "virtual reality" search, this option would retrieve a document only if it contains the exact phrase "virtual reality."

KEY TERM

proximity operator
A word or character that you insert between two key words to specify how close the words should be positioned in order for the document to be retrieved.

FROM HERE

You've learned the fundamentals of deep searching! With this conceptual knowledge in hand, it's time to learn the specifics of the Web's most powerful search engines. As you'll find, each of them enables most of the features discussed in this chapter and the previous one—but in different ways (naturally). In addition, each has its own unique features, which may make it more or less useful for a given search. Chapter 9 gets started with one of the best, Open Text.

CHAPTER 9

SEARCHING OPEN TEXT

The first of the Web search engines discussed in detail in this book, Open Text is a cooperative venture between Open Text, Inc., the makers of the Open Text search software, and UUNET Canada Ltd., an Internet service provider. And it's a good place to start, particularly if you're anxious to try out all those cool deep-search techniques you've just learned.

Indexing the full text of more than one million Web documents, Open Text combines a large database with the best search engine currently available. It's fast, but what's more, it provides the searcher with a level of deep-search control that is difficult to equal with competing search engines. Once Open Text's database reaches the size of Lycos, it will be hard to beat.

To search Open Text, you choose among the following options:

- **Simple Search**. You type your key words in a text box. By default, Open Text performs a phrase search. You can also choose to link all your key words with AND (all of these terms) or OR (any of these terms).

- **Power Search**. You type key words in separate text boxes, enabling you to choose varying Boolean operators (for example, you can search for Daguerreotype AND photography BUT_NOT Brady). You can also select the document components you want to search (the default is All).

- **Weighted Search**. You type key words in separate text boxes and specify a search weight for each. For example, in a search for "astronomy" and "astrophysics," you could give "astrophysics" a higher weight than "astronomy." In this search, you can also select the document components you want to search.

Open Text offers several advanced features that ought to be emulated by other search engines, including the following:

- **Search Refining**. If you get too many documents in your retrieval list (a common occurrence), you can click **Improve Your Search** button to specify additional key words (which are ANDed by default).

- **Find Similar Documents**. In the retrieval list, each item includes a link that initiates a search for similar documents. This search uses a word frequency analysis to determine the most significant words in the sample document, and performs a search to find documents matching this frequency profile.

The following sections show you how to use all of these features to full advantage.

OPEN TEXT AT A GLANCE

URL: http://www.opentext.com:8080/omw/f-omw.html
Internet Services Indexed: World Wide Web pages

continued…

continued...

Size of Database: 1.0 million documents

Web Document Components Indexed: All (URL, title, headings, all content, hyperlinks)

Restricted Field Searching: Yes (Summary, Title, First Heading, Hyperlinks)

Default Search Setting: Phrase search

Boolean Operators: AND, OR, BUT_NOT

Truncation: Automatic

Phrase Search: Yes

Proximity Operators: NEAR and FOLLOWED BY

Case-sensitive Search: Only if key words are capitalized and have been indexed as a proper noun (for example, "Million Man March")

Relevancy Ranking: Yes

Output Content: Title, URL, first five lines of text

Special Features: Search refining, find similar pages

PERFORMING A SIMPLE SEARCH

By default, Open Text displays the Simple Search page (see Figure 9.1). Available are three search options:

- **This Phrase**. The default choice, this option initiates a phrase search.

- **All of These Words**. This option inserts an AND operator between all the key words you type. If the key words you're using don't make up a phrase, use this option for a focused search.

- **Any of These Words**. This option inserts an OR operator between all the key words you type. Tip: Use this option if you're searching for synonyms attributable to variations in spelling ("CD-ROM OR CDROM," "Sarajevo OR Sarayevo").

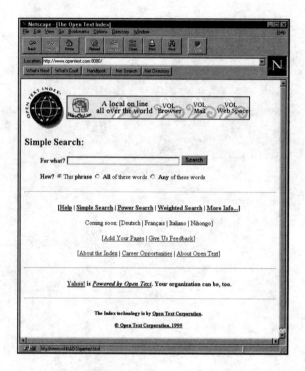

Figure 9.1 Simple Search Page.

SEARCH TIP

By default, Open Text searches with automatic truncation, which means that a search for "pear" will retrieve documents containing "pearl," "pearly," and more. To disable automatic truncation, use the Power Search or Weighted Search options, and type a space after each key word that you don't want truncated.

To search using the Simple Search page, type your key words, select one of the three search options, and click the **Search** button. You'll see a search output page, described later in this chapter in the section titled "Viewing the Search Output."

PERFORMING A POWER SEARCH

In the Simple Search screen, you can use Boolean operators—but you must use the same operator between each of your key words, and you can't use the BUT_NOT operator. In addition, you can't specify which part of the document Open Text searches (by default, it searches the entire text of the document). To gain more flexibility and control in your search, use the Power Search option. With Power Search, you can construct a search question that says, in effect, "Show me all the documents in which the title contains 'Massachusetts' and the document text contains 'Cape Cod' and 'Vacation Rentals,' but not 'Condos.'"

To initiate a **Power Search**, click the **Power Search** link. You'll see the Power Search page, shown in Figure 9.2.

Choosing Document Components

Note that this page enables you to type up to five key words. In the Within box, you can choose the following document components:

- **Anywhere**. Searches the entire document's text, including title, first heading, Web location (URL), hyperlinks, and all document text.
- **Title**. Searches only the title.
- **First Heading**. Searches only the first heading.
- **Summary**. This refers to the first four or five lines of text, which may or may not summarize the document's content.
- **Web Location (URL)**. Searches only the document's URL.
- **Hyperlinks**. Searches only the hyperlinks included in the document.

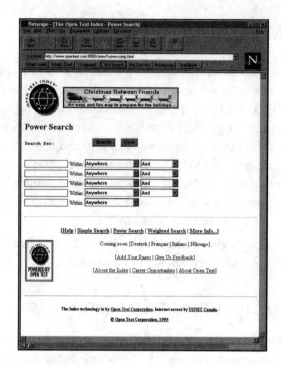

Figure 9.2 Power Search page.

Choosing Boolean and Proximity Operators

In the next box, you can choose from the following operators:

- **AND**. In order to be retrieved, the document must contain both of the terms linked with this operator.

- **OR**. In order to be retrieved, the document can contain either of the terms linked with this operator (or both).

- **BUT NOT**. In order to be retrieved, the document must not contain the second term of the two linked with this operator.

- **NEAR**. In order to be retrieved, the two terms linked with this operator must appear within several lines of each other.

- **FOLLOWED BY**. In order to be retrieved, the two terms linked with this operator must occur as a phrase.

Case and Truncation

As you construct your Power Search, bear the following in mind:

- **A search isn't case-sensitive unless you type capital letters.** Enter your key words in lowercase letters unless you want to restrict the match to the capitalization pattern you type.

- **Truncation is automatic unless you type a space after a key word.**

Performing a Weighted Search

The third of Open Text's search options, the Weighted Search, enables you to assign numerical weights to each of the key words you type. To initiate a Weighted Search, click the **Weighted Search** link. You'll see the Weighted Search page, shown in Figure 9.3.

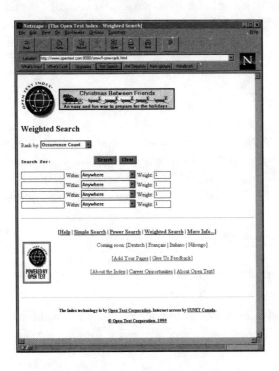

Figure 9.3 Weighted Search page.

Specifying the Ranking Method

In the Rank By box, you have the following choices:

- **Occurrence Count**. The search engine counts the number of occurrences of the term in each document, giving a higher rank to documents in which the search term occurs repeatedly.
- **Presence/Absence**. The search engine ignores the number of occurrences of a term; the document is scored by the presence or absence of the term.

Assigning Weights

For each key word you type, assign a weight. You can use any whole number (no decimal). To give the first term ten times more weight than the second, assign the first term a weight of 10 and leave the second term weighted 1 (the default). To initiate the search, click the **Search** button.

VIEWING THE SEARCH OUTPUT

When Open Text reports the results of a search, you see the search output page (shown in Figure 9.4). The documents are ranked in order, based on a score computed by Open Text's search engine. By default, Open Text displays the first ten matches. You can display more, if you wish.

The Output Page Header

At the top of the page, you see a report listing the total number of pages matching your search question.

To add key words to this search, click the **Improve Your Search** link, and see "Refining a Search" later in this chapter. To start a new search, click **Start a New Search**.

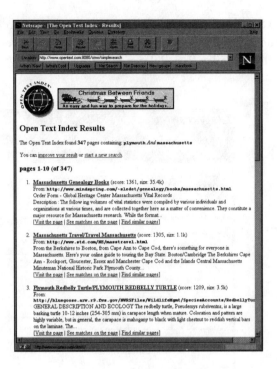

Figure 9.4 Search output page.

Understanding the Items in the Retrieval List

Each retrieved document is numbered to reflect its rank in the retrieval list, and includes the title, the score, the size of the document, the URL, and the first four or five lines of text.

Using the Retrieval List Hyperlinks

Beneath each retrieved document, you see the following hyperlinks:

- **Visit the Page**. Click here to access this page.
- **See Matches on the Page**. Click here to see a key-word-in-context (KWIC) list of the lines containing matches for your key words (for an example, see Figure 9.5).

- **Find Similar Pages**. Click here to initiate a search that uses the word frequency profile of this document. For more information, see "Finding Similar Pages" later in this chapter.

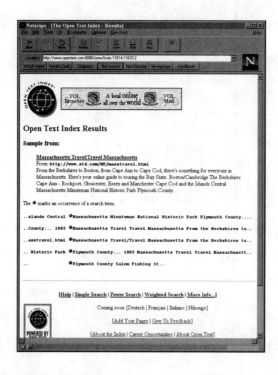

Figure 9.5 Key-word-in-context (KWIC) list of matches.

REFINING A SEARCH

Did you find a lot of false drops in your retrieval list? Take advantage of an excellent Open Text feature that enables you to add additional key words to your search question. This feature is found on only one other Web search engine, excite NetSearch, but it's something that *should* be included in all of them.

To refine your search, click the **Improve Your Search** link. You'll see a page that echoes your current search settings (see Figure 9.6). As you can see, Open Text proposes to add a new search term with the restrictive AND operator—a good choice, under most circumstances. Try adding a key word, and click **Search**.

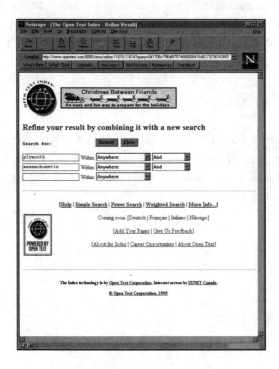

Figure 9.6 Refining your search.

FINDING SIMILAR PAGES

A unique feature of Open Text is the Find Similar Pages hyperlink, which you'll find at the bottom of each retrieved document. If you click this link, Open Text performs a word frequency analysis on this document, and then searches its database in an attempt to find documents that match this word frequency profile. You then see a new output page listing the documents that match this profile, in rank order.

You may be somewhat surprised by the results of this search—the documents retrieved might be wildly out of kilter with your search topic. Here's why. When Open Text performs its word frequency analysis, it looks for words occurring frequently and ranks the documents accordingly—even if the most frequently occurring words turn out to be irrelevant to your search interests. Still, it's worth a try.

FROM HERE

Now that you've mastered Open Text, try your search with the next search engine this book discusses: Lycos. As you'll see, Lycos is also a very powerful and useful search engine—but it, too, has its idiosyncrasies!

CHAPTER 10

SEARCHING LYCOS

Lycos, the search engine discussed in this chapter, lays claim to the Web's largest URL database. At this writing, it contained references to 10 million URLs, covering an estimated 91% of the Web's content. What's more, Lycos' database is growing at the rate of 300,000 documents per week. That's faster than the Web's growth (if only just), so Lycos will eventually index 100% of the Web.

Or so Lycos claims. Competitor Inktomi (Chapter 12) claims that Lycos doesn't mention that, of the 10 million URLs indexed, only a fraction have been fully analyzed. And even for those documents, Lycos does not index the full text. Instead, it indexes words found in the URL, the title, the header fields, the first 20 lines (or the first 20% of the document, whichever is smaller), the 100 most statistically significant words contained in a document, and words found in hyperlinks. This means that Lycos may not retrieve a document that mentions your search topic only peripherally.

A project initially based at Carnegie Mellon University (CMU), Lycos has made the move into the private sector, as have many of the Web's popular services that had their origins at universities. The search engine is the product of research performed by Michael L. Mauldin, of CMU's Computer Science faculty. Still affiliated with CMU, Lycos has been purchased by CMB Information Services, Inc. But don't worry about being charged for Lycos searches: CMB plans to make its money through on-site advertising and by licensing the Lycos database. One of its first customers: Microsoft Corporation, which makes its own copy of Lycos available for Microsoft Network subscribers.

Is Lycos worth searching? You bet. Despite its shortcomings, I find it to be one of the best search engines on the Web—it's fast and produces reasonably high recall. But you'll be well advised to read this chapter carefully. Lycos's default settings virtually guarantee an imprecise retrieval list; you'll need to learn some tricks—and to use several of your deep searching techniques—to get good results from Lycos.

LYCOS AT A GLANCE

URL: http://www.lycos.com

Internet Services Indexed: World Wide Web pages, FTP file archives, Gopher pages.

Size of Database: 7.98 million documents.

Web Document Components Indexed: URL, Title, first 200 words in header fields, 100 most statistically significant words occurring in the document, the smaller of the first 20 lines or 20% of the document text, up to 16 hyperlinks included in the document.

Restricted Field Searching: No.

Default Search Setting: OR. (In effect, default searches function as phrase searches because documents in which the key words occur together receive a higher score than documents in which the key words are separated by intervening text.)

Boolean Operators: AND, OR.

continued...

continued…

> **Truncation:** Automatic. To restrict the search to just the characters you type (exact match search), place a period *after* the word (for example, "Mac.").
>
> **Phrase Search:** None (but the search software prefers documents in which the key words appear together).
>
> **Proximity Operators:** None.
>
> **Case-sensitive Search:** No.
>
> **Relevancy Ranking:** Yes.
>
> **Output Content:** Title, rank, number of key words found in document, "abstract" (first 3–8 lines of text), URL.
>
> **Special Features**: Choose the format for search output (Standard, Summary, Details); prefix matching with $ operator.

LYCOS SEARCH OPTIONS

You have three basic options for your Lycos search:

- **Formless Searching**. Like most Web search engines, Lycos assumes that the majority of people searching the Web have little interest in learning advanced search techniques. For this reason, Lycos' default search page displays nothing more than a simple text box in which you type the key words for which you're searching. In Lycos' terminology, this is "formless searching."

- **Form-based Searching**. As an alternative to the formless search page, you can search using a form that enables you to use Boolean operators. You can also specify a variety of output options.

- **Searching with Lycos' "Hidden" Search Tools**. Unbeknownst to most Lycos searchers, and scarcely documented in Lycos' on-line help files, are three powerful operators that you can use to disable Lycos' default truncation, enable prefix matching, and devalue documents containing unwanted terms. You can use these "hidden" search tools in the formless or form-based search pages.

The following sections discuss these three options in detail.

PERFORMING A SIMPLE SEARCH WITH LYCOS

When you access Lycos, you see the "formless" search page, shown in Figure 10.1. The term "formless" isn't quite accurate, since there's a text box (generated by a FORM command in HTML) in which you type your search words. What's meant is that there are no search options. In short, this page is like open text's Simple Learn Page (see Chapter 9).

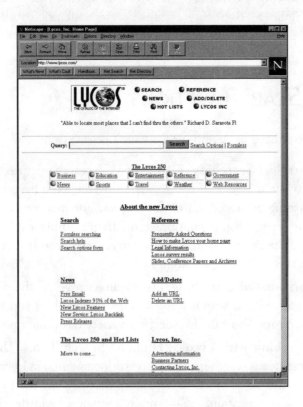

Figure 10.1 Lycos "formless" search page.

To search using the Lycos formless search page, type your key words and click the **Search** button. You'll see a search output page, described later in this chapter in the section titled "Viewing the Search Output."

PERFORMING A FORMS-BASED SEARCH WITH LYCOS

With a forms-based Lycos search, you have more options than with the "formless" search page. You can:

- **Choose Boolean operators**. You can choose to insert an AND operator between all the key words in the search question (the default is OR).

- **Limit search output**. You can limit the display by relevancy ranking, and you can also choose among three output formats.

To access Lycos' form-based search page, click the **Search Options** link. You'll see the forms-based search page, shown in Figure 10.2.

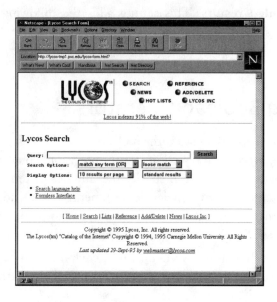

Figure 10.2 Lycos forms-based search page.

Choosing Display Options

When you initiate a search with the forms-based search page, you can choose the number of documents that Lycos displays on each retrieval list page (10 is the default). You can choose to display 20, 30, or 40 items per page, if you wish. No matter which option you choose here, you can always see additional hits by clicking a link at the bottom of the search page.

You can also choose the format that Lycos uses to display documents in the retrieval list. Choose from the following options:

- **Summary results**. You see a numbered list of document titles, sorted by relevance rank. This is a good choice if you want to get a quick overview of the document titles retrieved by your search. In the first Display Options text box, display 40 results per page so that you can see a lengthy list of titles.

- **Standard results**. This is the default setting. You see a numbered list of document summaries, sorted by relevance rank. The summaries include the title, the relevance score, the first significant heading, an "abstract" (actually the first three to nine lines of text), and the URL.

- **Detailed results**. This setting adds the following to the standard results: Number of links to outside resources, search words matched in this page, and a description of the document's content,

Choosing Boolean Operators

By default, Lycos searches with an OR operator, which is inserted between all the key words you type. For greater precision, you can search with the AND operator, or you can specify the number of terms that the system must match in order to retrieve a document. There's no way to construct a search that mixes OR and AND, and Lycos does not offer a NOT operator (but see "Excluding Unwanted Documents," later in this chapter).

To search with the AND operator, click the **Search Options** list box and choose **Match all terms (AND)**. Lycos will insert the AND operator between all the terms.

In the Search Options list box, you can also choose the following options:

- Match any 2 terms
- Match any 3 terms
- Match any 4 terms
- Match any 5 terms
- Match any 6 terms
- Match any 7 terms

These options enable you to specify how many of the search terms must be matched for a document to be retrieved. For example, suppose you type four search words. If you choose Match any 3 terms, Lycos will retrieve only those documents containing at least three of the four words you typed.

Choosing the Match Strength

In the next list box in the Search Options area, you can choose the "strength" of the match, with a number of options ranging from "loose" (the default) to "strong." Actually, this option does not affect the search; it affects the output. By choosing one of these options, you tell Lycos the relevancy rank level at which you want the service to cut off the display of documents. For each of the following options, a document must have a relevance rank of at least the cited number in order to be retrieved:

- Loose match: .10
- Fair match: .30
- Good match: .50
- Close match: .70.
- Strong match: .90.

What's the point of changing the match strength? Lycos' documentation says that you can save downloading time by choosing a stronger match—this will reduce the number of documents retrieved—but I don't see the point. Lycos downloads documents in sets of 10, by default, and you can tell pretty quickly whether a search question worked or not. If the retrieval list is full of false drops, you can redo the search without downloading more than 10 documents.

HIDDEN SECRETS OF SUCCESSFUL LYCOS SEARCHING

The Lycos search language is flexible and powerful, but that's not at all apparent from the help and reference pages available from the Lycos search page. In actuality, you can perform exact match searches, free prefix matching, exclusions, and inclusions. The following sections explain how to perform these search tricks.

Performing an Exact Match Search

One of the best things you can do to improve your Lycos search is to force an exact match search in which you disable automatic truncation.

Here's why. Suppose you're searching for "city." When Lycos evaluates this expression using automatic truncation, it automatically includes in the retrieval list documents containing "citylink," "citynet," "cityscape," and an astonishing 570 additional words. The search software ranks documents containing "city" higher than those containing "citynet" or "cityscape," but it's still a safe bet that you'll see plenty of false drops in the retrieval list.

To force an exact match, type a period after the key word (as in the following example): **city**.

The retrieval list will contain only those documents in which this word appears by itself.

Performing a Free Prefix Match Search

In the previous section, you learned that Lycos searches for all the words that begin with the characters you've typed (automatic truncation).

However, the search software gives the highest rank to those documents containing the word the way you typed it.

Sometimes it's preferable to see all the documents that contain variations on the root word you've typed. For example, suppose you're searching for "surf." You're probably equally interested in documents containing "surfin'," surfers," and "surfing." If you search with the prefix operator ($), Lycos will reduce the penalty for failure to conform to the root you've typed.

To enable prefix matching, type a dollar sign ($) before the key word, as in the following example:

```
$surf
```

Excluding Unwanted Documents

Although Lycos does not offer the Boolean NOT operator, you can decrease the rank of documents containing an unwanted term. To do so, use an exclusion operator. Unlike a Boolean NOT operator, an exclusion operator does not really exclude a document from the retrieval list—it just reduces its relevance rank. In Lycos, the exclusion operator is a minus sign, which must directly precede the excluded term, as in the following example:

```
telecommunications -radio
```

This search retrieves everything concerning telecommunications, but those documents that also mention radio are given a lower score.

Bringing Desired Documents to the Top of the Retrieval List

Lycos also offers an inclusion operator, which gives a higher rank to documents containing a specified term. In Lycos, the inclusion operator is a plus sign, which must directly precede the included term, as in the following example:

```
telecommunications +TV
```

This search retrieves everything concerning telecommunications, but it places those documents mentioning TV at the top of the retrieval list.

VIEWING THE SEARCH OUTPUT

When Lycos reports the results of a search, you see the search output page (shown in Figure 10.3). The documents are ranked in order, based on a score computed by Lycos' search engine. By default, Lycos displays the first ten matches; with a forms-based search, you can display up to 40 matches on one page. To see additional matches, scroll to the bottom of the page and click the hyperlink **Next *n* hits**. (The number *n* is the number you selected in the Display Options area of the forms-based search page; the default is 10.)

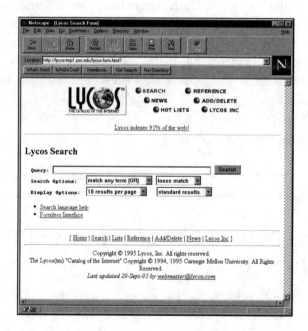

Figure 10.3 Lycos search output page.

The Output Page Header

At the top of the page, Lycos indicates the number of documents that contain at least one of the search terms you typed. You then see a message such as the following:

```
Printing only the first 10 of 578 documents with at least
scores of 0.100.
```

This message is based on your search choices. If you use the forms-based search page, you can control the number of documents printed per page (up to 40) and the match strength (up to .9).

Below this message, you see a list of the key words matched by this search, as in the following example:

```
Found 1300 matching words (number of documents): power
(32003), boats (3326), recommended (11303), first
(37086), ...
```

SEARCH TIP

Did Lycos match too many words? Remember that Lycos employs automatic truncation, which means that the program will retrieve many variations on the word's root that aren't relevant to your search. Try repeating the search with the exact match symbol (a period).

DEALING WITH UNSATISFACTORY SEARCHES

If your Lycos search didn't work as well as you would have liked, consider the following:

- **Too few documents retrieved?** Use synonyms and variations of your key words. For example, try searching for "CDROM" as well as "CD-ROM." Also, check your spelling.

- **Too many documents retrieved?** Try searching with the exact match operator (a period), and use the forms-based interface to select the Boolean AND operator.

FROM HERE

OpenText and Lycos are two of the three best search engines on the Web—Infoseek is the third. The next chapter explains how to use Infoseek.

CHAPTER 11

SEARCHING INFOSEEK

One of the Web's most popular search engines (the service currently performs three million searches each day), InfoSeek permits free searches of its Web database, currently containing 400,000 documents. Easy to use for simple searches, InfoSeek is very popular—a fact that has something to do, no doubt, with its presence at the top of Netscape's Search page, which appears when you click the **Search** button on Netscape's omnipresent button bar.

Another reason for InfoSeek's popularity: The search engine is designed to enable inexperienced searchers to achieve high-precision searches. It does so by defaulting to a case-sensitive phrase search, without truncation. For example, if you search for Outer Banks, you'll see documents containing this phrase at the top of the retrieval list; a document referring to the Long Island Savings Banks' quest for "out-going people" doesn't pop up until you've seen a solid 40 relevant documents.

But there's a price to pay for this ease of use. InfoSeek may be easy to use for quick, pinpointed searches, but for deep searching it's another matter: InfoSeek's search syntax is the most difficult and quirky of all the Web's search engines. Yet the payoff is well worth the effort you'll expend learning how to perform a deep search with InfoSeek. In this chapter, you'll learn everything you need to know to get outstanding results from your InfoSeek search.

Is There a Charge for Searching InfoSeek?

InfoSeek is really two search services, one available for free and the other charging a fee:

- **The Free Service (InfoSeek NetSearch).** You can search InfoSeek's database of Web documents for free and retrieve up to 100 documents.

- **The Fee-Based Service.** You can receive up to 200 Web documents for free. In addition, you can search a variety of databases for which varying fees are charged. Included are Usenet postings, magazine articles, movie reviews, and a variety of medical and technology-related databases.

This chapter focuses on InfoSeek's Web search services.

HELP

My 11-year-old kid just downloaded a bondage graphic from InfoSeek! Bear in mind that InfoSeek does not censor Usenet newsgroups, which are available for searching with an InfoSeek subscription. More than 10,000 newsgroups are included—and the number includes some of the more *outré* groups, such as alt.binaries.pictures.erotica.bondage, alt.binaries.pictures, erotica.fetish, and more. If you share your home computer with curious kids, it might be wise to keep your InfoSeek password to yourself. Note: Recognizing that some of the material on the Internet isn't suitable for children, InfoSeek requires that all subscribers be 18 years of age or older.

INFOSEEK NETSEARCH AT A GLANCE

URL: http://www2.infoseek.com

Internet Services Indexed: World Wide Web pages (free service); see Table 11.1 for a list of the fee-based services.

Size of Database: 400,000 documents.

Web Document Components Indexed: All (URL, title, headings, all content, hyperlinks).

Restricted Field Searching: Not currently implemented, but slated for future development.

Default Search Setting: OR. (In effect, default searches function as phrase searches because documents in which the key words occur together receive a higher score than documents in which the key words are separated by intervening text.)

Boolean Operators: None, but see Special Features, below.

Truncation: Key words default to stems (for example, *agrees*, *agreed*, *agreeing*, and *agree* all produce identical retrieval lists, since all are stemmed to *agree*).

Phrase Search: Optional (type the phrase in quotation marks).

Proximity Operators: Link two terms with a hyphen (Internet-access) to retrieve only those documents in which these words occur very near each other; surround two terms with brackets ([SCSI interface]) to retrieve documents in which the two words appear close to each other, in either order.

Case-sensitive Searches: Yes. Note that two capitalized words next to each other are treated as a proper name (Charles Smith).

Relevancy Ranking: Yes.

Output Content: Title, URL, first three lines of text.

Special Features: To require that a document contain a key word, type a plus sign (for example, +biomedicine). To require that a document *not* contain a key word, type a minus sign (for example, -biomedicine).

Table 11.1 Fee-based Database Services (InfoSeek)

Collections with Free Document Retrievals

WWW Pages (info)

InfoSeek Help (Frequently Asked Questions) (info) free queries!

Standard Collections

Usenet News (since the preceding Sunday).

A database of current Usenet postings.

Usenet News (last 7 weeks).

A larger, retrospective database of Usenet postings covering seven weeks.

Cinema Movie, Book, and Music Reviews.

Reviews of current books, films, musical recordings, and video tape releases.

FrameMaker 4.0 Help Notes.

A collection of support documents for the professional desktop publishing program.

Wire Services.

A database containing the full text of news reports from AP Online, PR Newswire, BusinessWire, Newsbytes News, and Reuters Business Report.

Computer Periodicals.

A database containing the full text of articles from *Computer Reseller News*, *Computer Retail Week*, *Communications Week*, *Communications Week International*, *Edge: Work-Group Computing Report*, *Edge: On & About AT&T*, *Electronic Buyer's News*, *Home PC*, *Information Week*, *Interactive Age*, *Network Computing*, *NetGuide*, *Newsbytes*, *OEM Magazine*, *VAR Business*, and *WINDOWS* Magazine.

Health and Medicine.

A database containing the full text of numerous health and medical newspapers, magazines, and journals, including the Medical Tribune News Service.

Corporate Information.

A database of information on U.S. corporations, based on Hoover's Master List and CorpTech reports.

Premium Collections

Hoover's Company Profiles (in-depth details) (info).

A database of more than 800 U.S. companies.

MDX Health Digest.

A database containing the full text of reports from this consumer-oriented health journal.

InfoWorld.

A database containing the full text of articles from *InfoWorld*.

CorpTech Directory of Technology Companies.

A database containing information on companies in high technology fields.

Microcomputer Abstracts.

A database containing bibliographic citations and abstracts from dozens of magazines and newspapers in the personal computer area.

CSA Biomedical Database.

A database of citations and abstracts in the fields of biomedical engineering, neuroscience, genetics, medicine, pharmacology, virology, and AIDS research.

CSA Computer and Engineering Database.

A database of citations and abstracts in computing, mechanical engineering, electrical engineering, communications, and information science.

CSA Worldwide Market Research Database.

A database of citations and abstracts of market research reports, derived from over 900 publishers worldwide.

PERFORMING A SIMPLE SEARCH WITH INFOSEEK

One of the best things about InfoSeek's Web search service is the ease with which one can perform a simple search. You'll get reasonably good precision thanks to the system's default settings, which are optimized for users who don't know how to use advanced search techniques.

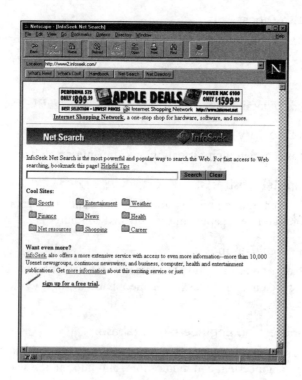

Figure 11.1 InfoSeek free Web search page.

To search using the InfoSeek search page, type your key words and click the **Search** button. You'll see a search output page, described later in this chapter in the section titled "Viewing the Search Output."

HARNESSING THE POWER OF INFOSEEK'S SEARCH ENGINE

InfoSeek departs from the search engine norm—it isn't Boolean-based, for one thing, and there's no truncation. These settings are good for simple, quick searches by untrained people, but those wishing to do more focused searches will have to learn InfoSeek's quirky syntax. The following sections provide detail about this syntax.

Adding a Required Term

Although InfoSeek does not use Boolean operators, you can implement an AND operator, in effect, by using the operator that forces the search software to retrieve only those documents containing a specified word.

To specify that a document *must* contain a key word in order to be retrieved, precede the term with a plus sign. For example, the following search question retrieves only those documents about the Outer Banks that mention "rentals":

Outer Banks +rentals

SEARCH TIP

Make sure that there's no space between the plus sign and the key word (this is correct: +Tibet). If you insert a space, the search software will ignore the plus sign.

Excluding Unwanted Documents

InfoSeek doesn't implement the Boolean NOT operator, but you can exclude unwanted documents by using an operator that forces the search software to exclude documents containing a specified word.

To specify that a document *should not* be retrieved if it contains a certain word, precede the word with a minus sign. For example, the following search question retrieves documents about the Outer Banks, except those that also mention "windsurfing":

Outer Banks -windsurfing

SEARCH TIP

Make sure that there's no space between the minus sign and the key word (this is correct: -Tibet). If you insert a space, the search software will ignore the minus sign.

Searching for Proper Nouns

An unusual InfoSeek capability is the program's capacity to retrieve proper nouns, such as personal and company names. The search software treats adjacent capitalized words as a single proper name, as in the following examples:

Susan Smith

Microsoft Windows

Apple Computer

If you wish to use additional key words in your search question, separate the proper names using commas:

Dalai Lama, human rights

Robert Frost, John Ashbery, John Keats

Performing a Phrase Search

As previously mentioned, InfoSeek gives the highest rank to those documents in which your key words occur as a phrase. For this reason, there does not appear to be a valid reason to use InfoSeek's phrase operators—quotation marks—when you're searching for two key words; searches with and without the marks produce the same retrieval lists.

That's not the case when you're searching with three key words, however. For example, a default search for "document imaging systems" produced a retrieval list in which the top-ranking documents did not contain the phrase "document imaging systems." When the search was repeated as a phrase search, the top-ranking documents contained this phrase.

To initiate a phrase search, enclose the key words within quotation marks, as in the following example:

"random access memory"

Using Proximity Operators

InfoSeek offers two proximity operators. You can specify limits for document retrieval in which the key words are:

- **Very close to each other, in the specified order.** Use a hyphen between the words, with no spaces (for example, "laser-printer").

- **Near each other, in any order.** Surround the two words with brackets (for example, [Amtrak timetable]).

VIEWING THE SEARCH OUTPUT

When InfoSeek reports the results of a search, you see the search output page (shown in Figure 11.2). The documents are ranked in order, based on a score computed by InfoSeek's search engine. By default, InfoSeek displays the first ten matches. You can display up to 100 with InfoSeek's free search service (200 if you subscribe).

The Output Page Header

At the top of the page, InfoSeek indicates the search terms that were used to construct the retrieval list.

SEARCH TIP
Look at the words that InfoSeek actually used to carry out your search. Occasionally, the search engine makes stemming errors, transforming your search word into a root that's not relevant to your search interests. If a stemming error should occur, try the search again using a proximity operator (separate the key words with hyphens).

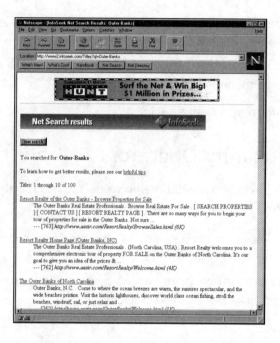

Figure 11.2 Infoseek's search output page.

Understanding the Items in the Retrieval List

Each retrieved document is numbered to reflect its rank in the retrieval list; it includes the title, the first three lines of text in the document, the score (in brackets), the document's URL, and its size (in parentheses).

DEALING WITH UNSATISFACTORY SEARCHES

If your InfoSeek search didn't work as well as you would have liked, look at the following checklist:

- **Check your spelling**. Look at the "words not used" entry on the output page. If you misspelled a search word, chances are it's listed here. Try again and spell the key words correctly.

- **Use the correct case**. If you're looking for a word that's normally capitalized, use capital letters.

- **Use commas to separate proper nouns**. If you're searching for names, use commas to separate the names so the search software doesn't get confused ("Clinton, Gore").

- **Use synonyms and variations of your key words**. For example, try searching for "labour" as well as "labor."

- **Check to see if you've placed a space after a plus or minus sign**.

- **Try using additional terms to bring relevant documents to the top of the retrieval list**.

FROM HERE

Open Text, Lycos, and InfoSeek are the Web's top three search engines. When you're deep-searching the Web, you should try all three of these search engines. If you haven't gotten the results you were hoping for, try some of the others. The best of the rest is, arguably, Inktomi (Chapter 12), although excite Netsearch (Chapter 13) is well worth a look.

With its (comparatively) tiny database and simple search engine, Webcrawler (Chapter 14) is suitable for a quick search just in case other engines missed a page or two.

CHAPTER 12

SEARCHING INKTOMI

Inktomi (pronounced "Ink-to-me") is one of the newer search engines on the Web, and it's one of the better ones. The search engine isn't as sophisticated as Open Text, but the service boasts a big, full-text database of Web documents. Plus, it's one of the faster search engines on the Web.

If you're performing a deep search, by all means give Inktomi a try—particularly if you've already learned to search with InfoSeek's rather quirky search syntax: Inktomi uses some of the same search operators.

INKTOMI AT A GLANCE

URL: http://inktomi.berkeley.edu/query.html.

Internet Services Indexed: Web documents.

Size of Database: 1.3 million documents.

Web Document Components Indexed: All (full text).

Restricted Field Searching: No.

Default Search Setting: OR.

Boolean Operators: None. Use + to precede a key word that must be in a retrieved document; use - to precede a key word that must not be in a retrieved document.

Truncation: None. Common endings (-ing, -ed, -s, -es, etc.) are stemmed and a root word is used for the search.

Phrase Search: None (but the search software prefers documents in which the key words appear together).

Proximity Operators: None.

Case-sensitive Search: No.

Relevancy Ranking: Yes

Output Content: Score, title, simple graph of relevance, count of relevant words in the document, and URL.

Special Features: None.

PERFORMING A SIMPLE SEARCH WITH INKTOMI

Inktomi's search page (Figure 12.1) is straightforward: just type up to ten words in the text box. Note the following:

- Don't use Boolean operators—Inktomi doesn't recognize them.
- Don't use punctuation or wildcards.

- Words of fewer than three letters are ignored.
- Words containing numbers are ignored.

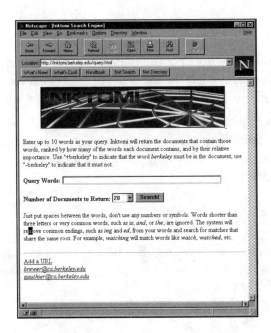

Figure 12.1 Inkomi's search page.

When you're finished typing your search terms, choose the number of documents you want to retrieve (the default is 20). To initiate the search, click the **Search** button. You'll see a search output page, described later in this chapter in the section titled "Viewing the Search Output."

USING INKTOMI'S INCLUSION AND EXCLUSION OPERATORS

Like InfoSeek, Inktomi departs from the search engine norm—it isn't Boolean-based, and there's no truncation. As noted in Chapter 11, these settings are good for simple, quick searches by untrained people, but those wishing to do more focused searches may want to use Inktomi's inclusion (+) and exclusion (-) operators. They work the same way InfoSeek's exclusion and inclusion operators work.

Adding a Required Term

Although Inktomi does not use Boolean operators, you can implement an AND operator, in effect, by using the operator that forces the search software to retrieve only those documents containing a specified word.

To specify that a document *must* contain a key word in order to be retrieved, precede the term with a plus sign. For example, the following search question retrieves only those documents about the Outer Banks that mention "rentals":

Outer Banks +rentals

SEARCH TIP

Make sure that there's no space between the plus sign and the key word (this is correct: +Tibet). If you insert a space, the search software will ignore the plus sign.

Excluding Unwanted Documents

Inktomi doesn't implement the Boolean NOT operator, but you can exclude unwanted documents by using an operator that forces the search software to exclude documents containing a specified word.

To specify that a document *should not* be retrieved if it contains a certain word, precede the word with a minus sign. For example, the following search question retrieves documents about the Outer Banks, except those that also mention "windsurfing":

Outer Banks -windsurfing

Make sure that there's no space between the minus sign and the key word (this is correct: -Tibet). If you insert a space, the search software will ignore the minus sign.

SEARCH TIP

VIEWING THE SEARCH OUTPUT

When Inktomi reports the results of a search, you see the search output page (shown in Figure 12.2). The documents are ranked in order, based on a score computed by Inktomi's search engine. The score is also represented visually by a bubble graph—the more dark bubbles you see, the better the match.

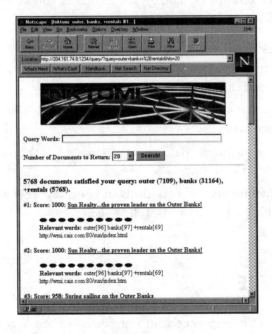

Figure 12.2 Inktomi's search output page.

By default, Inktomi displays the first 20 matches. At the top of the page, Inktomi indicates the search terms that were used to construct the retrieval list.

SEARCH TIP

If you see a message that some of the query words were not in Inktomi's index, note that you may have used excluded words (such as "is," "and," or "the"), short words (fewer than three letters), words containing numbers, or words that do not appear in Inktomi's database. Check your spelling and try again, possibly using variations or synonyms.

DEALING WITH UNSATISFACTORY SEARCHES

If your Inktomi search didn't work as well as you would have liked, look at the following checklist:

- **Check your spelling.** Look at the "words not used" entry on the output page. If you misspelled a search word, chances are it's listed here. Try again and spell the key words correctly.

- Repeat the search using the exclusion operator (-) to exclude unwanted documents.

- Use the inclusion operator (+) to force relevant documents to the top of the retrieval list.

- **Use synonyms and variations of your key words.** For example, try searching for "labour" as well as "labor."

FROM HERE

In the next chapter, check out the newest of the Web's search engines: excite (yes, it's spelled with a lowercase "e"). It's one of the best!

CHAPTER 13

SEARCHING EXCITE NETSEARCH

The newest of the Web's search engines, excite NetSearch, is a venture of Architext, Inc. And what's the payoff for Architext? It's a way of demonstrating the power of Architext's novel search engine for UNIX servers: try it out on a database of 1.5 million documents!

Is the search engine good enough to show off in this way? You be the judge, but there's one thing about Architext's search engine that you won't find on the other Web search engines discussed in this book: *concept searching*.

In brief, concept searching is very much like key word searching in that you search by typing one or more key words. However, a concept search can retrieve documents in which one or more of the key words isn't present— and there's a good chance that this document will be relevant to your search interests. How is this accomplished? By means of statistics. In a concept search, the retrieval list includes not only these documents that contain the key words you typed, but also those documents whose word frequency profiles closely resemble those of documents that contain all of the key words.

Here's an example of concept searching. Suppose you're searching for documents related to the social impact of the Internet. In an ordinary key word search, documents containing "social" *and* "impact" *and* "Internet" will top the list. But there may be documents out there that speak of the social *implications* of the Internet, without actually mentioning "impact." In a concept search, such a document would probably appear fairly near the top of the retrieval list. In a key word search, it might not appear at all.

This search engine offers a number of other plusses, including a database of some 30,000 reviews of Web sites and the ability to search Usenet newsgroups and the Web with the same search. It's worth a try, but you'll run into a major drawback for deep searching: You can retrieve a maximum of 40 documents. This makes sense for most searchers—after all, if you can't find a few good documents in the top 40 then you ought to redo the search. If you're trying to put together a comprehensive bibliography, though, it means you may have to do a number of well-focused searches to find everything that's relevant to your subject.

KEY TERM

concept searching
A method of retrieval from a full-text database that retrieves statistically similar documents, even if they lack one or more of the key words you've typed.

SEARCH OPTIONS WITH EXCITE NETSEARCH

To search excite NetSearch, choose among the following options:

- **Key Word Search**. You type your key words in a text box. By default, excite searches with an implied OR operator, giving preference to documents in which all the key words appear.

- **Concept Search**. You initiate this search the same way you initiate a key word search—by typing one or more key words. Some of the documents retrieved may not contain one or more of the key words you've typed, but their statistical profiles closely match the top-ranking documents.

In addition, you can select the following databases:

- **Web Documents**. The database currently contains 1.5 million documents.

- **Usenet Discussion Groups.** The full text of Usenet articles posted to thousands of newsgroups over the past two weeks.

- **Usenet Classified Ads.** This search focuses on Usenet newsgroups containing classified ads.

EXCITE NETSEARCH AT A GLANCE

URL: http://www.excite.com/

Internet Services Indexed: World Wide Web pages, Usenet newsgroups.

Size of Database: 1.5 million documents.

Web Document Components Indexed: All.

Restricted Field Searching: No.

Default Search Setting: OR, operator implied, but ranking preference is given to documents in which all key words appear.

Boolean Operators: None.

Truncation: Words are stemmed to their apparent roots (for example, "imagination" is stemmed to "imagine").

Phrase Search: No.

Proximity Operators: None.

Case-sensitive Search: None.

Relevancy Ranking: Yes.

Output Content: Title, URL, first 1–5 lines of text.

Special Features: Concept searching, Usenet discussion groups, search refining, query-by-example. Also, document summaries are generated by a proprietary algorithm that isolates sentences related to the document's thematic content and places them into the summary that appears in the retrieval list.

PERFORMING A SIMPLE SEARCH WITH EXCITE NETSEARCH

After accessing excite NetSearch's default page (Figure 13.1), do the following to start a search:

1. Choose a concept or key word search by clicking the appropriate option box.
2. Type one or more keywords, leaving a space between them.
3. Select the database you want to search.
4. Click **Search**.

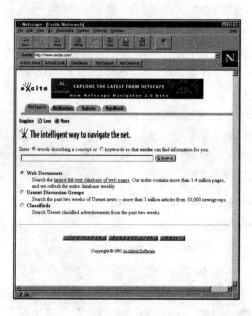

Figure 13.1 excite NetSearch Search Page.

By default, excite NetSearch stems your key words. If you type "properties," the search engine will give equal weight to documents containing "property."

After you click the **Search** button, you'll see a search output page, described in the next section.

VIEWING THE SEARCH OUTPUT

When excite NetSearch reports the results of a search, you see the search output page (shown in Figure 13.2). The documents are ranked in order, based on a confidence (relevance) percentage computed by the search engine. A document with a 100% confidence level is dead-on for your subject; a document with a 50% confidence level has only a 50-50 chance of being relevant to your subject.

The icons shown to the left of each retrieved item give you a quick index to the confidence level: The red icons indicate a good level of confidence that this document pertains to your search subject; an item flagged with a black icon probably isn't relevant.

You see ten documents, out of a maximum of 40. To see additional documents, if any are available, click the **Next Documents** button.

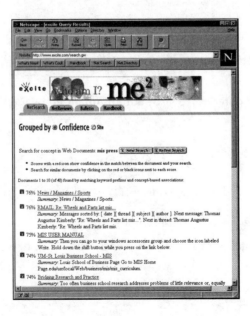

Figure 13.2 Search output page (excite NetSearch).

Sorting the Retrieval List by Web Site

A unique characteristic of excite NetSearch is the ability to display the retrieved documents in two ways. By default, you see a retrieval list sorted by confidence. By clicking the **Site** option button at the top of the retrieval page (in the Grouped By area), you can view the list sorted by the Web server from which the documents originate (see Figure 13.3).

Figure 13.3 Search output organized by Web server site.

The Output Page Header

At the top of the page, you see a report listing the following items:

- The key words used in your search.
- The total number of documents found (out of a maximum of 40).

Understanding the Items in the Retrieval List

Each retrieved document is preceded by a confidence icon (a red icon indicates high confidence that the document is relevant to your search interests, while a black icon indicates low confidence). Also shown is the confidence percentage, the document's title, and a brief summary (consisting of two or three lines of text surrounding the first instance of one of your key words).

REFINING A SEARCH

Like InfoSeek, excite NetSearch enables you to refine your search by adding additional key words to the ones you've already typed. This may increase precision if your retrieval list included many false drops.

To refine your search, click the **Refine Search** button. You'll see a page that echoes your current search settings. Try adding additional search terms, then click **Search**.

FINDING SIMILAR PAGES

If you click a confidence icon next to one of the documents in the retrieval list, excite NetSearch will display a new retrieval list consisting of documents that closely match the current document's word frequency profile.

SEARCH TIP

Try searching for similar pages. To do so, click one of the red or black confidence icons. Unlike a similar feature in InfoSeek, this one does a convincingly good job of retrieving interesting and relevant documents, including many that weren't retrieved by your original search.

FROM HERE

The next chapter brings this section to a close by examining WebCrawler, the last—and arguably the least—of the search engines discussed in this book.

CHAPTER 14

SEARCHING WEBCRAWLER

The two most important things about WebCrawler are that it's very fast, but the database isn't very big (only 250,000 documents). These facts make WebCrawler less than perfect for deep searching, but it's still worth a visit—particularly if you're after some fast results or are hoping that WebCrawler's spider has catalogued a document that escaped the spiders of other Web search engines.

Currently operated by America Online, WebCrawler may be headed for growth if its parent company decides to put some money into it. The investment's needed: WebCrawler's database lags far behind those of competing Web search engines. As for the search software, it's passable—it's easy to use for a rough-and-ready search, but it's very difficult to get a precise retrieval list out of a WebCrawler search. This chapter surveys the few things you can do to improve a WebCrawler search.

WEBCRAWLER AT A GLANCE

URL: http://webcrawler.com/

Internet Services Indexed: World Wide Web pages, Gopher, FTP.

Size of Database: 250,000 documents.

Web Document Components Indexed: All.

Restricted Field Searching: No.

Default Search Setting: AND operator applied between all key words.

Boolean Operators: OR, AND.

Truncation: Words are stemmed to their singular form.

Phrase Search: No.

Proximity Operators: None.

Case Sensitivity: None.

Relevancy Ranking: Yes.

Output Content: Title, URL, first 1-5 lines of text.

Special Features: None.

PERFORMING A SIMPLE SEARCH WITH WEBCRAWLER

WebCrawler's search page (Figure 14.1) displays this service's rather thin offerings: You can type search words, choose Boolean operators, and select the number of documents to display.

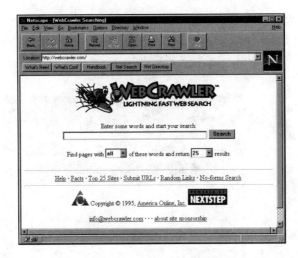

Figure 14.1 WebCrawler search page.

To choose Boolean operators, select one of the following from the list box:

- **All**. WebCrawler inserts AND between all the search words you type.
- **Any**. WebCrawler inserts OR between all the search words you type.

There's no way to perform a search that mixes OR and AND, and you won't find a NOT operator.

Note that WebCrawler does not automatically truncate words: If you type "rock," WebCrawler will not retrieve documents containing "rockets" and "rocketry." However, the program does strip common plurals to their root (for example, "boats" is changed to "boat").

After you click the **Search** button, you'll see a search output page, described in the next section.

VIEWING THE SEARCH OUTPUT

A WebCrawler retrieval list isn't anything to write home about (see Figure 14.2)—it's just a list of document titles preceded by their relevance rank.

But hey, it's fast. Just don't count on high precision! A search for "power boats for sale" produced a list in which the fifth listed document described a new technology in coffee brewing.

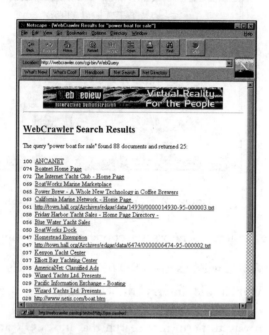

Figure 14.2 WebCrawler search output.

FROM HERE

This chapter concludes the book's survey of Web search engines. In the next section, you'll learn about the many specialized search services on the World Wide Web. If you're in search of a particular kind of information—reference, people, jobs, and more—be sure to check out the chapters to follow.

CHAPTER 15

FINDING GENERAL-INTEREST REFERENCE INFORMATION

If you can't find what you're looking for by using the Web's subject trees, search engines, and trailblazer pages, you may need a more specialized reference resource. Among the Web's treasures are hundreds of searchable databases of information in specialized resource areas, covering everything from the gods of antiquity to the jargon of modern-day computer hackers. In this section of Web Search Strategies, you learn how to take advantage of these specialized reference resources. We'll start with reference works then subsequent chapters discuss searchable Web resources covering news and weather, stocks and investments, periodical literature, jobs, and email addresses. This chapter and the next discuss Web-based reference works.

What are reference works? Walk into any library, and you'll see a reference shelf, filled with directories, encyclopedias, dictionaries, and other general reference works. These frequently-consulted works answer commonly-asked questions of the following sort: "What's the meaning of 'ambrosia'?" "Where is Earlysville, Virginia?" and "How much is 4.8 liters, in U.S. liquid measurements?"

Although the Web can't take the place of a good library, you'll find that some excellent general reference works can be found among the Web's searchable offerings. This chapter discusses the following general reference works:

- Acronyms
- Calendars
- Dictionaries
- Encyclopedias
- FAQs ("Frequently Asked Questions" from Usenet newsgroups)
- Phone Numbers (Yellow Pages and business directories)
- Quotations
- Thesaurus
- Zip Codes

SEARCH TIP

Looking for searchable databases on the Web? The place to start is The Internet Sleuth (http://www.intbc.com/sleuth/), which is nominally a unified search interface like the other ones discussed in Chapter 2. Using the Internet Sleuth, you can search Lycos, InfoSeek, WebCrawler, and other search engines—but as Chapter 2 argues, you're better off using these services directly. What's so special about the Internet Sleuth is the page's directory of subject-oriented databases in a huge variety of fields, ranging from agriculture to veterinary medicine. Take a browse through the Internet Sleuth's database list—you'll be glad you did.

HOW TO USE THE STEP 5 CHAPTERS

The fifth step of the Web search strategy is exploring specialized search resouces. In Chapters 15 through 25, you'll find many searchable sites listed (and a good dose of sites that use subject tree organizations). Where there's more than one site in a given category, the sites are listed in order of quality—the four-starred sites go first.

REFERENCE TRAILBLAZER PAGES

If you're starting a Web research session, you'll want to visit a reference trailblazer page first. These pages serve as guides to other Web resources, and can save you hours of aimless browsing. The good reference trailblazer pages—the Internet Public Library Reference Center is the best available—can promptly direct you to the information you need.

The Internet Public Library Reference Center

Imagine that you've just stepped into the reference room of a cozy public library. To the left, there's a librarian sitting at a desk. The bookshelves are jammed with dictionaries, encyclopedias, and other reference works. There's a comfortable couch to sit on. To use any of these reference works, just reach out—and click! That's the appeal of the Internet Public Library Reference Center, which ought to be the first stop in your reference work. There are other trailblazer pages that have more information, to be sure, but this one's very easy to use and comes with clear, concise explanations of the Web reference resources you can access. Figure 15.1 shows the welcome page.

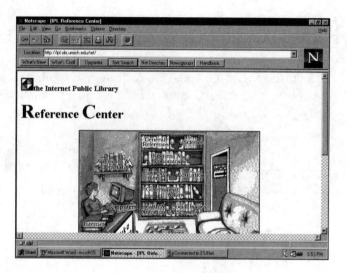

Figure 15.1 The Internet Public Library Reference Center welcome page.

Interactive features make this site stand out: You can even ask a live reference librarian a question using the Internet Public Library MOO (derived from object-oriented MUD games, no less). If there's no librarian in the MOO, you can ask your question via a form or email.

> ## THE INTERNET PUBLIC LIBRARY REFERENCE CENTER ★ ★ ★ ★
>
> **URL:** http://ipl.sils.umich.edu/ref/
>
> **Capsule Review:** For anyone who wishes to use the Web for reference purposes, this is the place to start. A University of Michigan project, this site uses the graphical metaphor of a public library; it's easy and fun to use.

Carol's Reference Desk

Maintained by Carol Oakes, a librarian at Boise State University, Carol's Reference Desk lacks the interactive features of the Internet Public Library Reference Center but otherwise competes favorably with it. Oakes has included links to lots of great Web resources, dealing with everything from the U.S. government to the weather. She's organized her links in a logical way, so finding the resource you need is a simple matter of scrolling through her subject headings until you find the one you want. Figure 15.2 shows Carol's Reference Desk.

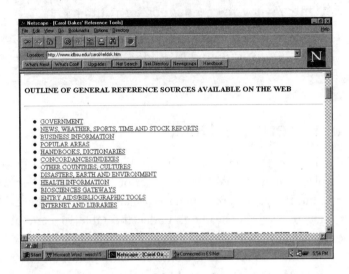

Figure 15.2 Carol's Reference Desk.

CAROL'S REFERENCE DESK ★ ★ ★

URL: http://www.idbsu.edu/carol/refdsk.htm

Capsule Review: A useful collection of Web reference resources, compiled by a librarian, with an easy-to-follow structure.

Virtual Reference Collection

Yet another nifty place to start a Web search session. This trailblazer page, maintained by the University of California at Irvine, references all the usual resources but distinguishes itself from the other trailblazer pages by its navigation features. Not only can you click headings in the table of contents to follow internal hyperlinks, you can also follow other internal hyperlinks throughout the page to return to the table of contents. This little feature makes it easy to find lots of resources in one session.

VIRTUAL REFERENCE COLLECTION ★ ★ ★

URL: http://www.lib.uci.edu/sources/vrc.html

Capsule Review: A reference trailblazer page with a good-sized collection of hyperlinks and a thoughtful internal-navigation scheme.

Virtual Reference Desk

Maintained by Purdue University, the Virtual Reference Desk is another great place to start a Web research effort. There's no key word or text search, but the page's creators have organized it with internal hyperlinks: just click one of the headings under the table of contents to see the resources listed under that heading. Purdue's librarians have loaded this site with links to everything from the United States Constitution to the periodic table of the elements. There's also a large collection of hyperlinks to obscure foreign-language dictionaries.

VIRTUAL REFERENCE DESK ★ ★ ★

URL: http://thorplus.lib.purdue.edu/reference/index.html

Capsule Review: A good place to start Web information searches, with an especially large collection of hyperlinks to foreign-language dictionaries.

University of Texas Library Online

This site isn't as good as the other reference trailblazer pages, but it's not a bad site to keep on your hotlist in case the other sites don't help you. At the University of Texas Library site, rely on the links to subject-specific trailblazer pages instead of on the key word search. The trailblazer pages contain a wealth of links to resources on a variety of subjects, while the text search—a WAIS gateway—can return some results that fall between puzzling and comical on the spectrum of usefulness. A search for "World Wide Web," for example, returned links to "World History" and "Australian Studies."

UNIVERSITY OF TEXAS LIBRARY ONLINE ★ ★

URL: http://www.lib.utexas.edu/

Capsule Review: A good collection of subject-specific trailblazer pages, but don't count on good results from the search tool.

ACRONYMS

Acronyms are words formed from the initial letters of a phrase, such as International Standards Organization (ISO). One of the problems with acronyms is that people often use them under the assumption that you know what they mean. If you run across an acronym that's Greek to you, you can get help from the Web.

Explain: The Ultimate Acronym Glossary

Here's the Web's best acronym server. When you type an acronym into Explain, the program will search an acronym database of over 22,000 entries, the largest on the Internet. The server is quite fast, and the retrieval list contains a plus—links (customized for the acronym you've just searched for) to all the other known acronym servers on the entire Internet. If you're not happy with Explain's results, you can click any of these links to search additional acronym servers.

To use Explain, just type the acronym whose meaning you don't know; case doesn't matter. When you've finished typing the acronym, press **Enter**.

EXPLAIN: THE ULTIMATE GLOSSARY ★ ★ ★ ★

URL: http//www.ihi.aber.ac.uk/cgi-bin/explain

Capsule Review: This is the place to start you search for an acronym's meaning. This acronym server offers a database of more than 22,000 acronyms, the largest on the Internet. The automatically-generated retrieval list can be used to initiate searches (using the acronym you typed) in as many as a dozen additional acronym databases.

WorldWideWeb Acronym and Abbreviation Server

Don't know what an acronym means? Check out the Acronym Server. You type the acronym, and the Acronym Server looks it up in a dictionary of more than 13,000 acronyms from a wide variety of fields. If the Acronym Server finds a match, you see a new Web page listing the words from which the acronym was constructed.

The Acronym Server is highly interactive—when a search fails, a list of recent acronyms is displayed that the Server couldn't identify. You're asked to supply the meanings if you should happen to know them. Using the Acronym Server is somewhat difficult because some pages lack internal navigation aids; you're supposed to use your browser's **Back** button to redisplay the initial page. This can be confusing to new users.

THE WORLDWIDEWEB ACRONYM AND ABBREVIATION SERVER ★ ★

URL: http://curia.ucc.ie/info/net/acronyms/acro.html

Capsule Review: If you can't find an acronym using Explain, try looking it up in the WorldWideWeb Acronym and Abbreviation Server, which has a smaller database but covers some different areas. You type the acronym, and the search engine attempts to expand the content. If it can't, you can click a link to try another acronym server.

SEARCH TIP

Couldn't find the acronym you're looking for? The WorldWideWeb Acronym and Abbreviation Server has a very nice feature: a hyperlink that, when clicked, automatically sends your query to another acronym server. If you didn't get results from this server, click the **search the INTT-ELEC database** hyperlink.

CALENDARS

What happened on a given day in history? Thanks to the calendar generators discussed in this section, you can find out by using the Web. You'll be able to answer lots of other questions, too, such as what day of the week a given day will fall on.

Britannica's Lives

Who was born on today's date—or for that matter, any other date, such as your birthday? Find out using Britannica's Lives, a free service of the subscription-based Britannica OnLine (the online edition of the famed Encyclopedia Britannica).

To use Britannica's Lives, picks a date and a month. At the bottom of the screen is the year, which you should leave set to the current year if you would like to know about today's famous people. Then pick an age range (for example, "Forties" or "Fifties"), and click **Show Biographies**.

To find out who was famous in a previous year, change the year, pick a date, pick an age range, and click **Show Biographies** again. I guarantee that you'll spend some time exploring this very interesting Web site!

BRITANNICA'S LIVES ★ ★ ★ ★

URL: http://www.eb.com/calendar/calendar.html

Capsule Review: Find out who was born on a given day, and read biographies drawn from the Encyclopedia Britannica. You can even type a given year, and find out who were the most famous contemporaries of that year. It's fun and mildly addictive!

Calendar

I was born on a Tuesday. The U.S. Declaration of Independence was signed on a Thursday. Christmas in the year 75 fell on a Monday. This is the sort of information with which you can amaze and baffle your friends if you're clued in to the U.S. Navy's Calendar site. Calendar lets you input a month and a year, and it returns a calendar for that month. Put your month and year into the text box in the form M/YYYY (2/1874 for February 1874, for example) and press **Enter**. You'll see a calendar for that month.

SEARCH TIP

As the instructions at the site say, try entering 9/1752. That's the month Pope Gregory decreed that thirteen calendar days would not occur in order to resynchronize the calendar with the celestial motion of the Earth.

CALENDAR ★ ★

URL: http://www.cmf.nrl.navy.mil/calendar

Capsule Review: Enter a month and year and see a calendar for that month, with days of the week labeled.

WWW Calendar Generator

The WWW Calendar Generator, based on a Common Gateway Interface script written by Dan Faules, builds calendars based on month, year, and heading information that you supply. For example, you can tell the program to make a calendar for June, 1944, with the heading "Key Dates in the Allied Invasion of France," and Faules' script will build such a calendar for you. What is more, the calendar is generated as an HTML table, so you can import it into your own Web publications. To import the HTML, use your browser to view the source code of the finished calendar; select all of the source code, copy it, and paste it into your document. Show appreciation for Faules' work by keeping his comments in the table source code intact in your document.

WWW CALENDAR GENERATOR ★ ★

URL: http://www.intellinet.com/CoolTools/CalendarMaker/

Capsule Review: If you need a calendar on your Web page, this site will do the dirty work of HTML coding for you. Enter the month, year, and heading you want, and a CGI script returns HTML code ready for pasting into your document.

DICTIONARIES

Dictionaries are a natural application of the Web. Unlike paper dictionaries, Web dictionaries take up no space on your desk and, in the cases of the dictionaries listed here, don't cost a dime. You don't even have to be familiar with alphabetical order to use a Web dictionary—just type in your word and see the results. Furthermore, Web dictionaries free you from having to find obscure foreign-language dictionaries for projects that require such resources.

Free On-Line Dictionary of Computing (FOLDOC)

A project of Denis Howe, a computing graduate student at the Imperial College, London, this impressive work contains 8611 definitions totaling 3.3 megabytes. It's searchable by key word. If you're having trouble getting through to the U.K. site, there's a mirror at Princeton University (http://wagner.Princeton.EDU/foldoc/contents.html).

To use FOLDOC, you can browse the subject headings—or better yet, you can search. Case isn't significant and truncation is automatic. However, you can perform a case-sensitive exact match search, if you prefer. The search returns a single entry whose complete heading matches your search string—or, if the search fails to find a match, a list of all entries that begin with your search string. The definitions may be somewhat brief—this isn't an encyclopedia, after all—but they're enlightening, and you'll be hard-pressed to find any computer dictionary, printed or otherwise, that contains so many terms.

FREE ON-LINE DICTIONARY OF COMPUTING (FOLDOC) ★ ★ ★ ★

URL: http://wombat.doc.ic.ac.uk/

Capsule Review: This impressive work contains 8611 definitions totaling 3.3 MB. It's searchable by key word. By default, searching is case-insensitive with automatic truncation, although you can perform an exact-match, case-sensitive search if you prefer. Definitions are brief but accurate and enlightening.

Hypertext Webster Interface

Based on the popular UNIX program called Webster, this Carnegie-Mellon University site lets you enter a word in a text box and click **Perform word lookup** to see the *Webster's Dictionary* definition of that word. Furthermore, the site hyperlinks nearly every word in the definition to other entries in *Webster's Dictionary*, making it easy to browse the dictionary and improve your vocabulary.

HYPERTEXT WEBSTER INTERFACE ★ ★ ★ ★

URL: http://c.gp.cs.cmu.edu:5103/prog/webster

Capsule Review: This site provides definitions of English words, and hyperlinks almost every word of the definitions to other dictionary entries.

Echo-Eurodicautom

A project of Felix Gaehtgens and Jens Kurlanda at the University of Frankfurt in Germany, Echo-Eurodicautom lets you enter a word in any major European language and see its translation in any other of those languages. Enter your word in the text box (be sure to see the chart at http://www.uni-frankfurt.de/~kurlanda/echo_umlauts.html for instructions on how to represent umlauts and other special characters), select a starting language and a target language, and click the **start query** button. If Echo-Eurodicautom has your word in its database, you'll see a definition of the word and its equivalent in the target language.

Note that Echo-Eurodicautom specializes in technical words, and therefore is not the place to look for general-usage words. The English word "film," for example, translates to a German word for bacterial cultures grown on the surface of a liquid. Figure 15.3 shows the Echo-Eurodicautom page.

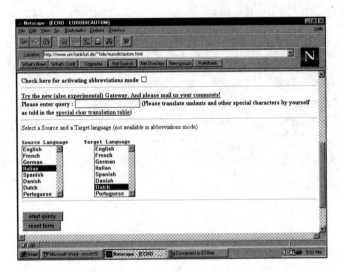

Figure 15.3 Echo-Eurodicautom.

ECHO–EURODICAUTOM ★ ★ ★

URL: http://www.uni-frankfurt.de/~felix/eurodictautom.html

Capsule Review: This site helps you translate a word in English, French, German, Italian, Spanish, Danish, Dutch, or Portuguese into any other of those languages. Though it claims to focus on technical words, this site has lots of general-usage words, too.

The Alternative Dictionaries

It had to happen—a site that enables Internet users themselves to build a dictionary of "Slang, swear words, and other 'bad language.'" What's especially intriguing about this site is its multi-lingual coverage: There are entries for dozens of languages, including Afrikaans, Arabic, Catalan, Lithuanian, Polish, and many more—including an astounding 25 entries for Esperanto, which I didn't suppose would have any swear words (but I suppose that's inevitable in an international language). What's not so great about The Alternative Dictionaries is the relatively sparse coverage—there are only 298 English entries, for example, and that's the largest of the dictionaries. There's no search facility; the site is browsable by alphabetical order only.

> **THE ALTERNATIVE DICTIONARIES ★ ★**
>
> **URL:** http://www.notam.uio.no/~hcholm/altlang/
>
> **Capsule Review:** An interesting experiment, The Alternative Dictionaries include slang and "bad language" definitions for dozens of languages. At present, coverage is sparse and spotty, but the site is lots of fun and will grow in value as more people contribute.

ENCYCLOPEDIAS

The Web has yet to see an encyclopedia that's both free and comprehensive. That may change in the future, but for now this is the weakest area of the Web—unless you're willing to fork over the hefty subscription fee for Britannica OnLine.

Britannica OnLine

The famed Encyclopedia Britannica, probably the most scholarly and assuredly the most expensive encyclopedia available, has an online version—but it's not free. A subscription will cost you $150 per year, at current pricing—well worth it, when you consider the cost of the print-based encyclopedia.

Moreover, you'll have the satisfaction of knowing that all the articles you're accessing are up-to-date, unlike the print-based version. If you're thinking about buying an encyclopedia for your home, consider Britannica OnLine. An enticement is a free trial, which is available by accessing the site's URL.

BRITANNICA ONLINE ★ ★ ★ ★

URL: http://www.eb.com:80/

Capsule Review: An excellent online version of the famed Encyclopedia Britannica. Thousands of illustrations and maps complement the text, which is accessible by means of browsing or searching. You'll need to subscribe in order to access this service, but a free trial is available.

CIA World Factbook 1995

Published by the U.S. Central Intelligence Agency (CIA), the CIA World Factbook is one of the most impressive and useful collections of country-based knowledge that you'll find anywhere. And the full text is available online. This is a valuable research resource.

The Factbook is actually only one of a series of intelligence resources that are available at this site; others include 1995 Factbook on Intelligence, CIA Maps and Publications Released to the Public, DCI and DDCIs of Central Intelligence, Chiefs of State and Cabinet Members of Foreign Governments, and Intelligence Literature: Suggested Reading List. You can search all of these publications (including the Factbook) by accessing the search page at http://www.odci.gov/Harvest/brokers/odciweb/query.html. The search engine, Harvest, is unusually powerful, offering a variety of search options. The result of a search is a ranked list of documents.

CIA WORLD FACTBOOK 1995 ★ ★ ★ ★

URL: http://www.odci.gov/cia/publications/pubs.html

Capsule Review: A useful collection of in-depth articles on most of the countries of the world, including maps and a wealth of statistics. An excellent research resource.

Global Encyclopedia

This encyclopedia represents a great concept, but one that has a long way to go before it competes in practice with subscription-based encyclopedias like the *Encyclopedia Britannica*. The Global Encyclopedia relies on submissions from volunteers to fill its database. Predictably, this has resulted in spotty quality. The entries for "immune system" and "India" fill several screens, while Winston Churchill merits a lone paragraph. While several article contributors provide references at the ends of their contributions, most do not, and there's no way to verify the accuracy of the articles.

To use the Global Encyclopedia, you can enter a search term in the text box and click the **Search** button. Alternately, click one of the hyperlinked letters on the welcome page to see articles available under that letter. You can add your own article by clicking the **Add Article** hyperlink on the welcome page.

GLOBAL ENCYCLOPEDIA ★ ★

URL: http://204.32.221.16/

Capsule Review: A growing encyclopedia built with contributions from volunteer article-writers. Coverage and article quality remain irregular, but this site has huge potential.

FAQs

Every Web and Usenet veteran knows that lists of frequently asked questions—FAQs—can contain the best information on any given subject. FAQs usually contain more up-to-date information than books, and more practical information than magazines. They're the place to look for information on any given subject. But how do you find the FAQ you need? The following site can help.

Oxford University FAQ Search Facility

Not only does this site provide an index of FAQs, it archives them too. Generally, that means you'll be able to access the FAQs you need anytime the search facility works. The archive is exhaustive, too: it contains FAQs on everything from model railroads to industrial music.

To search for a FAQ, enter a key word in the text box and click the **Search** button. The site will return a list of hyperlinks to FAQs that match your specification. The server isn't too picky about the links it returns: A search for FAQs about any particular genre of music will return links to FAQs for just about every other type of music, too. Still, lots of hits are better than too few.

OXFORD UNIVERSITY FAQ SEARCH FACILITY ★ ★ ★ ★

URL: http://www.lib.ox.ac.uk/search/search_faqs.html

Capsule Review: This page searches an extensive archive of FAQs for the ones you want, and returns hyperlinks to them.

PHONE NUMBERS

Though electronic mail is rapidly eroding the monopoly long held by the telephone for instant long-distance communication, you'll still want to use the phone frequently. Voice communications allow a more personal touch than email messages, and the telephone leaves no doubt that the person with whom you're communicating has received your message. The Web abounds with searchable databases of telephone numbers—mainly for businesses, but increasingly for individuals, too.

AT&T 800 Directory

Looking for a business that has a toll-free 800 number? Check this site, which lists every number included in the AT&T 800 directory (that's the same database the operators at 800-555-1212 use). Just enter the name of the business you want to reach in the text box and click the **Get Results** button to see numbers listed for that company. Alternately, click one of the hyperlinked letters to see a list of categories starting with that letter— this makes the site useful if you want a certain kind of company, but don't know which one in particular.

AT&T 800 DIRECTORY ★ ★ ★ ★

URL: http://www.att.net/textonly.html

Capsule Review: This page allows you to search the AT&T 800 directory—the same one used by directory-assistance operators. You also can search by category, making this site useful as a set of yellow pages.

Central Source Yellow Pages

Currently listing over 10 million businesses in the U.S., the Central Source Yellow pages (Figure 15.4) provides a national alternative to local phone book listings. There's no charge for a free one-line listing. So how does this site make money? You can purchase listings in additional categories, or purchase bold or extra bold listings; you can also purchase display advertising.

Don't expect to find every business in the country in the Central Source Yellow Pages. 10 million listings sounds like a lot, but that's still only a fraction of the total business listings to be found in printed directories. If you're really interesting in finding all the dealers in a given area, you'll need to rely on printed phone books.

To search for a business listing in Central Source Yellow Pages, you can choose from searches by company name, phone number, or category. These searches use a fill-in-the-blanks search form which is easy to use. For example, if you search by Category, you'll see a screen that enables you to search for a key word (such as "boats"); supplying additional information (such as "VA") narrows the scope of the search. The result is a list of matches, if any were found. You can click one of these matches to see a list of company names; click one of these to see the company's address and telephone number. If you'd prefer to browse, there's an alphabetical listing.

CENTRAL SOURCE YELLOW PAGES ★ ★ ★

URL: http://www.telephonebook.com/

Capsule Review: With over 10 million listings, this business directory is searchable by category, phone number, and business name. It's a worthwhile place to search for business names, addresses, and telephone numbers, but don't expect 100% coverage.

Figure 15.4 Central Source Yellow Pages.

NYNEX Interactive Yellow Pages

Though NYNEX is the regional Bell operating company for New York and New England, this site lists business telephone numbers for all 50 states. Coverage isn't perfect, but it's good, especially for companies with 100 or more employees. You'll find this site useful if you need to call a distant business associate but don't have phone books for other regions of the country.

To search for a particular business in the NYNEX Interactive Yellow Pages, click the **Biz Name** hyperlink on the welcome page. You'll see a form in which you choose one or more states to narrow your search to, and a text box where you enter the name of the business you're interested in. Click the **SEARCH** button to start the search process. Alternately, you can hunt for particular kinds of businesses by entering a business category in the Business Type text box. Figure 15.5 shows the NYNEX Interactive Yellow Pages welcome page.

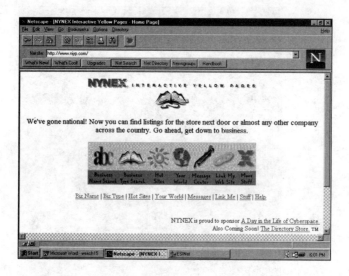

Figure 15.5 The NYNEX Interactive Yellow Pages.

 You can select several states in which to search, or you can select several states and click the **All but the selected states** check box to search for the business in all states but the ones you selected.

SEARCH TIP

NYNEX INTERACTIVE YELLOW PAGES ★ ★ ★

URL: http://www.niyp.com/

Capsule Review: Here, you can hunt for business telephone numbers in any, several, or all of the 50 states. You can also search for businesses of a particular type.

AmeriCom Long Distance Area Decoder

If you've forgotten the area code for Minneapolis, or if the country code for Estonia has slipped your mind, pay the AmeriCom Long Distance Area Decoder a visit. Just enter the city, state, and country in the proper text boxes and click the **SUBMIT** button. The AmeriCom site will return the area, city, or country codes you need. If you're not familiar with the two-letter country codes AmeriCom uses to identify countries, pay a visit to http://www.ics.uci.edu/WebSoft/wwwstat/country-codes.txt.

AMERICOM LONG DISTANCE AREA DECODER ★ ★

URL: http://www.xmission.com/~americom/aclookup.html

Capsule Review: With city, state, and country information, this site returns needed area, city, and country dialing codes.

QUOTATIONS

Whether you're an amateur toastmaster or you are just looking for a quote to add the right flavor to your home page, the Web's quotation servers can be lifesavers. Whatever kind of quote you need—humorous, inspirational, or whatever—the Web has something to suggest. Remember, as Shakespeare wrote in *All's Well that Ends Well*, "The web of our life is of a mingled yarn, good and ill together."

Bartlett's Familiar Quotations

Few reference works are, well, as familiar as *Bartlett's Familiar Quotations*. You'll find this Web site as useful as the traditional bound volume, and probably more so, as the interface makes it easy to find the perfect *bon mot* for every occasion. You can enter a key word (like "faith" or "boat") in the text box and click the **Search** button to find quotes related to that word, or you can browse the list of famous writers and speakers—each entry of which is hyperlinked to lists of that speaker's quotes—to find quotes you like.

Bear in mind that the Web version of Bartlett's is the First Edition, published in 1901. Don't look here for quotes from Winston Churchill, JFK, or Maya Angelou. Figure 15.6 shows the Bartlett's Familiar Quotations welcome page.

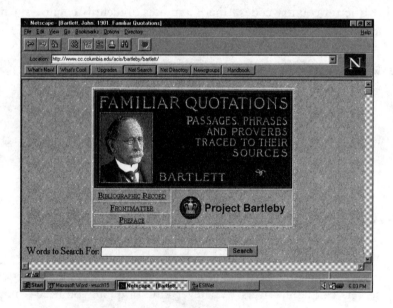

Figure 15.6 Bartlett's Familiar Quotations.

BARTLETT'S FAMILIAR QUOTATIONS ★ ★ ★ ★

URL: http://www.cc.columbia.edu/acis/bartleby/bartlett/

Capsule Review: Enter a key word and see a list of relevant famous quotes, or browse a database of quotes, organized by the names of the people to whom the quotes are attributed.

The Quote Archive

In close competition with Bartlett's Familiar Quotations is a resource backed by a much less well-known entity: Graham Ollis of the University of Arizona. The Quote Archive offers more extensive search capabilities than the Bartlett's site, offers a nifty random-quote service, and lets you add quotes of your own to the database.

To search the quote server, click the **Search** hyperlink on the welcome page. Then enter the text or source of the quote you want in the proper text box. You can specify a type of quote (movie, political, sports, etc.) by choosing a category from the drop-down list box. Click the **Search** button to generate a list of quotes that match your specifications.

THE QUOTE ARCHIVE ★ ★ ★ ★

URL: http://apsc7.rescomp.arizona.edu/~ollisg/quote/

Capsule Review: A very versatile page that lets you explore a large archive of quotes in a variety of ways.

THESAURI

With Web thesauri under your belt, you'll no longer have to think about which words to use in electronic mail you write. Instead, you'll be able to ponder the phrasing of your ethereal epistles.

Roget's Thesaurus

Right up there in the pantheon of reference tools with *Webster's Dictionary* and *Bartlett's Familiar Quotations* is *Roget's Thesaurus*. This site brings the vocabulary-widening power of this age-old resource to the Web. Enter a word in either of the two text boxes (the word entered in the "full text" box will more likely find a hit than one entered in the "headwords" box) and click the corresponding search button. You'll see the relevant passage from the 1911 edition of Roget's, with hyperlinks to other related entries.

ROGET'S THESAURUS ★ ★ ★ ★

> **URL:** http://tuna.uchicago.edu/forms_unrest/ROGET.html
>
> **Capsule Review:** A Web tool that finds synonyms and antonyms for words you provide, and makes it easy to browse the Roget's database of words.

WordNet

Here's a thesaurus with a twist. It's an online lexical reference system that's designed in accordance with current theories of how people remember words. You type in a root word, and you see a report listing the various senses of the words and the words that are typically associated with these senses. Try it!

If you like WordNet, you can download the entire system for installation on your computer (UNIX, PC, or Mac). The PC files take up 5.8 MB.

WORDNET ★ ★ ★

> **URL:** http://www.cogsci.princeton.edu/~wn/w3wn.html
>
> **Capsule Review:** An online version of WordNet, a lexical reference system that incorporates the latest psycholinguistic theories of how people remember words. Nouns, verbs, and adjectives are incorporated into synonym sets, which represent a single, underlying concept. An excellent aspect of this site is its ability to distinguish among, and define, the varying senses of a word.

ZIP CODES

Looking for a zip code, those numerical postal codes used in U.S. addresses? There are several Web services that provide zip code look-up, but the best of them comes from the U.S. Postal Service itself.

U.S. Postal Service Zip+4 Lookup

The U.S. Postal Service maintains a huge database of addresses and zip codes, and it's searchable from the Web. In the form that you'll see on-screen, you enter as much information about the address as you can find; the service then consults the huge database, and displays the correct zip code with the four-letter addendum.

USPS ZIP+4 LOOKUP ★ ★ ★ ★

URL: http://www.usps.gov/ncsc/lookups/lookup_zip+4.html

Capsule Review: Here's the only zip code lookup service that you'll ever need. You type in as much of the address as you can, and this page tells you the correct zip code. It's fast and easy to use.

CHAPTER 16

FINDING SPECIAL-INTEREST
REFERENCE INFORMATION

Dictionaries and thesauri are great, but they're usually only the beginning
of most people's reference tool kits. In addition to the resources in
Chapter 15, you may want to add maps, census tools, literature-search
engines, and a religious text or two to your arsenal of Web search
weapons.

- Authors
- Book Publishers
- Colleges and Universities
- Disasters
- Literary Works
- Maps
- Measurements
- Movies
- Religious Texts
- Scientific Constants
- Tax Forms

AUTHORS

Most public libraries have a copy of *Contemporary Authors*, a multi-volume refererence work containing information on thousands of published authors. There's nothing quite as comprehensive on the Web just yet, but you might want to take a look at the following site.

Internet Directory of Published Writers

The Internet Directory of Published Writers is a typical Internet creation: It's expanded and updated by writers themselves. Give me a few minutes, OK, while I create my entry?

You'll find hundreds of authors listed in this database, which you can browse or search. An added feature is a database of literary agents, which you can search by category. If you've been thinking of selling that cookbook or mystery, this is a good place to start looking for an agent.

INTERNET DIRECTORY OF PUBLISHED WRITERS ★ ★

URL: http://www.bocklabs.wisc.edu/ims/wri-full.html

Capsule Review: Far from comprehensive, this database of published writers depends on authors themselves for the entries. As such, it's probably not a very useful reference tool. Of more value (at least to aspiring authors) is the database of literary agents—again, it's far comprehensive, but at least you'll know that the agents listed are actively looking for business (not all are).

BOOK PUBLISHERS

More and more publishers are establishing a presence on the Web, enabling you find addresses and telephone numbers, and even to order books online.

AcqWeb's Directory of Publishers and Vendors Web and Gopher Sites

This site provides the ultimate trailblazer page of publishers and library vendors on the Web. It lists hundreds of publishers sites, grouped according to the categories shown in Table 16.1. A drawback—accounting for the site's three-star rating, despite its excellence—is the lack of a search engine.

ACQWEB'S DIRECTORY OF PUBLISHERS AND VENDORS WEB AND GOPHER SITES ★ ★ ★

URL: http://www.library.vanderbilt.edu/law/acqs/pubr.html

Capsule Review: Organized as a subject tree, this site lists hundreds of book publishers that have established an Internet presence.

Table 16.1 Publisher Categories (AcqWeb)

General and Multiple Subject Publishers
    Associations and Institutes
    Electronic Publications including online & CD-ROM
    Reference
    University Presses
Art
Business and Economics
Education
    Textbooks
Government Publications
Law
Library and Information Science
Literature and Fiction
    Children's Literature
    Poetry
    Science Fiction and Fantasy
Music
Religion
Science, Engineering and Mathematics
    BioMedicine
    Computing and Computer Science
Specialty Publishers
    Audio Books and Tapes
    Videos
Library Vendors
    Document Delivery
    Rare and Antiquarian Books

CENSUS DATA

The U.S. Bureau of the Census doesn't have a glamorous mission, but it has an important one. The Census' information determines the allotment of Congressional seats among the states, and speaks volumes about the social fabric of the United States. The Census Bureau's Web site makes it easy to access much of the information the office gathers every ten years. Click **Search** button at the bottom of the imagemap on the welcome page to start your search. On the page that appears, you can choose from among several searches:

- **Word Search**. The Word Search allows you to search for words and phrases in the Census Bureau's library of documents related to the U.S. Census. Choose from among the listed indices (special indices exist for press releases, graphics files, and other information categories) by clicking the hyperlinked name of the index you want. Then, in the text box, enter your terms and press **Enter**. The search engine will return a hyperlinked list of resources that match your terms. Click an item to display its full text.

SEARCH TIP

The Census Bureau search engine supports nested Boolean searches, which are useful tools. In the search engine's text boxes, you could enter, say, "(chicano and dallas) or (latino and phoenix)" to cull from the database all records containing both "chicano" and "dallas," or "latino" and "phoenix."

- **Place Search**. One of the most powerful features of the Census site, the Place Search tool combs the Census Bureau's U.S. Gazetteer for information about any incorporated city or town—from Philadelphia, Pennsylvania, to Cut And Shoot, Texas—you specify. In the text box, enter the city name, city and state name, or ZIP code of the place you're studying and press **Enter**. The search engine will return capsule summaries of each census year) and physical location. The capsule summaries also include links to maps, and links to more detailed census information including racial, age, and family-status breakdowns.

- **Map Search**. For those who like their information presented graphically, or who require county- or congressional district-level information, the Census Bureau offers Map Search, an imagemap-based interface to information about different parts of the United States. To use Map Search, click the state or district you're interested in. You'll see a map of that state, divided into counties (parishes, census districts, whatever). If you want, you can click the **Congressional Districts** hyperlink below the state map to see a list—not a map— of county or other division you want, and you'll see a capsule summary of the county's statistics, complete with links to detailed maps and census forms.

- **Staff Search.** You also can look for Census Bureau employees here. Enter your person's first name in the top box, his or her last name in the bottom box, and click the **Submit** button.

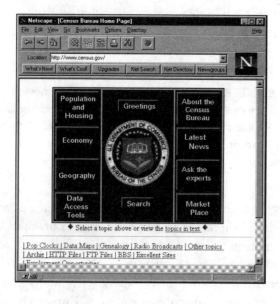

Figure 16.1 The U.S. Census Bureau welcome page.

U.S. CENSUS BUREAU ★ ★ ★

URL: http://www.census.gov/

Capsule Review: A guide to the 1990 U.S. Census, including search engines that allow you to search for statistics on particular towns and cities. There's also a great map-based interface to the Census data.

COLLEGES AND UNIVERSITIES

Selecting a college is one of the most important decisions of a person's life, so it's a great idea to take advantage of all the information you can find. Unfortunately, the Web is surprisingly weak in this area. You can find thousands of college and university home pages, but these are designed for utilitarian purposes (such as providing faculty addresses and course lists) rather than admission purposes, in the main. There's an on-line version of the famed *Peterson's College Guide*, but the coverage isn't nearly as comprehensives as the print-based version.

Peterson's Education Center

This site brings together information about schools at every conceivable level, from K-12 through graduate school. You can search for information, and even apply to schools of your choice. A drawback of the site is that there's no search tool; you have to access information using an alphabetical or geographical guide. Note, too, that coverage isn't complete; schools must pay a fee to be listed here. Also, the entries are pretty thin. You'd have a tough time selecting a school from the information contained here.

> **PETERSON'S EDUCATION CENTER ★ ★ ★**
>
> **URL:** http://www.petersons.com/
>
> **Capsule Review:** This service is a good place to start if you're looking for college admissions information, but note that the coverage isn't complete—not every college has paid a fee to be included here—and some of the articles seem pretty thin.

American Universities

A trailblazer page that provides links to official and unofficial college and university home pages, this site doesn't offer advanced features—for example, there's no search engine. Coverage is spotty, too. You'll find links to Canadian and international universities.

AMERICAN UNIVERSITIES ★ ★

> **URL:** http://www.clas.ufl.edu/CLAS/american-universities.html
>
> **Capsule Review:** A useful trailblazer page that provides links to hundreds of U.S. universities. The site lacks a search engine, but it's easily browsed. Note that the pages may not be official ones, and quality varies.

National Liberal Arts Colleges

This trailblazer page provides an index of liberal arts colleges (as defined by the Carnegie Foundation for the Advancement of Teaching) that maintain home pages—official or unofficial. The quality and coverage varies, but it's worth taking a look—especially if you're thinking about investing $100,000 in your kid's college education at one of these pricey schools!

NATIONAL LIBERAL ARTS COLLEGES ★ ★

> **URL:** http://www.aavc.vassar.edu/libarts.colleges.html
>
> **Capsule Review:** A useful trailblazer page that provides links to hundreds of liberal arts colleges. Although there's no search engine, the list is easily browsed. The quality of the listed sites varies, and there's no search engine.

EARTHQUAKES

Given the strong presence of science and scientists on the Internet, it's not surprising that you'd find high-quality scientific information on the Web—and that's especially true of earthquakes. The two sites listed here will occupy anyone interested in these terrifying disasters

Earthquake Info from the U.S.G.S. in Menlo Park, CA

Here's the ultimate earthquake site. You'll find earthquake lists, maps, and news. The Current Earthquakes page catalogs large earthquakes all over the world. The Weekly Reports cover northern California, the US, and the world. The Hot News page allows extended discussion of recent events. You'll even find maps that predict the earthquake danger for future quakes in the shaky San Francisco Bay Area.

EARTHQUAKE INFO FROM THE U.S.G.S. IN MENLO PARK, CA ★ ★ ★ ★

URL: http://quake.wr.usgs.gov/

Capsule Review: The ultimate site for news and information about earthquakes, both recent and historical. The site offers up-to-date news and discussions of recent seismic events, informative graphics, and detailed statistical information. There's a Northern California focus, naturally that's where the site is located, and there are lots of earthquakes there—but you'll find news and data of earthquakes elsewhere.

Global Earthquake Information

This site isn't fancy—it doesn't have the depth of the U.S.G.S. site—but it does have one interesting feature: A map that displays the most recent top ten seismic events. Well worth a look if you're interested in a quick overview.

GLOBAL EARTHQUAKE INFORMATION ★ ★

URL: http://128.95.24.1/globaleq.html

Capsule Review: This site provides a quick overview, both in a list and in a graphic, of the top recent seismic events. If you're looking for a quick overview of recent earthquake patterns, this is a great place to look.

LITERACY WORKS

Aside from being useful to literary scholars, these sites are some of the most fun on the Web for those who love language. How many times does Shakespeare use the word "love" in *Romeo and Juliet*? In what books of the *Iliad* does Penelope speak? What does Hippocrates have to say about surgery? Did any famous Classical writers have characters with your name? These sites answer those questions. Also take a look at the "Religious Texts" section later in this chapter; the sites there do much the same thing.

Searching the Works of the Bard

Jeremy Hylton, a Webmaster at *The Tech*, a student newspaper at the Massachusetts Institute of Technology, has done a favor for every under-graduate who has to analyze imagery in the speeches of Iago or classical allusions in the words of King Lear. The Complete Works of William Shakespeare enables you to search the text of all of William Shakespeare's plays, sonnets, and other poems for search terms of your choice. Never again will you have to go without a classy epigraph for an essay.

To search The Complete Works of William Shakespeare, click the **Search the Texts** hyperlink on the welcome page (Figure 16.2). Enter your search terms in the top text box ("Feast of Crispian," for example, if you're looking for King Henry's stirring speech to his troops before the Battle of Agincourt in *Henry V*). Click one of the radio buttons below the key word to specify whether the search terms are to be joined with the Boolean oper-ator AND or OR. In the second text box, enter the number of letters by which results can differ from your search terms, and click a radio button to indicate whether you want the search engine to look for your search terms alone, or as part of larger words, too. Click the **Submit Query** button. The search engine will return a list of hyperlinks—complete with your search terms in context—to places in the text where your terms occur.

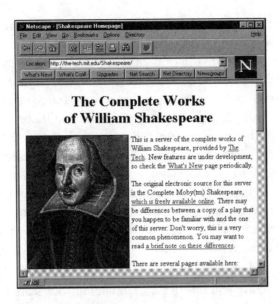

Figure 16.2 The Complete Works of William Shakespeare welcome page.

THE COMPLETE WORKS OF WILLIAM SHAKESPEARE ★ ★ ★ ★

URL: http://the-tech.mit.edu/Shakespeare/

Capsule Review: Search the plays and poems of William Shakespeare for words you specify, or just browse the texts, using the helpful glosses to improve your understanding of the works.

Examining the Classics

Here's a monumental work that gives a simple way of accessing 375 works by ancient Greek and Roman authors, including Homer, Virgil, Plutarch, Herodotus, and Aristotle. Webmaster Daniel Stevenson, another MIT student, has taken electronic texts from all over the Internet and built a search engine that can tell you what Homer had to say about ships or what Tacitus wrote about the Roman Senate.

To search The Tech Classics Archive, click the **search the complete body of work** hyperlink on the welcome page. Enter your search terms in the text box at the top of the page, and click radio buttons to describe how the Glimpse search engine should interpret your key words. With the first set of radio buttons, you can tell the search engine to look for any of your words (effectively putting a Boolean OR between them), all of your words (the equivalent of a Boolean AND), or your words exactly as you entered them. The next sets of radio buttons allow you to tell the search engine to look for whole words only or to pay attention to capitalization in your search terms. You also can de-select authors whose works do not interest you by clicking the check boxes in front of their names. The search engine will not examine the works of any unchecked authors for your search terms.

Click the **Run Search** button to submit your search. The Tech Classics Archive will return lines containing your search terms, organized by the titles of the works in which they appear. Click the title of a work to see the full text of that work, or click the **[text]** hyperlink at the end of each returned line to see that line in context.

THE TECH CLASSICS ARCHIVE ★ ★ ★ ★

URL: http://the-tech.mit.edu/Classics/index.html

Capsule Review: A means of searching 375 classical texts, with a number of search-customization options.

MAPS

The Web makes geography transparent, but most of the human experience takes place off-line. Airplanes fly from one city to another, battles are fought over real hills and rivers, and refugees live in tent cities outside real-life political boundaries. Fortunately, the Web makes it easier to understand the layout of the physical world.

Browsing Maps of the World

The Perry-Castañeda Library Map Collection at the University of Texas has no search engine, but that's part of the site's appeal. Organized as a subject tree—a Yahoo of maps—the PCL Map Collection encourages you to discover resources among its scanned-in maps that you hadn't considered looking for.

To use the PCL Map Collection, scroll down the welcome page until you see the headings "Maps of Current Interest" and "Maps of General Interest." The former section contains maps relevant to current world news—Bosnia, the Gaza Strip, and the West Bank at this writing—while the latter section contains the real meat of the collection. Click the hyperlink for the area of the world for which you want maps. You can tell this is a collection at the University of Texas when you see that Texas gets two headings, while Europe and Asia each get one.

The pages for each region display hyperlinks to maps related to that region. The Middle East page, for example, includes links to maps of most Middle Eastern countries, as well as maps of population distribution, water-distribution projects, and other special-interest maps. Click a hyperlink to display the map it represents.

SEARCH TIP

If the PCL Map Collection doesn't have what you need, click the **Other Map-Related Sites** hyperlink at the bottom of the welcome page. It leads to a trailblazer page full of hundreds of cartographic resources, including ones maintained by nearly every country in the world and many U.S. government scientific agencies.

THE PERRY-CASTAÑEDA LIBRARY MAP COLLECTION ★ ★ ★

URL: http://www.lib.utexas.edu/Libs/PCL/Map_collection /Map_collection.html

Capsule Review: A subject tree of maps, including more than 275 maps of different parts of the United States.

Xerox PARC Map Viewer

It sounds like a cool idea: This sites is an interactive map viewer that begins with a map of the world, and lets you zoom in using ever-greater magnifications, until you see the area of the world you're looking for. But the implementation leaves a great deal to be desired. When you zoom in, there's no detail. No roads, or cities, or airports—just rivers, mainly. The people who created this site were interested in the computer technology they were developing, not geography.

XEROX PARC MAP VIEWER ★

URL: http://pubweb.parc.xerox.com/map/color=1/features=all-types/ht=175.00/lat=38.74/lon=16.52/wd=225.00

Capsule Review: An interactive Web site, the Xerox PARC Map Viewer is an experimental project that lets you "zoom in" on any area of the world, to see ever-more-detailed maps. The concept's exciting—you can click "down" to see more detail—but the payoff isn't; when you zoom in, you find that there's no detail. Worth visiting if you're interested in the basic concept, but a waste of time otherwise.

MEASUREMENTS

Measurements are useful, except when you and someone else use different ones. Whether you deal with time or acceleration, you have to understand what others are saying, and you need to make yourself understood to them. These sites can help you accomplish that goal.

Managing Time Zones

The Time Zone Converter, a service of Rensselaer Polytechnic Institute, makes it easy to figure out what time it is at a particular point on the globe. By means of a couple of lists of cities and a fast conversion program, the Time Zone Converter can tell you what time it is in Abu Dhabi when it's tea time in York.

To use the Time Zone Converter (Figure 16.3), enter a time in 24-hour format (i.e. 15:34:21, not 3:34:21 p.m.) in the Time text box. Enter a date, using the drop-down list box for the month and entering day and year values in text boxes. Select a city from the upper list box—this is the city in which the time you entered is valid. Select another city from the lower list box—this is the city whose time the program will yield. Click the **Convert** button; the Time Zone Converter will display the date and time in the target city.

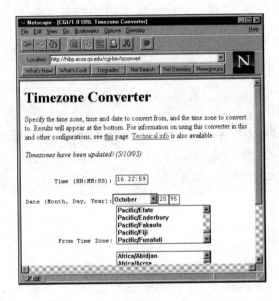

Figure 16.3 The Time Zone Converter.

TIME ZONE CONVERTER ★ ★

URL: http://hibp.ecse.rpi.edu/cgi-bin/tzconvert/

Capsule Review: Converts the time and date in one city to the time and date in another city.

Converting Measurements

Quick, how many kilometers per hour equal sixty furlongs per fortnight? Legacy Systems Convert2 won't help you with this problem, but it will assist you with more mundane measurement-conversion tasks, such as changing metric (SI) accelerations to English ones or converting an obscure angular momentum figure to a more easily understood measurement.

To use Legacy Systems Convert2, select a category (such as current, force, or magnetic flux) from the list box on the welcome page and click the **Select Category** button. Select a starting unit from the upper list box, and select a target unit from the lower list box. If you want, you can enter a value (in the units you selected from the upper list box) for Convert2 to convert for you. Click the **Process Conversion** button. Convert2 gives you the conversion factor you'd use to convert the units, and, if you specified a value, displays that value in terms of the target units.

> **LEGACY SYSTEMS CONVERT2 ★ ★ ★**
>
> **URL:** http://www.webcom.com/~legacysy/convert2/convert2.html
> **Capsule Review:** Converts measurements in one units system to another units system.

MOVIES

You'll find hundreds of Internet sites related to motion pictures, but there are two search services that you won't want to miss: The Internet Movie Database, which contains an astonishing amount of information about films, and the Movie Review Query Engine, which enables you to find substantive, high-quality reviews of contemporary and classic films.

The Internet Movie Database

Don't look for professional reviews here—this is an example of "how the Internet can provide for itself," according to the team that created the

Internet Movie Database. In fact, don't look for reviews at all—there's just a numerical, 1 to 10 rating. The ratings aren't idiosyncratic; they're based on votes—sometimes several thousand of them!—cast by the Internet Movie Database's users themselves. Big surprise: Their favorite film is *Star Wars*. Well, most of the voters are computer people, for whom science fiction is literature writ large.

No matter—the strength of the Internet Movie Database is the wealth of information that's recorded for each film. You can search in a vast number of ways: by movie title, cast/crew, cast character name, MPAA rating, country of origin, filming location, quotes, plot summaries, and more.

INTERNET MOVIE DATABASE ★ ★ ★ ★

URL: http://www.msstate.edu/Movies/

Capsule Review: If you're looking for information about movies—directors, actors, release dates, names of cast members, names of characters, and much more—this is the place to search. There's an automated "review" system, which is nothing more than a compilation of Internet users' votes—not much more than a "personality contest," without substance. Look elsewhere for reviews, but look here for tons of substantive information about the people involved in film-making.

Movie Review Query Engine

This site shows what Internet technology can do. You type the title of a film—if you're not quite sure of the title you can type key words—and the Query Engine ransacks the Internet, searching for reviews. A search for reviews of *Belle de Jour* netted nearly 20 full-text reviews, appearing originally in magazines ranging from *Entertainment Weekly* to *Dimension X Reeltalk*. A creation of the Pittsburg Cinema Project, this is one of the most interesting sites on the Web, and a good counterfoil to the Internet Movie Database's lack of substantive reviews.

MOVIE REVIEW QUERY ENGINE ★ ★ ★ ★

URL: http://www.cinema.pgh.pa.us/movie/reviews/

Capsule Review: This search service provides a query interface for movie reviews in various locations all over the Internet. Whether you're looking for reviews of a current or classic film, this site is the place to start.

RELIGIOUS TEXTS

Religious texts always have been on the cutting edge of information technology. Islamic religious documents were kept in some of the first libraries during the Middle Ages, and the Bible was the first publication of Johan Gutenberg's press in the 1500s. Today, searchable Web versions of sacred books make them accessible to even more people, and make the job of interpretation much easier.

Searching Various Bible Versions

This site's so good a dozen other Bible-related sites use it as an information source called by CGI scripts. Here, you'll find versions of the Christian scriptures in German, Swedish, Latin, French, Spanish, and Tagalog, as well as five different English translations (the New International Version, the Revised Standard Version, the King James Version, the Darby translation, and Young's Literal Translation). Not only will you find the full text of all these versions organized for browsing (by book and by chapter), you can search for specific words and phrases as well.

To search the Bible Gateway (in English; click one of the languages at the top of the welcome page to search in another tongue), scroll down to the bottom of the welcome page (Figure 16.4). Select a version of the Bible from the drop-down list box, and fill in at least one text box.

Figure 16.4 The Bible Gateway welcome page.

The text boxes are:

- **Passage**, in which you enter a book, chapter, and verse (i.e., Ruth 4:6).

- **Search word(s)**, in which you enter key words (i.e., olive).

- **Restrict search**, in which you enter a range of books to search (i.e., Matthew–John). If you leave this box blank, the search engine will search the whole Bible.

- **Max verses to display**, which limits the output of your search.

Click the **Lookup** button to execute your search. The search engine will return either the verse you requested or verses that contain your search terms. The verse titles are hyperlinked to the rest of the book in which they appear, if you wish to see more context, and to the other Bible versions, if you want to compare translations.

Just as a point of entertainment, the word "web" appears four times in the King James Version of the Bible: Twice in the book of Judges, and once each in the books of Job and Isaiah. Judges 16:14 gives some insight into Samson as an early Web surfer (and probable laptop user): "And she fastened it with the pin, and said unto him, The Philistines be upon thee, Samson. And he awaked out of his sleep, and went away with the pin of the beam, and with the web."

BIBLE GATEWAY ★ ★ ★ ★

URL: http://www.gospelcom.net/bible

Capsule Review: A tool for searching the Bible, in a slew of different languages and translations.

Searching the Qur'an

The University of Texas maintains this searchable version of Islam's holy book. With this resource, you can search the Qur'an for passages relevant to practically any occasion and discover relationships among passages you might not otherwise have identified. Aside from the search feature, this site lets you browse the full text of each of the 114 surahs of the Qur'an, and lets you download them to your computer for further study or manipulation.

To search the Qur'an, click the **Search the Holy Qur'an** hyperlink on the welcome page. In the search form, enter the terms for which you want to hunt. Adjust the options to fit your needs: you can require the search engine to return only those items that match your search terms exactly, or, if you're unsure of the spelling of your search term, allow it to retrieve files containing similar key words, too. Click the **Submit** button to start your search.

The search engine returns hyperlinks to each passage in which your search term appears. To make it easier for you to pick the passage you want, the search engine displays the sentence from each passage that contains the search word.

THE HOLY QUR'AN ★ ★ ★

URL: http://www.utexas.edu/students/amso/quran_html/

Capsule Review: A searchable version of the Qur'an, Islam's sacred text.

SCIENTIFIC CONSTANTS

Once the exclusive playground of academics and scientists, the Internet and the Web are still rife with resources for scientists. One such resource is scientific constants–the numbers that describe the relationship of one thing to another, but which are always slipping the minds of esteemed scientists and high-school students alike.

WebElements

The Periodic Table of the Elements is a basic instrument of scientific knowledge. And it's perfectly suited to the Web. You click on one of the elements, and you see a table giving the atomic weights and additional data—get the idea? It's here, and it's perfectly implemented in WebElements, a project based at the University of Sheffield in South Yorkshire, England

The Berkeley mirror of WebElements contains links to data for the first 109 elements. The names of the elements from 104 through 109 are currently bones of contention between the IUPAC and the American Chemical

Society. At Berkeley, we are using the ACS suggestions for the names in honor of Professor Seaborg's accomplishments.

On the way at this book's writing was WebElements 2.0, a significant effort involving a 30 megabyte collection of 5500 files. Currently in beta, the site's URL is http://www.shef.ac.uk:80/~chem/web-elements/web-elements -home.html.

WEBELEMENTS ★ ★ ★ ★

URL: http://www.cchem.berkeley.edu/Table/index.html

Here's a periodic table of the elements that's browsable by clicking on a map. Very neat, and just the thing for anyone studying chemistry.

Fundamental Physical Constants

The Fundamental Physical Constants page, maintained by the National Institute for Standards and Technology, offers a quick reference to the generally accepted values that physical scientists use in calculations. Such constants include the speed of light in a vacuum, the Planck constant, and G, Newton's gravitational constant.

To search this resource, use your browser's search function, or scroll manually down the page (it's not too long). Click the name of the constant you want, and you'll see the generally accepted value for it. One big problem: the constants are really graphics–scanned pages from a reference book. As such, they can't be copied for pasting into a spreadsheet or other calculation.

FUNDAMENTAL PHYSICAL CONSTANTS ★

URL: http://physics.nist.gov/PhysRefData/codata86/codata86.html

Capsule Review: A guide to generally accepted values for basic physical constants.

TAX FORMS

It isn't fun. Every April 15th, Americans turn in their self-reported tax forms, sometimes running to 25 or more pages of IRS-approved pages. And every one of them must conform to IRS regulations about layout and format. What happens if it's April 14th, and you're short a form? You came to the right place: the Web.

IRS Tax Forms

It's straight from the Internal Revenue Service—and it could save you a last-minute, panicked trip to the county office building, where you find out that alas—they don't have the form you need. From this site, you can download hundreds of IRS forms, and—thanks to Adobe Acrobat—you can print these forms in an IRS-approved format, which means you can include these forms with your tax return. (If you don't thave the Adobe Acrobat reader, you can download the software from the site.)

IRS Tax Forms ★ ★ ★ ★

URL: http://www.ustreas.gov/treasury/bureaus/irs/taxforms.html

Capsule Review: This useful service could save you a trip to the county office building, or a long wait while the IRS mails you a needed form. You can access any of the tax forms or instructions the IRS publishes. Using Adobe Acrobat, you can download and print correct, picture-perfect versions of these forms. (If you don't have Acrobat, you can download a free copy of the Acrobat viewer from this site.)

CHAPTER 17

FINDING CURRENT NEWS AND WEATHER

An important part of any comprehensive research strategy is keeping up with news reports. In the past, you had to do so by clipping news papers or by forking over some serious money for fee-based newspaper databases. Happily, the Web has stepped in with some great full-text news article search services.

This chapter opens with trailblazer pages—pages that can help you find the specific resources you want. The chapter lists and describes news sites where you can search for full-text news articles, and then describes sites relevant to the weather.

TRAILBLAZER PAGES

These pages point you in the right direction when you're looking for information about the news and weather. Though you'll probably want to use these pages to identify a few sites you like and put them on your bookmark list or home page, you may want to refer back to these trailblazer pages if you're called upon to search for information you can't find at your favorite pages. For example, WeatherNet may come in handy if you normally use the Weather Channel site for forecasts, but suddenly are called upon to explain to a child what a cold front is.

The Electronic Newstand

This is an excellent trailblazer page for Web-based magazines, newsletters, newspapers, and catalogs. Categories covered include business, computers and technology, entertainment, automotive, health, politics, travel, sports and recreation, books, catalogs, news services—and, of course, newspapers. The newspaper list (http://www.enews.com/papers.html) isn't as extensive as some of the trailblazer pages discussed in this section, but it hits the highlights.

THE ELECTRONIC NEWSSTAND ★ ★ ★ ★

URL: http://www.enews.com/

Capsule Review: Here's an excellent trailblazer page for all kinds of Internet-based periodicals, including magazines, newsletters, and catalogs as well as newspapers. The newspaper page contains up-to-date links to most of the active newspapers publishing on the Web.

The Daily News

Here's a bare-bones trailblazer page that has links to dozens of on-line newspapers worldwide. It's fast (no flashy graphics), up-to-date, and very comprehensive. If you're interested in world news, this is a great place to start.

THE DAILY NEWS ★ ★ ★ ★

URL: http://www.cs.vu.nl/~gerben/news.html

Capsule Review: This site, created by Gerben Vos of the Netherlands, contains links to dozens of newspapers worldwide that have established Web presences.

The Newsroom

If you're interested in fast-breaking news stories, this is a good place to begin your exploration of Web-based newspapers. You'll find links to most of the major newspapers that publish on the Web, as well as US and world headlines from the Reuters news service. Emphasis is placed on the big players in the business.

Don't miss The Newsroom's many features, business and finance news, and resources (including the U.S. Constitution). A wonderful new feature: This Is True, a compilation of unusual and downright bizarre events.

THE NEWSROOM ★ ★ ★ ★

URL: http://www.auburn.edu/~vestmon/news.html

Capsule Review: Here's a convenient, high-quality trailblazer page that contains links to some of the best news sources on the Web.

United States: Newspaper Services on the Internet

With links to the sites of virtually every nonacademic on-line paper in the United States, this site's a great starting point for researchers hunting information about municipalities. Part of the Web edition of *Editor & Publisher* magazine, this site has links to papers ranging from the *Chicago Tribune* to the *Southern Maine Coastal Beacon* of Saco, Maine, and to the *Beloit Daily News* of Beloit, Wisconsin.

Using this unimaginatively named resource is a no-brainer: just click the name of the state in which the community you want is located, and pick the paper you want from the resulting list. The names of the papers are hyperlinked to the papers' Internet resources—typically Web sites, but a few Gopher servers appear here, too. This site's welcome page is shown in Figure 17.1.

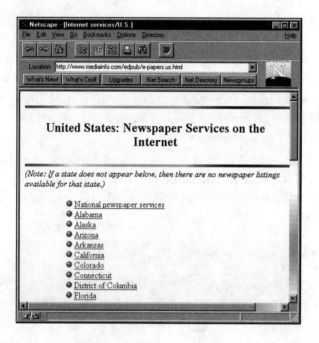

Figure 17.1 The United States: Newspaper Services on the Internet welcome page.

UNITED STATES: NEWSPAPER SERVICES ON THE INTERNET ★ ★ ★

URL: http://www.mediainfo.com/edpub/e-papers.us.html

Capsule Review: A directory of U.S. newspapers, small and large, with presences on the Internet.

Compilation of News Services Provided by the Inet-News Listserv

A mailing list called Inet-News exists to provide journalists and researchers with directions to resources of interest to them on the World Wide Web and elsewhere on the Internet. This mailing list format is kind of tedious—all you can do is delete the messages containing resources for which you have no use, and then wish you hadn't deleted them when you later find a reason to use them.

The Inet-News information archive on the Web helps solve the problem. On the welcome page (Figure 17.3), click the area of news you're interested in (business, government, world news, etc.). You'll see a page of links to on-line resources related to that topic. Unfortunately, there's no search engine and the pages aren't well organized or laid out, but they contain links to some obscure resources you'll have trouble finding elsewhere. Furthermore, Jonathan Maier updates the pages with information to the list—though when I visited, the pages hadn't been updated for more than eight weeks.

Figure 17.3 The Compilation of News Services Provided by the Inet-News Listserv welcome page.

COMPILATION OF NEWS SERVICES PROVIDED BY THE INET-NEWS LISTSERV ★ ★

URL: http://www-leland.stanford.edu/~jmaier/inetnews.htm

Capsule Review: A series of pages containing links to mainstream and obscure Web and Internet news sites worldwide.

NEWS

These sites deal with news—that is, events that have taken place in the past week, or that took place long ago and have just recently come to light. Turn to these pages for information just as you'd turn to the news radio station at the top of the hour to keep current on the news of your community, country, and world. The best of them offer search services, which let you locate and read the full text of current and past news articles.

CNN Interactive

Cable News Network's CNN site is what you'd expect from the company that changed the public's perception of modern warfare with real-time reports from downtown Baghdad in 1991. This site is both incredibly slick—with lots of sound and video—and heavy on content. Here, you'll find both current news and an archive of the past month's news, complete with a flexible search tool.

To search CNN Interactive, click the **Search** button at the bottom of the lead graphic (Figure 17.4). You'll see the search form, where you can enter your search term in the text box. The search engine treats multiple words as if they were joined with the Boolean operator AND; that is, the search engine won't return items that don't contain all your search terms. This doesn't guarantee accuracy, as a search for "green party" will return an item that contains the sentence, "Members of the band Green Day threw a party upon the release of their new album..." Also be careful of plurals—using "computers" as a search term won't return stories in which "computer" occurs but "computers" does not. Press the **Enter** key, and the search engine will return a hyperlinked list of hits.

Figure 17.4 The CNN Interactive welcome page.

SEARCH TIP

You can speed up your search by de-selecting categories on the search form. Make sure there are no Xs in the check boxes of subjects unrelated to your search word. There's no reason to waste time searching the Sports database for information about actress Angela Lansbury, for example.

CNN INTERACTIVE ★ ★ ★ ★

URL: http://www.cnn.com/

Capsule Review: Lots of current news, complete with sound and video. There's also a searchable archive of the past month's news.

The Electronic Telegraph

The Telegraph is one of London's best daily newspapers, between the *Times* and the *Guardian* politically. The electronic edition is very nicely produced, and best of all, there's a search engine that enables you to retrieve the full text of past news articles. Chances are you'll find a lot of false drops in the retrieval list, but that's intended—to find more documents, click the check box next to the one that matches your search interests, and click the **Expand** button. You'll see a list of statistically-related words that you can add to the query. Check one or more words, and click **Add Selected Words to Query**.

THE ELECTRONIC TELEGRAPH ★ ★ ★ ★

URL: http://www.telegraph.co.uk/

Capsule Review: One of London's best dailies, the Telegraph makes the full text of past news articles available in this searchable service. The search engine is unusually capable.

PathFinder's News Now

One of the best daily news services on the Web, PathFinder's News Now integrates the feeds of Reuters, Sports Ticker and Quote.Com, enabling you to keep up with current news, sports, and stock market information. The news feeds are updated hourly, while the sports feed is updated continuously. Stock and mutual fund quotes have about a 15-minute delay. An excellent feature is a link to the News Now Search service, which enables you to search previous Reuters news articles (as well as daily news articles provided by several Times-Warner magazines, including *Time*).

PATHFINDER NEWSNOW ★ ★ ★ ★

URL: http://pathfinder.com/@@kRAC9PGPlgIAQAJU/News/news.html

Capsule Review: This news search service enables you to search the full text of current and past Reuters news articles as well as news stories supplied by Time-Warner magazines. An excellent database of news stories that is searchable with a high-quality search engine.

San Francisco Chronicle

This page provides a search interface to *San Francisco Chronicle* news articles from all sections of the newspaper (except the Classifieds,) dating back to November, 1994. The capable search engine enables you to use Boolean operators (AND, OR, NOT) and a proximity operator (ADJ). You can also perform a phrase search by enclosing the phrase in quotation marks. The result of the search is a relevancy-ranked list of items; if you find one that looks good, click it to see the full text of the article. Excellent!

SAN FRANCISCO CHRONICLE ★ ★ ★

URL: http://www.sfgate.com/wais-chron.html

Capsule Review: A full-text database of news articles dating back to November 2, 1994, searchable using a flexible and fast WAIS search engines, makes this site one of the best on the 'Net for anyone looking for in-depth news analysis.

San Jose Mercury-News Library

OK, first the good news. Here's a fantastic search resource—a database, containing nearly one million full-text news articles published since 1985 by one of the country's most interesting and innovative newspapers. If you're searching for news reports, this is the place to start. The bad news is that you have to subscribe—the charge is currently $4.95 per month—and each search will cost you an additional 25 cents per retrieved article

MERCURY-NEWS LIBRARY ★ ★ ★

URL: http://www.sjmercury.com/library/index.htm

Capsule Review: A subscription-based service that offers searchable access to a full-text database of over one million news articles, dating from 1985.

ABC News

This site isn't searchable at all, but it has absolutely current news from one of the most respected news-gathering outfits in the world. Furthermore, ABC News employs RealAudio technology, a scheme by which you can play sound almost as fast as you can download it. This means you can call up the latest ABC News broadcast (updated hourly) and have it play in the background as you work on other tasks.

To use this site, click the **Internet Hourly News** hyperlink on the welcome page (Figure 17.6) and enter your username and password in the dialog box that appears. (Don't have a username and password for this site? Click the **free user account** hyperlink to set up a free user account.) The ABC Radio news broadcast will start downloading, and you'll start hearing it right away if you have a properly configured RealAudio Player on your computer. You can get the RealAudio Player from the RealAudio site (http://www.realaudio.com/).

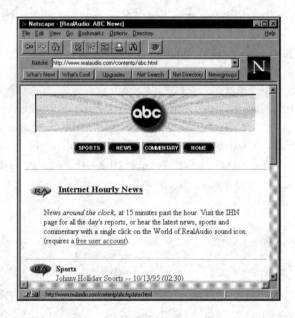

Figure 17.6 The ABC News welcome page.

ABC NEWS ★ ★ ★

URL: http://www.realaudio.com/contentp/abc.html
Capsule Review: ABC Radio news broadcasts in RealAudio format, updated hourly.

Associated Press on Trib.Com

Ever wonder what happened to those huge clattering teletype machines you see in old movies about newspapers? They went digital, and now newsrooms feature rows of computers pulling stories from wires, ready to be incorporated into newspapers without ever being printed out before the final press run. Most of these wire services are subscription-only arrangements, but the Associated Press, the oldest and perhaps the most respected news service makes some of its stories available on the Web via this resource, provided by Howard Publications and the *Casper Star-Tribune* of Casper, Wyoming.

You have to register to use this service, but there's no associated charge. Click the **registration form** hyperlink on the welcome page (Figure 17.5) to register. Once you've signed up, you can access the service by entering your username and password in the text boxes and clicking the **sign on** button.

There's no search feature for AP stories, and there's no archive: you just get access to the ten most recent stories in six categories. The biggest problem with this site is that its automatically generated hyperlinks to stories are truncations of stories' "slugs"—the brief descriptions at the top of the stories. The truncation leaves some doubt about the contents of stories: a story about a Pennsylvania mine fire had the headline "Old Timers Won't Be Driven From.HTM." The story's full headline was, "Old Timers Won't Be Driven From Homes by Underground Mine Fire." Still, this site provides current information from one of the world's top news services.

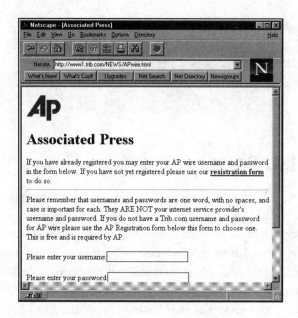

Fig. 17.5 The Associated Press at Trib.Com welcome page.

ASSOCIATED PRESS ON TRIB.COM ★ ★ ★

URL: http://www1.trib.com/NEWS/APwire.html

Capsule Review: Sixty of the most recent stories from the Associated Press, organized into six categories including Sports and Business.

USA Today

Known for changing the newspaper industry forever with its introduction of large-circulation, heavily illustrated, full-color national print news, *USA Today* finds itself right at home on the Web. Its illustrations serve to enhance otherwise dry text, and hypertext organizes this notoriously choppy paper admirably. USA Today isn't the place to go for in-depth coverage of any issue, but it's a fine resource for current news, weather, and financial information in capsule form.

To get an idea of what's available at the USA Today site on a particular day, click the **Click here for a complete guide to USA TODAY content** hyperlink on the welcome page (Figure 17.7). You'll see the Index page, which contains hyperlinks to all the paper's resources. Pay special attention to the "Scores" hyperlink: it leads to a page of sports scores that's updated every two minutes. Also note the "Continuing Stories" hyperlinks: they lead to pages containing links to several stories on a common subject, such as the war in Bosnia or the Oklahoma City Federal Building bombing.

Figure 17.7 The USA Today welcome page.

USA TODAY ★ ★ ★

URL: http://www.usatoday.com/

Capsule Review: News organized for browsing rather than searching, but with some excellent illustrations and nearly real-time sports scores. The USA Today site also features links to historical stories on big news issues.

WEATHER

If you're planning a trip and want to know what the weather is like at your destination, or if you work in the bowels of some giant office and want to know whether you need your umbrella when you head home, take a look at these sites. They can provide you with everything from radar images of the entire world to forecasts for your local area. Many of these sites also are useful as educational tools: they offer pages that explain the "how" and "why" of weather to students and amateur meteorologists alike.

If these sites don't answer your questions, refer to WeatherNet (http://cirrus.sprl.umich.edu/wxnet/) for a link to a site that does.

Intellicast

With nearly real-time satellite imagery and weather condition information for cities around the world, Intellicast represents the resource of choice for Web users who know what an isobar is and what the furry white regions on satellite maps represent. This site should be on the hotlists of frequent travelers and amateur meteorologists alike.

To use Intellicast, click one of the three buttons at the top of the welcome page (Figure 17.8): "USA Weather," "Around the World," or "Ski Report." You'll find that the United States weather reports are the most current and complete, as Intellicast cooperates with television stations around the country. Once you're on one of the three main pages, click one of the internal hyperlinks at the top of the page to go to the material you want—and be sure to check out the "images and movies" hyperlink for quick access to satellite imagery. On the U.S. page, you can click the names of certain cities to see separate pages containing detailed weather information for those cities.

INTELLICAST ★ ★ ★

URL: http://www.intellicast.com/

Capsule Review: A large and up-to-date collection of information about the weather, including past conditions, predictions, and a great collection of satellite imagery.

Figure 17.8 The Intellicast welcome page.

WeatherNet

Looking for weather information on the Web or elsewhere on the Internet? Start at WeatherNet. This trailblazer page (Figure 17.2) includes links to every major weather resource, and practically every minor one, on the Internet—including Gopher and Telnet sites as well as Web services. Like most trailblazer pages, this one contains little information of its own. It does, however, organize other sites' information so well that it seems as if it's all part of the WeatherNet site.

A good example of WeatherNet's exemplary organization is its WeatherCam page. This page provides links to cameras in more than two dozen cities all over the United States. When you click the name of a city, the WeatherCam page shows you a live (or nearly live) image from the camera in that city, allowing you to ascertain the weather there the old-fashioned way. There's no need to wade through the welcome pages of the weather stations in the various cities; you see the images immediately.

WeatherNet also boasts a large selection of satellite imagery sites, and a great clickable-map interface to radar images across the country.

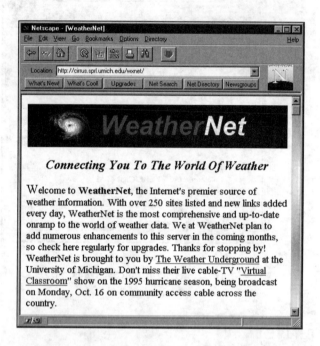

Figure 17.2 WeatherNet welcome page.

WEATHERNET ★ ★ ★ ★

> **URL:** http://cirrus.sprl.umich.edu/wxnet/
>
> **Capsule Review:** An interface to virtually every Internet weather resource, including Web sites, Gopher servers, and Telnet services. WeatherNet integrates weather resources from all over the U.S. nearly seamlessly.

The Weather Channel Online

If you like your weather with a little bit more interpretive backup than Intellicast provides, check out The Weather Channel Online. This site provides less raw data than the Intellicast site and replaces it with handy graphics and less arcane terminology. For example, hurricane tracking on the Weather Channel site features four-color graphics and friendly icons, as opposed to Intellicast's black-and-white satellite photos of cloud vortices. The Weather Channel site provides no information about weather outside the United States.

To use The Weather Channel Online to get current weather information, click the **Weather Information** hyperlink (or click the **Weather** graphic, which shows a bolt of lightning striking the ground) on the welcome page (Figure 17.9). On the Weather Information page, you can choose from a series of services, including current weather maps, forecasts for the next 24 hours, and special aviation weather reports.

Figure 17.9 The Weather Channel Online welcome page.

If your question can't be answered with the Weather Channel's standard on-line services, try "Met on the Net," a service that lets you send weather-related questions to Weather Channel meteorologists. The meteorologists reply to some of the questions they receive by posting answers in a public forum (http://www.infi.net/~wxmike/metnet.html). This interactive feature adds to The Weather Channel Online's value as an educational tool.

THE WEATHER CHANNEL ONLINE ★ ★ ★

URL: http://www.infi.net/weather/

Capsule Review: A weather site that provides less information than Intellicast, but which provides more interpretation of the on-line information. This site also allows you (or your kids) to ask questions of Weather Channel meteorologists.

CHAPTER 18

Finding Government Information

As part of a campaign to make government more accessible, increasing numbers of government bodies at all levels are creating Web pages. Some of the most impressive efforts are those of the V.I. Federal Government. You'll find reams of government related information on–line, including current legislation, Supreme Court decisions and more.

This chapter begins with trailblazer pages that lead to government resources of all kinds. On these pages, you'll find links to the other resources in this chapter, as well as to other interesting sites. The second section of this chapter deals (mainly) with searchable databases with which you can retrieve Supreme Court opinions, legislative information, and data about governments outside the United States. These sites also will help you retrieve information you need from the mountains of *stuff* governments put out each year.

Government Trailblazer Pages

These trailblazer pages contain hyperlinks to government resources of all kinds. Attach these pages to your home page if you're frequently called upon to find unusual bits of information related to U.S. federal or state governments.

Also, remember that your Web browser most likely is equipped with a search function of its own. To use it, choose **Find** from the Edit menu on the menu bar (in Netscape), enter a search term in the dialog box that appears, and click **OK**. You can also usually click a toolbar button or use a keyboard shortcut, such as **Ctrl-F** in Netscape. Browsers' search tools come in handy when you're trying to find one line of information in large, minimally indexed documents—like most of these trailblazer pages.

The Federal Web Locator

A service of The Villanova Center for Information Law and Policy at Villanova University, The Federal Web Locator is the easiest way to find the U.S. government resources you want. If you're familiar with *The United States Government Manual*, a printed directory of government branches, offices, bureaus, and agencies, you'll find this site familiar, as the two reference tools follow the same organizational plan.

To use The Federal Web Locator, scroll down the welcome page (shown in Figure 18.1) past the instructions and notices of new material. You'll see sections for each branch of the U.S. government, as well as for independent government entities (such as the Federal Reserve) and international organizations. Within each section, there are headings for major entities within that branch. The Executive Branch section contains headings for the Executive Office of the President and the Office of Management and Budget, for example. Click the resource you want. You'll see a page containing hyperlinks to all the Internet resources maintained by that government entity.

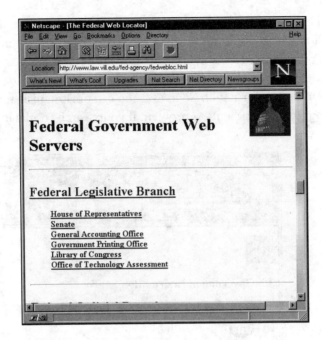

Figure 18.1 The Federal Web Locator welcome page.

The Federal Web Locator ★ ★ ★ ★

URL: http://www.law.vill.edu/fed-agency/fedwebloc.html

Capsule Review: A comprehensive index of all U.S. federal government Internet servers, organized in the manner of The United States Government Manual.

The World Wide Web Virtual Library: U.S. Government Information Sources

Broken down into four sections—one for federal branches, one for Cabinet-level departments, one for independent agencies (like the Voice of America and the Smithsonian Institution), and one for miscellaneous government entities—this site offers links to practically every U.S. federal government resource on the Web. The hyperlinks appear in hierarchically organized lists, making it easy to find the one you need.

This site features a searchable index, but it's not especially good. Scroll down to the bottom of the welcome page (shown in Figure 18.2) and enter search terms in the text box. You'll get results, but every hit appears as a hyperlink to "The World Wide Web Library: Links to US Government Information Sources." You can't distinguish among the links without following them—a problem if your search results in a dozen hits.

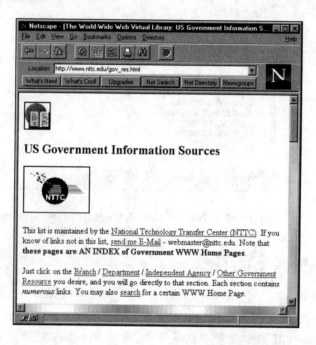

Figure 18.2 The World Wide Web Virtual Library: U.S. Government Information Sources.

The World Wide Web Virtual Library: U.S. Government Information Sources ★ ★ ★

URL: http://www.nttc.edu/gov_res.html

Capsule Review: A hierarchically organized list of federal government information resources, with a search engine, albeit a fairly poor one.

State and Local Government on the Net

State and Local Government on the Net provides links to most, if not all, state and local government on-line resources in the United States. Whether you're looking for the Honolulu Fire Department site or the Idaho Public Utilities Commission site, State and Local Government on the Net has the hyperlink you need. This site should be especially useful to you if your state or municipality has an on-line resource, as state and local government policies probably affect your life more than federal policies, which tend to receive more attention.

You'll have to put your browser's search function to use when searching State and Local Government on the Net. Use it to search the welcome page (Figure 18.3) for the name of the state for which you want resources. Then click that state's hyperlink and examine the state's page, which contains hyperlinks to that state's on-line resources.

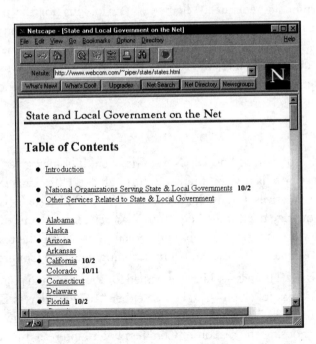

Figure 18.3 The State and Local Government on the Net welcome page.

If a hyperlinked letter G follows a hyperlink to a resource, it means that resource is available on Gopher, too. Click the G if you prefer the Gopher interface, or if you think the Gopher may have more current information.

State and Local Government on the Net ★ ★ ★

URL: http://www.webcom.com/~piper/state/states.html

Capsule Review: Hyperlinks to state and local on-line resources, from the well-known to the absolutely obscure.

SEARCHABLE GOVERNMENT RESOURCES

These sites let you search for what you need among the gigabytes of data governments generate. Whether you're looking for the name and electronic mail address of the Senator who introduced a bill you oppose, or the per capita gross national product of Egypt, these sites can help. Call up the right document, enter the right search terms, and you'll find information that's more up-to-date than any you'd find in paper reference works.

Thomas

An idea of House Speaker Newt Gingrich, Thomas gives you access to the text of bills making their way through the U.S. Senate and House of Representatives. Granted, the language of the bills usually is quite arcane, and you may need some help from a lawyer to figure out the significance of the various subparagraphs and codicils, but having the text available on the Web makes it easier to begin decoding what the Congress is up to.

To use Thomas—which was named for President and popular-education fan Thomas Jefferson—you choose either "103rd Congress Bills" or "104th Congress Bills" from the hyperlinks on the welcome page (Figure 18.4). After choosing the session of Congress you're interested in, enter a search term in the text box. The search term can be either a bill's alphanumeric identifier (such as S 314) or popular title (such as the Communications

Decency Act). You can limit your search, with the radio buttons on the search page, to Senate bills, House bills, bills passed and sent to the President, or bills on which action has occurred outside of committee. After entering your search terms, click the **RUN QUERY** button. You'll see a list of hyperlinks to matching bills. Click the one you want and you'll see the text of that bill, organized under hypertext headings.

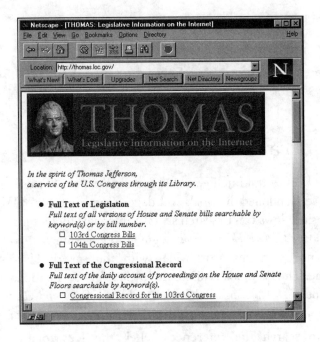

Figure 18.4 The Thomas welcome page.

SEARCH TIP

Frequently, when a member of Congress speaks on a topic of current popular interest, he or she will cite an academic journal, newspaper, or magazine. To make sure the cited text is available to other members for reference, the speaking member will include it in the *Congressional Record*, the official record of what happens in Congress. These addenda are called Extensions of Remarks. You can search the *Congressional Record*, including Extensions of Remarks, with Thomas. This way, you can use the Web to get the full text of newspaper articles relevant to current bills.

Click the **Congressional Record for the 103rd Congress** or **Congressional Record for the 104th Congress** hyperlink on the Thomas welcome page. Enter search terms in the text box. You can limit your search to the Extensions of Remarks by clicking the "Extensions of Remarks Only" radio button. You can also limit your search to portions involving only certain members of Congress, or to either house.

Thomas ★ ★ ★

URL: http://thomas.loc.gov/

Capsule Review: A searchable database of all the bills in the 103rd and 104th Congress.

CIA Publications

The U.S. Central Intelligence Agency, in the wake of the Cold War, seems to have abandoned the cloak-and-dagger game in favor of Web publishing. This site allows you to search six CIA reference tools—including the near-legendary *CIA World Factbook*, a guide to governments, politics, economics, and geography worldwide—with the superb Harvest text-search engine. The Factbook is discussed in Chapter 15. Additional research tools include *CIA Maps and Publications, Chiefs of State and Cabinet Members of Foreign Governments* and *Intelligence Literature: Selected Reading*.

To search the references, click the **Keyword Search C.I.A. Publications** graphic on the welcome page (Figure 18.5). Enter your search terms in the text box. You can set options for your search, including the number of spelling errors allowed in your query and whether Harvest should perform a case-sensitive or case-insensitive search. Click the **Submit** button to start your search. Harvest returns a list of hyperlinked hits, each of which is followed by the lines of text in which your keyword appears, which makes it easier to determine if your topic is central or tangential to the hyperlinked documents.

Figure 18.5 The CIA Publications welcome page.

CIA Publications ★ ★ ★

URL: http://www.odci.gov/cia/publications/pubs.html

Capsule Review: A search tool that combs six excellent reference tools, including the CIA World Factbook, with the Harvest search engine.

Decisions of the U.S. Supreme Court

The U.S. Supreme Court is arguably the most powerful branch of the federal government, and operates under the most secrecy. Thanks to a database of Supreme Court information (with cases decided as early as 1990) at Case Western Reserve University and an index to that database managed by the Legal Information Institute at Cornell University, the Web makes it easier to study the opinions of this powerful body.

At the site's welcome page (Figure 18.6), click the **Key Word Search** hyperlink. In the text box at the top of the search page, enter your search terms. Your search terms can be the name of a party to a case, such as "Rosenberger" or "Dobson," or a legal issue you're interested in, such as "copyright" or "firearms." Press your computer's **Return** or **Enter** key to start the search. The search engine will return a list of hits, indexed by date of decision. Furthermore, it provides separate hyperlinks to the syllabus and various opinions for each case. Unfortunately, it doesn't label the hyperlinks with Justices' names—there may be several "concur" hyperlinks for a given case, leaving you to figure out which one is Justice O'Connor's opinion and which is Justice Thomas'. You can, however, click the **About the Court** hyperlink, then click the **Gallery of the Justices** hyperlink to see biographies of the Justices and hyperlinks to their recent and important opinions.

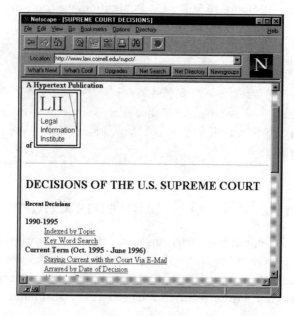

Figure 18.6 Decisions of the U.S. Supreme Court.

Decisions of the U.S. Supreme Court ★ ★ ★

URL: http://www.law.cornell.edu/supct/

Capsule Review: A searchable database of U.S. Supreme Court decisions from 1990 to the present.

Contacting the 104th Congress

The Founding Fathers were into interactivity long before the Web made possible CGI scripts and VRML. They intended for the citizenry to take an active part in the maintenance and operation of government, both during election seasons and in the daily mechanics of developing laws and policy. Contacting the 104th Congress, a site maintained as a public service by Juan E. Cabanela at the University of Minnesota, makes it easier for you to participate in the legislative process by lobbying your Senators and Representative on issues of importance to you.

To use this site, click one of two hyperlinks on the welcome page (Figure 18.7). If your browser can interpret tables, click the one leading to the table-wise database; click the other link if you run an older browser. On the index page, click the name of the state, territory, or district for which you want information. You'll see a page containing Senators' and Representatives' electronic mail addresses, telephone numbers, and fax numbers. If a member maintains a Web page, his or her name is hyperlinked to it. Note that if you click the name of a state at the top of the page containing the contact information, you'll see the state's CapWeb page, which includes information about the committees on which that state's legislators sit.

Congressional email Directory ★ ★ ★

URL: http://ast1.spa.umn.edu/juan/congress.html

Capsule Review: A list, indexed by state, of Congressional electronic mail addresses, telephone numbers, and fax numbers.

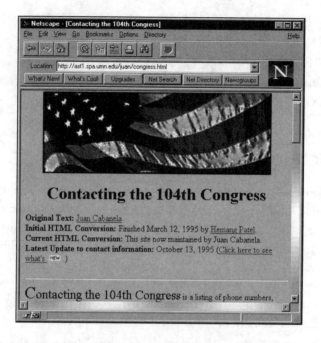

Figure 18.7 Contacting the 104th Congress welcome page.

United Nations Scholars' Workstation at Yale University

A front end to a WAIS system, the search facility at Yale's United Nations Scholars' Workstation doesn't always provide high-quality hits, but it does ease your search for information in the fairly large Yale archive of United Nations information. To use the search tool, click the **Search** hyperlink on the welcome page (Figure 18.8). Enter your search terms in the text box and click the **Search** button. You'll get a list of hyperlinks to resources that match your keyword.

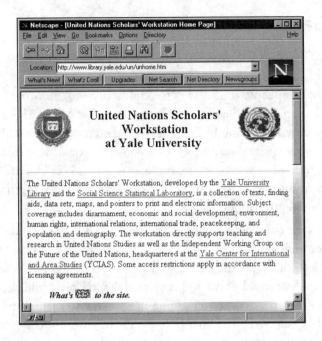

Figure 18.8 The United Nations Scholars' Workstation at Yale University welcome page.

You'll find that certain documents tend to show up in many different searches. A document on the future of the United Nations only touches on genocide as an issue that international peacemakers have to confront, and does not explore the issue in depth. The document appears, however, as a hit on the keyword "genocide."

United Nations Scholars' Workstation at Yale University ★ ★

URL: http://www.library.yale.edu/un/unhome.htm

Capsule Review: A front-end for a WAIS search tool that combs the full text of an archive of United Nations documents for words you specify.

GPO Gate

Every day, the U.S. federal government pours out tons of information. Most of it falls in the category of mundane and irrelevant—unless you're one of the people it affects. The University of California at San Diego's GPO Gate site provides a searchable index to all the output of the Government Printing Office, the official recordkeeping body of Congress and other federal entities. The Congressional Record for any day Congress is in session, for example, is posted to GPO Gate by 11 o'clock the next morning. You can use GPO Gate as a news resource to keep up on federal government issues.

To use the search facility, click the **Search GPO Databases** hyperlink on the welcome page (Figure 18.9). From the list box at the top of the search form, select the databases you want to search. To select more than one database, hold down your computer's **Ctrl** key while clicking database names with your computer's mouse. Then enter a search term in the first text box below the list box. If you want to enter more search terms, you can enter them in the second and third text boxes. You must select Boolean operators (AND, OR, or NOT) from the drop-down list boxes that separate the text boxes. If you want, you can limit your search further by entering words that must appear in the title of selected documents in the lowest text box. Click the **Search** button *at the top of the page* to execute your search. GPO Gate, like other WAIS front-ends, will return a list of hyperlinks to documents that match your search terms.

You may want to use Thomas to search the Congressional Record instead of GPO Gate, since Thomas allows you to search Extensions of Remarks as well as Remarks themselves. Extensions of Remarks usually include newspaper articles cited by Congresspeople in their speeches. See the Thomas entry in this chapter for more information.

SEARCH TIP

Some documents have a "PDF" hyperlink listed after the main hyperlink. These hyperlinks lead to versions of the document in Adobe Acrobat Portable Document Format—a flexible cross-platform file format you can read with the Adobe Acrobat Reader program, available free from http://www.adobe.com.

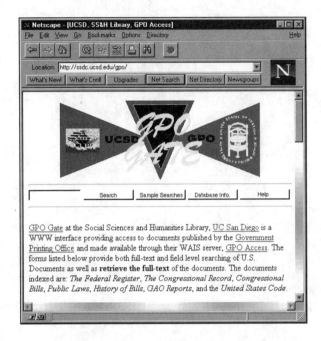

Figure 18.9 The GPO Gate welcome page.

GPO Gate ★ ★

URL: http://ssdc.ucsd.edu/gpo/

Capsule Review: A WAIS interface to Government Printing Office documents—including the Congressional Record and Federal Register—from 1994 through the present.

Chapter 19

Finding Stock Market and Investment Information

Financial and investment information is worth plenty of money—because it makes plenty of money for the people who are able to obtain it. Until the Internet came along, much of that information was inaccessible, even though some of it was created by public regulatory agencies funded with taxpayers' money. For example, all publicly traded companies in the United States must submit reams of financial reports to the Securities and Exchange Commission (SEC), and a variety of information providers have been making good money repackaging this information and reselling it on computer networks.

With the advent of the Web, this picture is beginning to change. Why not make taxpayer-funded information available on the Net? A number of free services offer investment-related information, such as current stock quotes and mutual fund prospectuses. Also found on the Web are commercial ventures of various kinds that offer free financial information as a means of marketing fee-based services.

All these services are valuable for any investor who wishes to be fully informed when forking over hard-earned dough for a stock or mutual fund. Just bear in mind that all of these services warn you that they can't be responsible for the quotes they give you; before purchasing a stock, you should check with a licensed broker to determine the correct price.

SEARCH TIP

Looking for more economic and investment information? Here's a world-class trailblazer page: http://www.cob.ohio-state.edu/dept/fin/osudata.htm. It's the Ohio State University Financial Data Finder, sponsored by Ohio State's Department of Finance. Folks, this is what a trailblazer page ought to look like!

CLOSING PRICES

For a quick look at the most recent closing numbers of the major stock exchanges, check out CNN's Wall Street page (http://www.cnn.com/BIZ/ WallStreet/). You'll find closing figures from all the major exchanges (Figure 19.1), highlighted by graphics that show whether the trend's up or down.

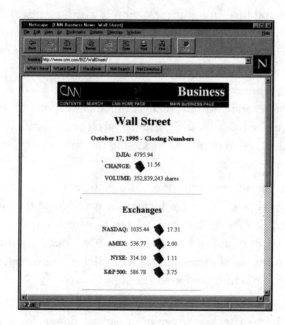

Figure 19.1 CNN's Wall Street page.

WALL STREET CLOSING PRICES ★ ★ ★

URL: http://www.cnn.com/BIZ/WallStreet/

Capsule Review: Access this site for a quick look at the most recently posted closing numbers from the major stock exchanges.

ECONOMIC CHARTS

Looking for excellent charts and graphs of current economic trends? Check out Dr. Ed Yardeni's Chart Room (http://www.webcom.com/~yardeni/economic.html). You'll find dozens of charts showing trends in inflation, U.S. economic performance, business indicators, business forecasts, flows of banking funds and the money supply, and economic trends in Asian and European economies. The U.S. Economy charts alone are amazingly comprehensive, covering inflation, consumer prices, business indicators, business surveys, employment trends, income, spending, borrowing, consumer opinion, housing indicators, money and credit, trade, and even economic history. For an example, see Figure 19.2.

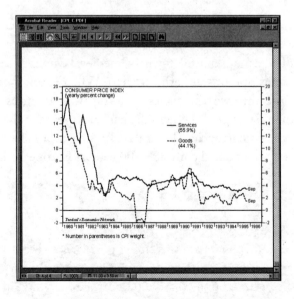

Figure 19.2 Consumer Price Index chart (Dr. Ed Yardeni's Chart Room).

To view the charts in Dr. Yardeni's excellent site, you'll need Adobe Acrobat Reader, a free program that you can download from http://www.adobe.com/Acrobat/AcrobatWWW.html.

SEARCH TIP

DR. ED YARDENI'S CHART ROOM ★ ★ ★ ★

URL: http://www.webcom.com/~yardeni/economic.html

Capsule Review: A wealth of charts, prepared for viewing with Adobe Acrobat, on virtually every aspect of the U.S. economy. A vital resource for anyone seeking to understand the economy's complex gyrations.

FOREIGN CURRENCY EXCHANGE RATES

Planning an overseas trip? You can get accurate, up-to-date information on currency exchange rates from these sites.

Foreign Exchange Rates

Here's a great service maintained by the Department of Computer Science at the Lund University in Sweden (Lund, in case you've never heard of it, is a beautiful town of medieval vintage, set in the gentle, rolling landscape of southern Sweden). When you log on to the service, you choose the two currencies that you want to measure against each other; the final page shows you the current foreign exchange rates, calculated for both currencies (Figure 19.3). The data tables for the site's 36 currencies are updated daily at 17:00 central European time.

FOREIGN EXCHANGE RATES ★ ★ ★

URL: http://www.dna.lth.se/cgi-bin/kurt/rates/

Capsule Review: From this site you can obtain reasonably recent currency quotes, cross-listed for 36 major world currencies. The data is updated daily (at 17:00 Central European Time).

Figure 19.3 Foreign Currency Exchange Server results.

XENON LABS UNIVERSAL CURRENCY CONVERTER

The Xenon Labs Universal Currency Converter tells you how many Bermudan dollars buy one Malaysian ringgit and how many Peruvian new sols equate to 1000 Irish punts. It can also handle more mundane currency-conversion tasks, such as determining the strength of the U.S. dollar relative to the Japanese yen and the German mark. This page's maintainers update the exchange rates once each business day, which is accurate enough for most purposes. If you're trading currencies for a living, though, look elsewhere for your data.

To use the Universal Currency Converter, choose a currency from each of the two list boxes and click the **Perform Currency Conversion** button. The Converter will convert one unit of the currency you chose from the left list box into one unit of the currency you chose from the right list box. If you want to convert more than one unit of currency, enter a value in the leftmost text box. Figure 19.4 shows the layout of the Currency Converter page.

Figure 19.4 The Xenon Labs Universal Currency Converter page.

XENON LABS UNIVERSAL CURRENCY CONVERTER ★ ★ ★

URL: http://www.xe.com/xenon/currency.htm

Capsule Review: This page will convert virtually any world currency into virtually any other currency. A page extremely useful to travelers and those interested in general trends in world currency markets.

MUTUAL FUND PERFORMANCE

Charts showing the long-term performance of dozens of leading mutual funds are available from the Experimental Stock Market Data Server at the MIT Artificial Intelligence Laboratory. The future of this service is in doubt, since the company that provided the data has stopped doing so and requests that visitors to the site register with their fee-based service (http://www.ai.mit.edu/stocks/funds/InterTrade.info).

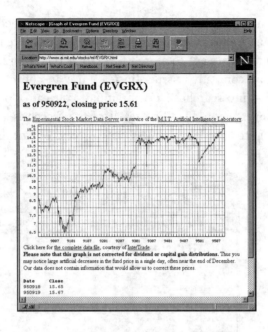

Figure 19.5 Experimental Stock Market Data Server results.

EXPERIMENTAL MUTUAL FUND CHARTS ★ ★ ★ ★

URL: http://www.ai.mit.edu/stocks/mf.html

Capsule Review: Detailed charts show the performance of leading mutual funds over a five-year period.

OBTAINING A MUTUAL FUND PROSPECTUS

Before investing in any mutual fund, you should obtain the prospectus and read it carefully. Normally, this involves calling the company and waiting for the prospectus to arrive via snail mail. If you'd like to see the prospectus right now, though, you may be able to find it in the Securities and Exchange Commission (SEC) database service, called Edgar. The Edgar Prospectus Report enables you to search for a given mutual fund, and—if an electronic version of the prospectus is available—to read it on-screen.

After accessing the site, you see the Edgar Prospectus Report search page (Figure 19.6). In the search box, type one or more key words describing the fund you want to search for. Don't type more than 20 words to describe the company's name—instead, use an abbreviation (Edgar performs substring searches). For example, you can type "fid" to identify Fidelity Investments Inc. The result of the search is a list of documents conforming to your search question; to access one of them, just click it.

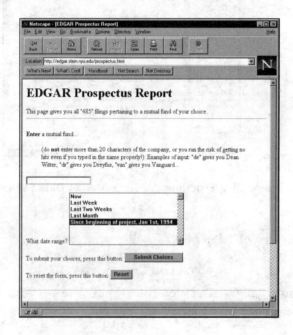

Figure 19.6 Edgar Prospectus Report search page.

EDGAR PROSPECTUS REPORT ★ ★ ★

URL: http://edgar.stern.nyu.edu/prospectus.html

Capsule Review: A good selection of mutual fund prospectuses is available here. If you can find one for the fund in which you're interested, you can save yourself the trouble of ordering it directly from the fund. Coverage is far from complete, though.

PUBLICLY AVAILABLE CORPORATE DATA

Before investing in a stock, it makes good sense to obtain all the financial information you can concerning the company. U.S. security regulations require companies to provide a variety of financial information, including quarterly performance reports, to the Securities and Exchange Commission (SEC)—and many do so in electronic format (all companies will be required to do so in 1996). Thanks to the Edgar Project, an NSF-funded effort at New York University (NYU), this information is now available from the SEC's Web server. At this writing, it's also available—with a much better search interface—at NYU.

EDGAR EXHAUSTIVE COMPANY SEARCH ★ ★ ★

URL: http://edgar.stern.nyu.edu/formco_array.html

Capsule Review: Careful investors will want to find out everything they can about a firm's financial state before buying stock—and here's where you can find a great deal of information about what's actually going on with a firm's finances. If information industry lobbyists get their way, this service will go down and you'll have to pay for this information—despite the fact that it has been assembled with taxpayers' money.

STANDARD & POOR'S 500 INDEX

This site, part of the Security APL service, displays a graph of the S&P 500's activity for the current day (see Figure 19.7). You can also view graphs for the last 12 months, the last 5 years, and the last 12 years.

SEARCH TIP

Note that most browsers cache this site, and some may not check to see whether the chart has changed before displaying it. For this reason, you could be looking at data from the last time you accessed the site, and not realize it. If you're not sure how your browser's cache function works, click the **Reload** button to make sure you're viewing the most recent version of the graph.

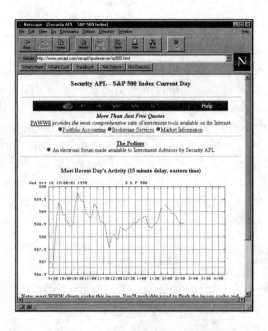

Figure 19.7 S & P 500 performance for October 18, 1995 (Security APL Server).

SECURITY APL S&P 500 ★ ★ ★ ★

URL: http://www.secapl.com/secapl/quoteserver/sp500.html

Capsule Review: Get a quick, graphical look at the S&P's performance throughout the trading day, for the past 12 months, the past 5 years, or the past 12 years.

STOCK PERFORMANCE

MIT's Artificial Intelligence Laboratory maintains this exceptional service, which provides on-screen graphs (see Figure 19.8) of recent price and volume performance for 392 stocks. The graphs cover a three-month period. In the background, you see the relative performance of the S&P 500 during the same period. Also available are indices of the S&P 500 and the NASDAQ Composite Index.

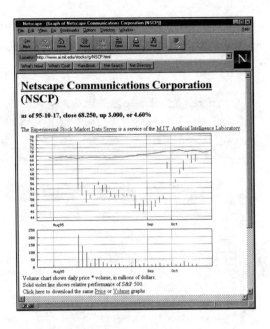

Figure 19.8 MIT's Experimental Stock Market Charts

EXPERIMENTAL STOCK MARKET CHARTS ★ ★ ★ ★

URL: http://www.ai.mit.edu/stocks/graphs.html

Capsule Review: If a stock in which you're interested is included in the list of 392 charts graphed here, take a look—you'll see price and volume graphs for the past three months.

STOCK QUOTES

Want to know how your stock is doing? You can get a quick quote from the APL Quote Server. Note that this isn't a real-time service—the quotes are at least 15 minutes old.

To use the APL Quote Server, log on to the site (http://www.secapl.com/cgi-bin/qs), type your stock's ticker symbol in the Ticker Symbol box, and click **Submit**. You'll see a response page showing the stock's complete name and lots of trading data (Figure 19.9), including the last trading price, the change (in dollars), the change in percentage, the day's low, the day's high, the 52 week low, and the 52 week high.

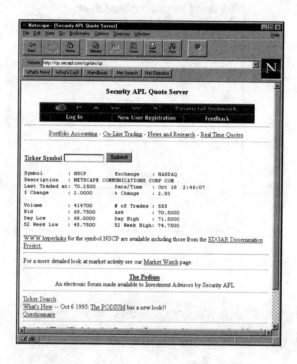

Figure 19.9 Security APL Quote Server.

Don't know your stock's ticker symbol? See the next section, "Ticker Symbol Lookup."

SEARCH TIP

SECURITY APL QUOTE SERVER ★ ★ ★ ★

URL: http://www.secapl.com/cgi-bin/qs

Capsule Review: This is the place to look for a current stock quote. It's not exactly up to the minute—the quotes are at least

15 minutes old. You'll need to know your stock's ticker symbol to use this service.

TICKER SYMBOL LOOKUP

Do you know the name of a company but don't know its ticker code? This site, part of the Security APL suite of on-line financial services, quickly produces the code. To search the site, select the "universe" of stocks you're looking for (stocks, Canadian stocks, money market funds, or mutual funds), type the company's name in the Search box, and click **Submit**.

SEARCH TIP

Note that the Security APL Ticker Lookup service indexes many company names using abbreviations, such as Intl Business Machines. In addition, the search software performs an exact match search. Therefore, if your search doesn't succeed, try again with another spelling or abbreviation. If all else fails, you can search with truncation (the operator is a period, as in *nova.*). Note that there's a limit of 50 items in the retrieval list.

SECURITY APL TICKER LOOKUP ★ ★ ★

URL: http://www.secapl.com/cgi-bin/lookup

Capsule Review: It's fast and useful—and does the advertised job!

CHAPTER 20

SEARCHING PERIODICALS

One of the key steps in research is to check out the periodical literature—scholarly and scientific journals, magazines, and other print-based publications that appear at weekly, monthly, or quarterly intervals. As you'll find in this chapter, the Web is a great place to look for periodical literature. You'll find a Web-accessible service called Uncover that indexes more than 17,000 periodicals, and you'll also find the *full text* of current and past issues of many popular magazines, including *Time*, *Sports Illustrated*, *NetGuide*, and more.

CAMBRIDGE SCIENTIFIC ABSTRACTS

One of the most important resources for university-level scientific and scholarly research are those big, thick, annual reference indexes which you'll find in the reference section of college and university libraries. Organized by subject area, these provide researchers with the means to cope with the huge amount of scientific literature that appears each year. They contain thousands of bibliographic citations and professionally written abstracts, which enable researchers to determine whether a given publication is worth retrieving and reading.

Many print-based abstracts have long been available in on-line versions, searchable through subscription-only services—and that's a good thing, since they're increasingly expensive and time-consuming to publish in print-based media. Researchers in scientific, technical, and medical fields need the latest information, and the producers of reference indexes can make it available on-line very quickly—often, it's only a matter of days from the publication of an article to its inclusion in the on-line database.

Wouldn't the broader public like to have access to this information? You would think so. A searcher with average competence could, in a matter of minutes, tell you whether most scientists think that soybeans are a healthful addition to your diet (they are, incidentally), and print out the latest theories about how to deal with surly adolescents.

Despite several unsuccessful attempts to market these databases to a wider audience, a mass market hasn't appeared. The databases are mostly used by university librarians and corporate information specialists. Why? The consensus of opinion has been that the services were too hard to use—you really had to speak Boolean—and that people just didn't have the time to plough through all that tedious scientific prose, loaded with the passive voice and the usual academic equivocations ("It has been the suggestion of this article that a limited salubrious effect can be assigned to the consumption of walnuts, but further research needs to be done to confirm this apparent pattern").

But now the Web has come along—and with it, the rather amazing phenomenon of millions of people actually performing computer searches using fairly sophisticated search tools (even, yes, Boolean operators). Is there a mass market for scientific reference information? Of all the players on the contemporary scene, Cambridge Scientific Abstracts (CSA), a privately owned company based in Bethesda, Maryland, may be best poised to find out. CSA has just launched a fee-based search service which allows on-line access to very high quality databases of information in the fields of the biological sciences, environmental sciences, engineering, and aquatic marine sciences.

CSA's Web site, called Internet Database Services (IDS), gets everything right—it's easy to use, and the search page doesn't drag you kicking and screaming through tons of unwanted search information. The search defaults make sense—you can do field-based searches (for title or author), or search the whole abstract—and the default setting is an exact-match phrase search with an implied AND operator (these are the settings chosen, you might recall, by the most popular Web search engines, such as InfoSeek—and for good reason).

IDS provides access to more than three dozen databases, grouped into four general fields of scientific and technical knowledge (see Table 20.1).

Table 20.1 Internet Database Services Databases

Aquatic Sciences and Fisheries Journals

ASFA Aquaculture Abstracts

ASFA Marine Biotechnology Abstracts

ASFA 1: Biological Sciences & Living Resources

ASFA 2: Ocean Technology, Policy & Non-Living Resources

ASFA 3: Aquatic Pollution & Environmental Quality

Oceanic Abstracts

Biological and Medical Science Journals

ASFA Aquaculture Abstracts

ASFA Marine Biotechnology Abstracts

ASFA 1: Biological Sciences & Living Resources

Agricultural & Environmental Biotechnology Abstracts

Algology, Mycology & Protozoology Abstracts (Microbiology C)

Animal Behavior Abstracts

Bacteriology Abstracts (Microbiology B)

BioEngineering Abstracts

CSA Neurosciences Abstracts

Calcium & Calcified Tissue Abstracts

Chemoreception Abstracts

Ecology Abstracts

Entomology Abstracts

Genetics Abstracts

Human Genome Abstracts

Immunology Abstracts

Industrial & Applied Microbiology Abstracts (Microbiology A)

Medical & Pharmaceutical Biotechnology Abstracts

Nucleic Acids Abstracts

Oncogenes & Growth Factors Abstracts

Toxicology Abstracts

Virology & AIDS Abstracts

Environment and Pollution Journals

Agricultural & Environmental Biotechnology Abstracts

ASFA 3: Aquatic Pollution & Environmental Quality

Bacteriology Abstracts (Microbiology B)

Ecology Journal

EIS: Digests of Environmental Impact Statements

Health & Safety Science Abstracts

Industrial & Applied Microbiology Abstracts (Microbiology A)

Pollution Abstracts

Risk Abstracts

Toxicology Abstracts

Engineering and Computer Science Journals

Computer & Information Systems Abstracts

Electronics & Communications Abstracts

Engineered Materials Abstracts

Materials Business File

Mechanical Engineering Abstracts

METADEX

Risk Abstracts

Solid State & Superconductivity Abstracts

IDS (Figure 20.1) is a fee-based service—there's a subscription fee, and it isn't cheap (to find out more about IDS subscriptions, send mail to sales@csa.com). To find out whether the service might meet your needs, though, there's a free demo which permits you to search the 1990 database. You'll need to fill out a registration form, which enables you to access the search form (Figure 20.2). You then choose from five general subject areas, and you'll see a page asking you to identify the specific databases you want to search (click all the ones that you'd like to search).

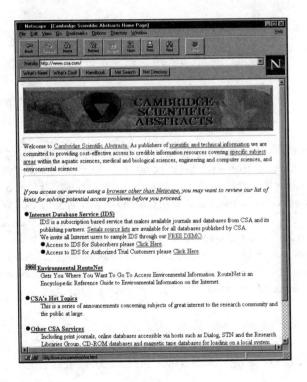

Figure 20.1 Cambridge Scientific Abstracts welcome page.

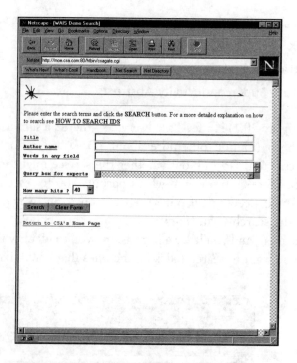

Figure 20.2 Internet Database Services search page.

SEARCH TIP

The IDS search defaults—an exact-match phrase search with an implied AND operator—are very good for unsophisticated searchers, but be aware that they could produce too few results. If you get too few documents, try broadening the search. If you would like to try truncation, you'll need to use a truncation operator (an asterisk). For example, "fish*" will retrieve *fishing, fisheries,* and *fished.* If you're searching for two words that aren't actually a phrase, defeat phrase searching by using the **OR** operator. Use **OR** to link alternative versions of a search term, such as "eutrophication" OR "deoxygenation."

The result of your search is a list of documents (Figure 20.3) that match your search query (if any were found). To view the citation and abstract for one of these documents (see Figure 20.4), just click the hyperlink.

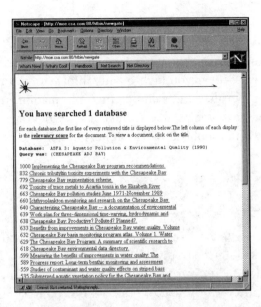

Figure 20.3 List of retrieved documents.

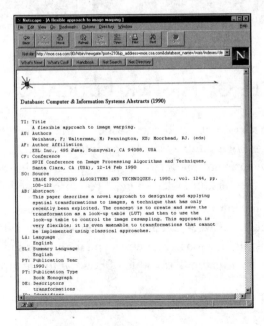

Figure 20.4 Citation and abstract (IDS).

Is IDS such a big deal? Yes, if you're a serious student or a professional in one of the fields covered by the IDS databases. You'll have to fork over some serious money to subscribe, but it's well worth it if your career advancement depends on high-quality information. In time, as more and more people realize the value of this information, the price will come down. For now, you're able to take a free look at a service that's well designed with unsophisticated searchers in mind.

INTERNET DATABASE SERVICES ★ ★ ★ ★

URL: http://www.csa.com/

Capsule Review: A fee-based service, IDS lets you search sample scientific data (from the 1990 databases). Take a look—you'll find out why universities and corporate researchers shell out subscriptions of up to $795 per year to gain access to the latest scientific, technical, and medical information. Note that you won't see the full text of the documents, but the professionally written abstracts enable you to determine whether it's worth the trouble to obtain the full-text version.

CHRONICLE OF HIGHER EDUCATION

The most important weekly newspaper of the academic community is the *Chronicle of Higher Education*. Its on-line edition, Academe This Week, offers summaries of the major articles appearing in the newspaper—but they're just teasers, intended to goad you into subscribing.

The only information of substance is the *Chronicle's* jobs listing (some 750 openings per week, on average), which is searchable by key word. If you're looking for a job in academia, you'll find this site of great interest—otherwise, it's a textbook example of how *not* to put a publication online.

MUTUAL FUNDS ONLINE

Mutual funds investors fork over lots of money for subscriptions to newsletters and magazines—and well they should, considering how many mutual funds are available (and how much their performance varies). Now there's a searchable on-line source of very high quality information concerning mutual funds, brought to Web users by the Institute for Econometric Research. If that sounds academic, you'll be very pleased by the polished look and excellent writing to be found in Mutual Funds Online's offerings.

To search Mutual Funds Online, access the search page (Figure 20.5) at http://www.mfmag.com/srchart.htm. Type your search term or terms in the text box, and click **Perform Search**.

SEARCH TIP

By default, Mutual Funds Online's search software performs an exact-match search—"Fidel" retrieves an article on Cuba rather than a complete list of Fidelity funds. But it's not case-sensitive. In addition, there's an implied AND operator—if you type "Magellan" and "Janus Fund," you get no hits, because there's no article that discusses both of them. It's best to type one well-focused search term.

The result of the search is a list of articles, which are listed in reverse chronological order, with the most recent articles at the bottom of the list. To view an article just click the link, and you'll see the full text of the article onscreen (Figure 20.6).

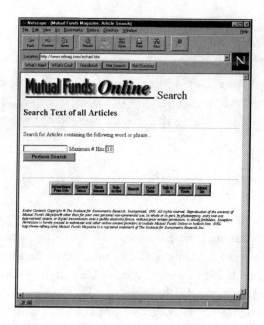

Figure 20.5 Mutual Funds Online search page.

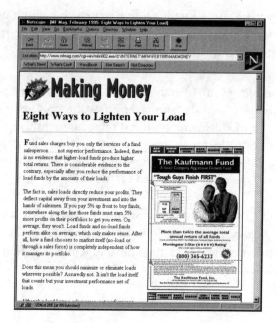

Figure 20.6 Mutual Funds Online article.

MUTUAL FUNDS ONLINE ★ ★ ★ ★

URL: http://www.mfmag.com/srchart.htm

Capsule Review: Excellent on-line version of a leading mutual funds magazine with good search capabilities (once you know the default search settings).

PATHFINDER

And now for the blockbuster—the very closest thing to a small public library's periodical room that you'll find on the Web. Actually, if you titled this site "The Time-Warner's Periodical Room," you'd be closer to the mark, since this site contains full-text Web versions of Time-Warner magazines. In these days of media mergers, Time-Warner's stock of magazines is pretty impressive, as you'll surely agree after looking at Table 20.2. But the best thing about this site is the fantastic search engine.

Table 20.2 Magazines Searchable with PathFinder

Asiaweek

Digital Pulse

Entertainment Weekly

Fortune

Money

People

Progressive Farmer

Southern Living

Sports Illustrated

Sunset

Time

Time Life Music

Time Life Photo Sight

Time-Warner Electronic Publishing

Vibe

Virtual Garden

After you click the **Search** button in PathFinder's welcome page (http://www.pathfinder.com), you'll see a page with three options. PathFinder enables you to search three ways:

- **Home pages within PathFinder**. Here, you search for the titles of "home pages" within PathFinder—that is, the main pages for each of the publications.

- **PathFinder databases by key word**. This is the option you want for a full-text search of the magazines' text.

- **Search the Net**. This option displays a rather out-of-date page of search engine URLs... c'mon, guys. Skip this one.

After you choose PathFinder databases by key word, you'll see the search page, the top portion of which is shown in Figure 20.7. We're told that searching is a process, not an event—which is pretty good advice. By default, PathFinder searches all the databases—which is a pretty good setting, actually, if you're looking for high recall. If you'd rather select one of the magazines, do so, and go on to the next step: typing your search terms.

In the second section of the PathFinder search page (Figure 20.8), you type the search terms you're looking for. To perform a simple search, just type one or more words.

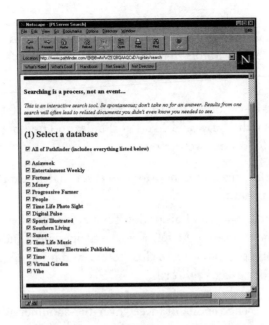

Figure 20.7 PathFinder full-text database search page (database selection).

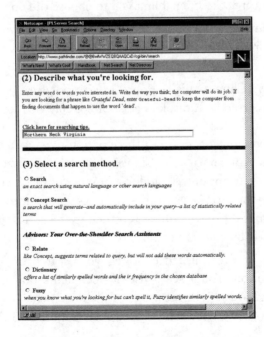

Figure 20.8 PathFinder key word and search method selection.

SEARCH TIP

By default, PathFinder performs an exact-match search with an implied OR operator. You can considerably refine and focus this search by using the many operators that PathFinder makes available. For more information, see the sidebar, "Searching PathFinder."

In the third section of the search page (see Figure 20.8), you choose the type of search you would like PathFinder to attempt. First, you choose from the following two options:

- **Search**. This option performs an exact-match search, with an implied OR operator.

- **Concept Search**. This option generates a list of words that frequently appear close to the terms you actually typed, and will retrieve documents containing these close terms even if the documents don't contain your exact key words.

You can also choose one of three "over-the-shoulder advisors":

- **Relate**. This option displays a list of the terms that would be used in a Concept search, enabling you to choose the ones you want to use.

- **Dictionary**. This option displays a list of words with similar spellings, enabling you to choose possible synonyms or variants of your key words.

- **Fuzzy**. Choose this option if you're not sure you've spelled a key word correctly. It displays a list of possible correct spellings.

If you choose one of these last three options, you won't see a list of documents, but rather a page that shows a list of the alternative key words generated by these options. To add one or more of these words to your query, hold down the **Ctrl** key and click the ones you want to use, and then click **Add Terms to Query**. You're returned to the search page, but this time these option buttons are blank.

When you've finished choosing your search options, click the **Go Search** button. You'll see a list of documents that match your search words (Figure 20.9). To view one of the documents, click the document's title, and you'll see the full text onscreen (Figure 20.10).

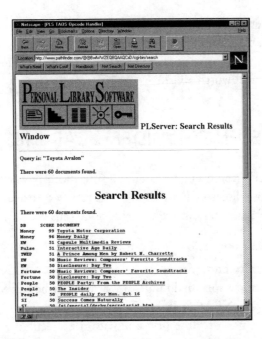

Figure 20.9 Documents retrieved by PathFinder search.

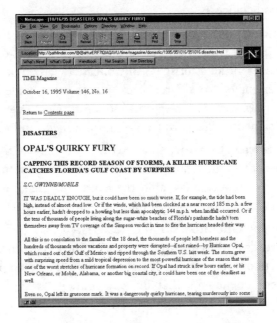

Figure 20.10 Full text of document retrieved by PathFinder.

PathFinder shows how it's done. With a huge amount of information available and a powerful search engine, virtually any Web user can find a great deal of information in short order. This is one of the Web's best sites, and well worth a visit.

ADVANCED PATHFINDER SEARCHES

PathFinder's search engine is among the more powerful—and complicated—of those discussed in this book. The following explains some of the most useful operators you can use to refine and focus your PathFinder search.

- **Boolean operators**. You can use AND, OR, and NOT.

- **Proximity and adjacency operators**. Use NEAR to link terms that fall within a specified range of words, in either direction (for example, "Simpson NEAR/4 Ito"). To match documents in which the second term comes after the first one within a specified word range, use the W operator (for example, "Simpson W/4 jury"). Use ADJ to link words that must appear next to each other in the specified order ("bloody glove").

- **Truncation**. By default, PathFinder uses an exact-match search. To search with truncation, use a question mark (?) to truncate by one character, or an asterisk (*) to truncate by any number of characters. For example, "rock?" retrieves *rock* or *rocks*, while "rock*" retrieves *rock*, *rocks*, *rockin'*, *rocket*, and lots more. To force stemming, type a plus sign after the word (run+ finds *run*, *runs*, and *running*).

- **Thesaurus Operator**. To force the search engine to replace your key word with all the synonyms for this word found in the database's word list, type an at sign (@) after the word. For example, "satellite@" initiates a search that uses all the synonyms for "satellite."

- **Concept Operator**. To initiate a search that automatically uses all the words that frequently occur with the key word you type, use the concept operator (an exclamation point). For example, "tattoo!" will retrieve documents that do not contain "tattoo" but do contain "bodyart."

- **Field Operators**. To restrict the search to a certain field in the retrieved records, type a colon followed by the name of the field (for example, "wall:author" retrieves documents in which the Author field contains *Wall*). You can also add a "year=" statement to your query (for example, "year=1994"). This will restrict the search to just those documents that were published in 1994.

PATHFINDER ★ ★ ★ ★

URL: http://www.pathfinder.com/

Capsule Review: One of the Web's best sites, this very searchable database of popular magazines is the Web's answer to the Reader's Guide to Periodical Literature. Sure, it's restricted to Times-Warner magazines, but there are lots of 'em! The search engine is very powerful, but tends to produce too many false drops unless you know what you're doing (but you do, by now, don't you?).

TECHWEB

Looking for information on computers and related technologies? If your focus is on professional computing, database management, system administration, enterprise networking, and other professional areas of computing, TechWeb is an excellent choice. Produced by CMP Publications, Inc., TechWeb includes searchable databases containing the full text of articles published in 16 leading computer magazines. Apart from *NetGuide* and *Windows Magazine*, the focus is on professionals in the field of computing rather than end users. (If you're a PC user looking for practical PC-related information, ZDNet might be a better choice.)

To search TechWeb, click the **Search** button that's available on several of the TechWeb pages, or use the following URL: http://techweb.cmp.com/techweb/programs/registered/search/cmp-wais-index.html. You'll see the TechWeb search page, shown in Figure 20.11.

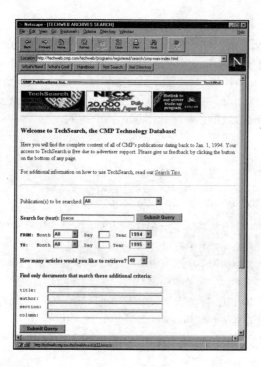

Figure 20.11 TechWeb search page.

Choose the database you want to search (the default is All). Type the key word or words you want to use in the Search for Text box. If you would prefer to restrict the search to a certain field in the retrieved record, type the key words in the Title, Author, Section, or Column boxes, below. Another option: You can restrict the search by date. To do so, choose dates in the From and To areas. If you would like to retrieve more or fewer articles than the default 40, make your choice. When you're finished, click **Submit**.

SEARCH TIP

By default, TechWeb performs an exact-match, case-insensitive search, with an implied OR operator. As you've probably already found from searching databases with similar default settings, these search settings are likely to produce a lot of false drops. To focus and refine your search, take advantage of the TechWeb search engine's many advanced features and operators, which are discussed in the sidebar titled "Searching TechWeb."

If TechWeb finds any matches for the key words you've supplied, you'll see a retrieval list such as the one shown in Figure 20.12.

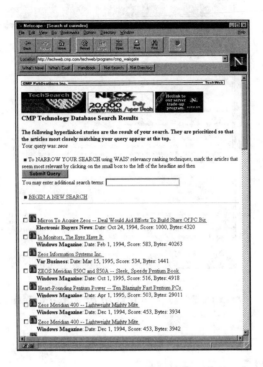

Figure 20.12 Documents retrieved by a TechWeb search.

SEARCH TIP

TechWeb uses a WAIS search engine, which offers two ways to refine your search. If the list of retrieved documents isn't focused enough, you can add additional search terms to your query. You can also click the check boxes next to documents that conform to your search interest; the search engine will retrieve documents whose word frequency profiles resemble those of the ones you've clicked. Nifty!

When you find a document you'd like to see, click its title, and you'll see it onscreen (Figure 20.13).

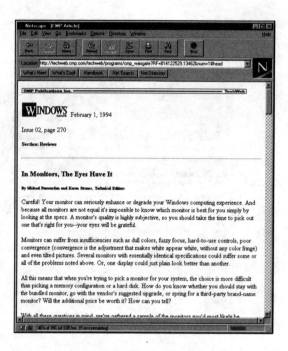

Figure 20.13 Full text of document (TechWeb).

SEARCHING TECHWEB

TechWeb's search engine is unusually flexible and powerful, so you can refine and focus your search by taking advantage of the many operators available. Here's an overview:

- **Boolean Operators**. You can use **AND, OR**, and **NOT**.

- **Proximity Operators**. Link two words with ADJ to force the search engine to retrieve only those documents in which the linked words appear together, in any order.

- **Phrase Searching**. To perform a phrase search, type the phrase in quotation marks ("postponed Shuttle launch").

- **Truncation**. By default, TechWeb's search engine performs an exact-match search. You can add truncation by cutting the word down to a root and adding an asterisk (*). For example, "tech*" retrieves *techie*, *technical, technician*, etc.

- **Parentheses**. Here's a great feature. By grouping key words in parentheses, you can refine your search even more. Here's an example: (vacation or holiday) AND (Hawaii or Tahiti). This query finds any document that mentions vacation or holiday, and also mentions Hawaii or Tahiti.

Table 20.3 Magazines Searchable on TechWeb

CommunicationsWeek

CommunicationsWeek International

Computer Reseller News

Computer Retail Week

Electronic Buyers' News

Electronic Engineering Times

HomePC

Informatiques

InformationWeek

InteractiveAge

Max CD-ROM

NetGuide

Network Computing,

OEM Magazine

VAR Business

Windows Magazine

TECHWEB ★ ★ ★ ★

URL:
http://techweb.cmp.com/techweb/programs/registered/search/cmp-wais-index.html

Capsule Review: Here's a great place to look if you're searching for trade and professional information concerning computers, communications, data processing, system administration, network management, and enterprise networking. TechWeb's unusually powerful search engine will enable you to focus your searches well.

UNCOVER

This is amazing! Here's a service that indexes more than 17,000 periodicals, enabling you to find bibliographic references to more than six million articles. And you can search the UnCover database for free!

What's in it for UnCover? UnCover offers a fee-based document delivery system. If you find an article in UnCover that you must have, and quickly, you can get it faxed to you in 24 hours or less. Don't worry about copyright—your UnCover fees cover clearance and payment with the Copyright Clearance Center. And the cost? Currently $8.50 per article, plus copyright fees (which can run as high as $12.50 per article). If you don't want to pay the fee, you can retrieve the article for free at your local library.

So what's the catch? UnCover is currently a Telnet-based service, meaning that you're back in the clunky world of text-only terminals. Still, the service is well designed (for a Telnet service), and you won't have any trouble learning how to navigate the displays.

SEARCH TIP

In order to use UnCover, you'll need to equip your browser with a Telnet helper application. You can obtain a Telnet helper for free by accessing The Consummate Winsock Apps List (http://cwsapps.texas.net/term.html). If you're using Windows 95, you'll find that Microsoft has provided a Telnet utility for you to use—and that Netscape is already configured to use it!

Accessing UnCover

To access UnCover, you have two options:

- **Logging on through UnCover's Web site**. Access http://www.carl.org/uncover/unchome.html, and click the link to open UnCover's database. If your browser has been properly configured, your Telnet helper program will start.

- **Logging on through Telnet directly**. Start your Telnet helper application, and use the Connect menu (or its equivalent in your program) to access database.carl.org.

After you access the service, follow these instructions to access the free UnCover service:

1. If you don't see anything onscreen, just press **Enter** once or twice. You'll see a list of terminal types.

2. Type the number corresponding to the VT-100 terminal type, and press **Enter**. You'll see a list of database options.

3. Type the number corresponding to UnCover—Article access & document delivery—No password required, and press **Enter**. You'll be asked to supply a password if you want to enter UnCover's password-based services.

4. Press **Enter**. You'll be asked whether you've set up a profile. A profile contains your name, address, and additional information that is used to send articles to you.

5. Just press **Enter**.

SEARCH TIP

If you're using UnCover, don't switch to another application and leave UnCover unattended. The system is programmed to log you off if there's no activity for a specified interval—and once you're logged off, UnCover won't let you log back on for an hour. Apparently, this setting is intended to discourage users from tying up the system if they're not serious searchers, but it's very frustrating to find that you're prevented from re-accessing the system after an idle period that's attributable to a legitimate reason (for example, visiting the men's or ladies' room).

Choosing the Search Method

With UnCover, you can search in three ways:

- **Word**. A word search is a key word search, just like those you've used in the Web's search engines.
- **Author**. You can enter the last name and first name, or just the last name.
- **Browse by Journal Title**. This search enables you to retrieve journal titles. You can then view the table of contents for any single issue.

To choose the search method, use the following UnCover screen:

```
To use UnCover, enter:  W for WORD or TOPIC search
        N for AUTHOR search
        B to BROWSE by journal title

For information, type:  ? to learn about UnCover
        ?C to learn about UnCover Complete
        ?R to learn about UnCover Reveal ALERT service
        QS to learn about searching short-cuts
To leave UnCover, type: S to STOP or SWITCH to another
database

Type the letter(s) of the UnCover service you want and
press <RETURN>
        SELECTED DATABASE: UnCover
```

Try a word search by typing **W** (uppercase or lowercase) and pressing **Enter**.

Searching for a Word

An UnCover word search retrieves words drawn from the title, subtitle, summaries, or the abstracts that appear on the contents page for each journal. You can also search for proper names of people mentioned in the text of the articles.

SEARCH TIP

If you type the name of a journal along with the other words in your Word search, you will limit the retrieval list to just those articles printed in that journal.

To perform a word search, type one or more words (but no more than one line), and press **Enter**.

Searching for an author

To perform a NAME search, just list the author's first and last name, as in "Calvin Trillin" or "Colin Powell." Be sure to separate the names with spaces, and press **Enter** when you're done.

Viewing the Retrieval List

If UnCover finds any matches for the search words you've used, you'll see a numbered list of articles, showing the titles, the periodicall's title, the author's name and the date of publication. If you'd like to get more information about a given article, you can view the full citation, which inclules a summary and additional bibliographical information.

ZDNet

ZDNet is the searchable on-line database of magazines in Ziff-Davis Publishing Co.'s formidable roster (see Table 20.4), which includes a good portion of the computing magazines you're likely to find on the super-market magazine shelf.

To search ZDNet, access the site at http://www.ziff.com/ and click the **Search** button. You'll see the search page shown in Figure 20.14. To initiate a search, select your database (by default, ZDNet searches all of the databases), type one or more search terms, and click **Start Search**. If ZDNet's search engine finds one or more matches, you'll see a retrieval list such as the one shown in Figure 20.15; click one of the titles to see a document such as the one shown in Figure 20.16.

Figure 20.14 ZDNet search page.

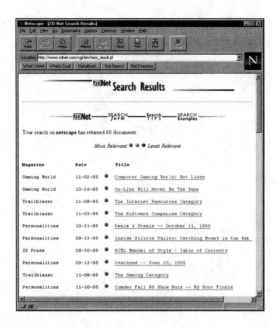

Figure 20.15 ZDNet retrieval list.

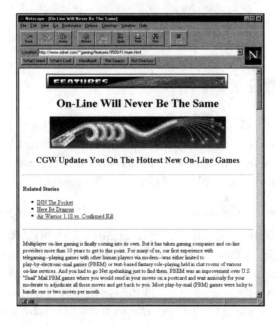

Figure 20.16 Full text of document (ZDNet).

Table 20.4 Magazines Searchable on ZDNet

Computer Life

Computer Shopper

FamilyPC

Gaming World

Inter@ctive Week

MacUser

MacWeek

PC Computing

PC Magazine

PC Week

Personalities

The Cobb Group

Trailblazer

Windows Sources

ZD Press

SEARCHING ZDNET

ZDNet's search engine offers many possibilities for refining and focusing your search. (By the way, these operators are almost identical to the ones you can use in PathFinder—and that's because the two sites got their software from the same place!) Here's an overview:

- **Boolean operators**. You can use **AND, OR**, and **NOT**.
- **Proximity and adjacency operators**. Use **NEAR** to link terms that fall within a specified range of words, in either direction (for example, "Macintosh NEAR5 Performa." Use **ADJ** to link words that must appear next to each other in the specified order ("Zeos Pantera"). You can also use the **W/n** operator to specify that the second word should

come within the specified number of words after the first word ("Zeos W/10 service").

- **Truncation.** By default, ZDNet's search engine uses an exact-match search. To search with truncation, use a question mark (?) to truncate by one character, or an asterisk (*) to truncate by any number of characters. For example, "rock?" retrieves *rock* or *rocks*, while "rock*" retrieves *rock, rocks, rockin', rocket*, and lots more.

- **Thesaurus Operator.** To force the search engine to replace your key word with all the synonyms for this word found in the database's word list, type an at sign (@) after the word. For example, "ram@" initiates a search that uses all the synonyms for "ram."

- **Concept Operator.** To initiate a search that automatically uses all the words that frequently occur with the key word you type, use the concept operator (an exclamation point). For example, "ram!" will retrieve documents that do not contain "ram" but do contain "random-access memory."

ZDNet ★ ★ ★ ★

URL: http://www.ziff.com/

Capsule Review: This is the place to search for information in personal computer-related periodicals. The search engine is powerful, the graphics are elegant, and the information is top-notch. Great site!

CHAPTER 21

SEARCHING LIBRARY DATABASES

In this chapter, you'll learn how to search one of the most amazing information resources you'll find anywhere on the Internet: the card catalogs of the world's leading research libraries, including the Library of Congress. What's more, you'll learn how to use the demo version of the exceptionally fine software that's included on this book's disk, called BookWhere.

BookWhere is a Web application that allows you to search huge library databases directly, without having to use clunky Telnet sessions. So put aside your Web browser for a while, and give BookWhere a try. Before long, you'll know how to track down just about any book on any subject published since the late 1970s, and many of those published before that date.

INTRODUCING THE Z39.50 PROTOCOL

During the past twenty years, libraries everywhere have been trying to get their card catalogs on-line—and for good reason. It's just too expensive to deal with alphabetizing and checking all those cards, and besides, library patrons are sufficiently computer literate nowadays that they can use a computer to look up holdings.

Unfortunately, most libraries chose to computerize their card catalogs using proprietary computer systems marketed by IBM and other manufacturers. These computers can't talk directly to the Internet; as a result, these library databases—containing millions of references to books, government documents, and much more—could be accessed only by means of clunky Telnet sessions. (In a Telnet session, you run a terminal program that turns your graphical Web browser into a text-only terminal for a distant mainframe computer.)

But along came the Z39.50 protocol, a standard established by the International Standards Organization (ISO) and—as yet—little recognized by the Internet community. That ought to change, as you'll see. I won't drag you through the technical details—suffice it to say that Z39.50 enables Internet-based applications to "talk" to library database systems without requiring you to abandon the graphical user interface for its text-based predecessor, Telnet. A Web application that incorporates the Z39.50 protocol can access any Z39.50 database, anywhere on the Internet.

In order to take advantage of the information stored on library databases, you'll need a Web browser or application that's conversant with the Z39.50 protocol. Where do you get it? You've already got it! BookWhere, a Z39.50 Web application that's designed to search library databases, is included with this book.

INTRODUCING BOOKWHERE

A product of a Canadian firm called Sea Change Corporation (http://www.seachange.com), BookWhere is a Web application that's designed to enable you to do the following:

- **Obtain and manage a list of Z39.50-accessible library database profiles.** You need these profiles in order to access distant databases.

The version of the program included on this disk offers dozens of huge library databases, including the biggest of them all, the U.S. Library of Congress.

- **Formulate a search query.** You already know enough about on-line searching to handle this with no problem. As you'll see, BookWhere's capabilities are outstanding—you can formulate complex Boolean search questions just by clicking a few buttons. Designers of Web search engines, take a look at how this is done!

- **Initiate the search.** When you click the **Search** button, BookWhere contacts the distant library database, performs the search, and obtains the results.

- **Display a list of documents matching your search question.** This is just an overview, which enables you to scan quickly for documents that might prove pertinent to your interests.

- **Examine the full bibliographic record.** Many of the records you'll retrieve from a BookWhere search conform to a standard bibliographic format. You'll find all the usual bibliographic information, including the author, title, publisher, date, and so on; but there's lots more, including subject descriptions, physical descriptions (for non-print-based media), and—perhaps best of all—libraries that actually possess a copy of the work you're looking for.

BOOKWHERE SYSTEM REQUIREMENTS

- Windows-compatible PC (486-33 or greater recommended) equipped with Windows 3.1 or Windows 95 (not compatible with Windows NT)

- 5 MB available hard disk space (more may be required if a high number of records are retrieved)

- Internet connection (PPP, SLIP, direct)

- Properly installed WinSock DLL

Hats off to Sea Change Corporation for enabling us to include a demo version of BookWhere on the disk enclosed with this book. You can use this program for 45 days from the time you first start it. If you wish to continue using BookWhere, you need to purchase a copy—and the price is reasonable (US$39.50, plus $5 for shipping and handling, but check with Sea Change Corporation for current prices).

INSTALLING AND STARTING BOOKWHERE

On the floppy disk that comes with this book, You'll find the BookWhere Setup program. You can run the program to install BookWhere on your hard disk, as explained in the following section.

Running the Setup Program

Run BookWhere's SETUP program to install the BookWhere software on your hard disk.

To install BookWhere with Windows 3.1, do the following:

1. From the File Manager's File menu, choose **Run**. You'll see the Run dialog box.

2. In the Run dialog box, type **a:\bkwr\setup.exe**

3. Press **Enter** or click **OK**.

4. Follow the on-screen instructions.

To install BookWhere with Windows 95, do the following:

1. From the Start menu, choose **Run**. You'll see the Run dialog box.

2. In the Run dialog box, type **a:\bkwr\setup.exe**

3. Press **Enter** or click **OK**.

4. Follow the on-screen instructions.

NOTE: After you've finished installing BookWhere, you can delete the files in the temporary directory. They're no longer needed.

STARTING BOOKWHERE

To start BookWhere, do one of the following:

- If you're running Windows 3.1, open the BookWhere program group and double-click the **BookWhere** icon.

- If you're running Windows 95, click the **Start** menu, click **Programs**, click **BookWhere**, and click **BookWhere** again.

You'll see BookWhere on-screen, as shown in Figure 21.1. A message will appear informing you how many days you can continue to evaluate the program; just click **OK**.

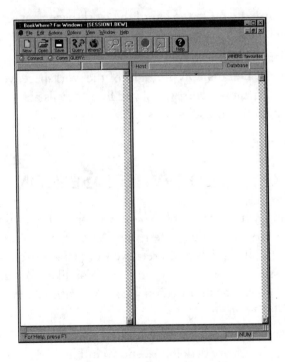

Figure 21.1 BookWhere.

Understanding BookWhere's Screen Features

When you start BookWhere, you see the Query dialog box, which enables you to form your search query. For now, click **Cancel** to close this dialog box and learn about the features of BookWhere's screen.

BookWhere's screen has the usual Windows features, including a title bar and a menu bar. Like all excellent Windows applications, it also has a button bar that enables you to initiate the program's most frequently chosen operations. You'll learn more about what these buttons do in this chapter.

Within BookWhere's application workspace (below the button bar), you'll find two panels:

- **Records List.** On the left of the workspace, you see the Records List panel. Here's where you'll see a summary list of the items your search retrieves.

- **Record Details.** On the right of the workspace, you see the Record Details panel. Here's where you'll see details about the record selected in the Records List.

Starting a BookWhere Session

Every time you search BookWhere, you begin by starting a new session, which has its own unique file name. All that transpires in the session—including all the goodies you retrieve from your search—will be recorded in the session file, which you can save if you like. You can then retrieve it later, and access the information it contains without having to perform the search all over again.

To begin your BookWhere session, choose **New** from the File menu. You'll see the Query dialog box, shown in Figure 21.2. In this dialog box, you'll formulate your query, as explained in the next section.

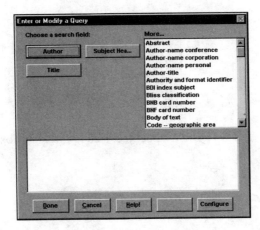

Figure 21.2 Query dialog box.

FORMULATING YOUR QUERY

BookWhere doesn't force you to learn complicated search protocols, although you will need to understand the mysteries of Boolean operators (see Chapter 7 if you need a brush-up). You construct a query by typing key words and clicking buttons, as you'll see.

Before you start, though, there's one point to notice. Unlike Web search engines, BookWhere always searches on a specific field, such as Author or Title. The Z39.50 protocol defines many fields for search purposes, but lots of them have very limited usefulness. You'll be wise to stick with Author, Title, and Subject Heading, which are accessible by means of the buttons within the dialog box.

Begin by trying a simple query using the **Subject Heading** button. Click this button, and you'll see the Subject Heading dialog box, shown in Figure 21.3. In this dialog box, type a well-focused search word, such as **hypothermia**. Click **Done**, and you'll see your query in the Query box. Click **Done** to confirm.

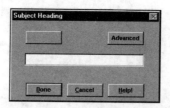

Figure 21.3 Subject Heading dialog box.

CHOOSING A DATABASE

A unique feature of BookWhere is its user-definable groups, which enable you to group two or more databases so that all are searched simultaneously. You'll learn more later about making your own groups, but begin by selecting the **Favourites** group. This group contains two of the most useful databases discussed in this book:

- **BIB.** A major bibliography of books at the Research Library Group (RLG), a California-based consortium of research libraries.
- **BOOKS.** This is it, folks—the Library of Congress's computerized bibliography of virtually everything collected by the Library since.

To choose Favourites, click the **Where** button on the button bar. You'll see the Target Group Selection dialog box, shown in Figure 21.4. In the left panel, highlight **Favourites**, and click **Add**. BookWhere adds the group to the Target Groups window. Click **Done** to return to the main window.

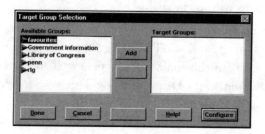

Figure 21.4 Target Group Selection dialog box.

Note that the line just below the button bar now indicates your search query (hypothermia) and the target database group (Favourites). You're ready to search!

SEARCHING AND VIEWING THE RESULTS

To begin your BookWhere search, click the **Search** button. BookWhere automatically contacts the databases you've selected, retrieves the records, and displays these records in the Records List panel (Figure 21.5, which shows a Subject Heading search for Netscape). By default, the list is sorted by Title. To sort the list by Author or Date, click the **Author** or **Date** button at the top of the Records List panel. Note that the Record Details panel contains a detailed view of the record that's currently selected in the Records List panel. To display another record, click the record for which you want to see details.

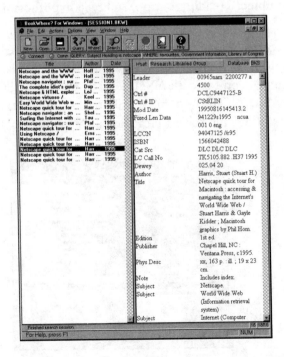

Figure 21.5 Records retrieved in Records List panel.

SAVING AND CLEARING QUERIES

Did you find some good stuff? If so, you may wish to save your query—which you can do in the full, licensed version of BookWhere (but not the demo). To do so, click the **Save** button. You'll see a Save As dialog box, enabling you to name the file and store it on your hard drive.

Once you've saved your retrieval list, or if it didn't produce anything of value, you may wish to search again. If so, click the **Clear** button. This button removes everything from both panels and lets you start anew.

FORMULATING MORE COMPLEX QUERIES

In the Query window, you can build complex queries using a variety of Boolean operators and multiple fields.

Build a complex query one step at a time. For example, begin by clicking the **Subject Heading** button, and type **hypothermia**. Click **Done**.

Then click the **Subject Heading** button again, and type **stress**. Click **Done**. As you'll see in Figure 21.6, BookWhere has entered your query using the default AND operator. If you wish to change this, select the operator; you'll see that you can click AND, OR, or AND-NOT (Figure 21.6). Try clicking **AND-NOT**. Your query will now say, in effect, "Show me all the documents where the Subject Heading says 'hypothermia' but not 'stress.'"

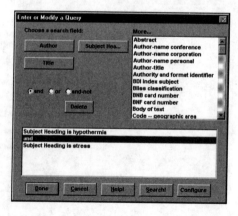

Figure 21.6 Query using the default AND operator

Experiment with this query-building technique. For example, you can create a retrieval list consisting of works in which the Title contains "Computers" but the Author *does not* contain "Pfaffenberger." I won't be terribly flattered by this, naturally, but I do want you to appreciate all the amazing things that can be done with the Query dialog box.

BookWhere Horizons

There's much more to say about BookWhere, but this chapter is intended to whet your appetite—which I hope it has done. As time goes on, more and more libraries are making their databases available to Z39.50 searching. If your local or university library has done so, you can add their profile to the database (to do this, you'll need the licensed version). What's more, Sea Change Corporation is constantly adding new sites, and you can download expanded library database files from their server (http://www.seachange.com/). Happy hunting!

CHAPTER 22

FINDING SOFTWARE

If you're using the Web, you own or otherwise have access to a computer. Therefore, you're constantly on the lookout for neat software to run on your machine. Whether you need a patch that will insert Barney the Dinosaur into the Doom dungeon, or a complete suite of Internet communications tools, the Web has what you need. Furthermore, software you get from the Web usually is either freeware—software you can use forever without paying any money to anyone—or shareware—software you can try free of charge, then register (if you want to continue using the program) by paying a modest fee to the developer.

There are not, however, many huge libraries of general interest software on the Web. This stands to reason, since software files, even compressed ones, can occupy many megabytes of disk space; few server owners can afford to tie up their disk space for purely altruistic purposes. You'll find only a handful of archives containing programs for a variety of purposes and from many different developers.

Instead, you'll find that software developers, both large and small, have their own Web sites. At their sites, developers make files available for download—and frequently provide documentation and support for their programs, too. This way, developers need only tie up their computers with resources related to their products.

This is one of the points at which the field-leveling power of the Web is most evident. You'll find that there's little difference in the appearance and function of Microsoft's site and the appearance and function of the sites of small-time shareware developers like JASC, which publishes Paint Shop Pro.

SOFTWARE TRAILBLAZER PAGES

There aren't that many software trailblazer pages on the Web—and for good reason: The searchable sites, discussed in the next version, can search many software libraries at once, saving you the trouble of visiting each one individually. So the typical trailblazer page, with its list of individual sites, isn't as useful for software as it is with other search subjects. Still, the following sites are worth a look—especially the Windows 95 Page.

The Windows 95 Page

As action in the Windows world shifts to Windows 95, lots of new freeware and shareware programs are becoming available. Here's a frequently-updated site (see Figure 22.1) that makes an effort to keep up with the best of the new software. You'll find the Windows 95 Page's selection of the "best" software for Win95, a list of 1001 keyboard shortcuts for Win95, a "must have" list, hardware and software compatibility lists, and much more. In addition, you'll find links to Windows 95-related publications, other Win95 sites, and information on programming for Windows 95.

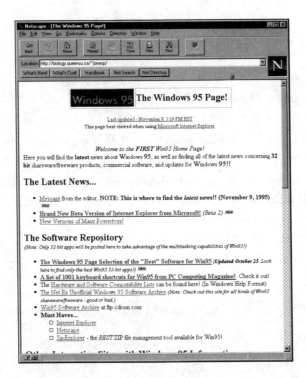

Figure 22.1 The Windows 95 Page

THE WINDOWS 95 PAGE ★ ★ ★ ★

URL: http://biology.queensu.ca/~jonesp/

Capsule Review: If you're using Windows 95, run, don't walk, to your computer and take a look at this page. It's a trailblazer page—don't expect to find fancy search tools—but it's kept up-to-date and you're sure to find lots of goodies.

Comprehensive List of Freeware and Shareware Sites

Nothing to write home about from a design viewpoint, this page nevertheless sums up some of the best shareware and freeware sites you'll find on the 'Net. A great place to start your search. Some of the highlights include the following:

- **McAfee Shareware.** Virus protection programs.
- **Popular Downloadable Files for the PC and FTP Sites.** Find out what everyone *else* is downloading.
- **Tucows Ultimate Collection of Winsock Software.** Just the thing to get your Windows system connected to the Internet.
- **Windows 95 InterNetworking Headquarters and Microsofts 32-bit Shareware Page.** If you're running Windows 95, you'll want to take a look at this page.
- **PC World's Win95 Shareware Library.** Here's a great trailblazer page for Windows 95 software.

COMPREHENSIVE LIST OF FREEWARE AND SHAREWARE SITES ★ ★ ★

URL: http://metro.turnpike.net/Rene/soft.htm

Capsule Review: A small selection of high-quality software sites makes this page a good place to start your search for software on the Web.

FTP Software and Support

A project based at Harris Semiconductor, this page lists shareware and commercial FTP sites for a variety of computing platforms, including DOS, Windows, Apple, UNIX, and OS/2. You'll also find links to some of the most popular search services.

FTP SOFTWARE AND SUPPORT ★ ★ ★

URL: http://mtmis1.mis.semi.harris.com/ftp.html

Capsule Review: Worth visiting if you're interested in locating and searching individual FTP sites. Most readers of this book will be better off using a comprehensive search service, such as the Virtual Software Library.

PC Software-Related Links

A self-described "feeble attempt" to keep up with the deluge of new *commercial* software sites, this page is a useful index to the many software publishers who have established Web presences. If you're looking for links to the likes of Adobe, Borland, and Microsoft, this is the place to start. A plus on this site is the subject-tree organization which is subindexed by program name.

PC SOFTWARE-RELATED LINKS ★ ★ ★

URL: http://alfred.uib.no/People/wolf/daniel/pc-eng.html

Capsule Review: This is a good place to start if you're looking for the Web page of a commercial software firm. The site is organized alphabetically.

SEARCHABLE ARCHIVES

The best place to look for software on the Web, especially if you're interested in something that's been out for a while, is an all-encompassing software archive. Though few of these sites exist due to the huge resource demands they place on their servers, you'll find the ones that are available to be invaluable in outfitting a computer with software from the Web.

The sites listed in this section are searchable; that is, you can enter a name or other key word into a text box and see a list of programs that match that keyword.

The Games Domain

Here's one of the most wonderful sites on the Web. A fabulous repository of information about computer games, the Games Domain offers a search interface that enables you to type one or more key words.

Included are gobs of information about commercial, shareware, and freeware games, including thousands of links to downloadable games that you can enjoy within minutes. Destroy the giant mutated killer hamsters from the planet Zog with your highly experimental zap-o-kill laser jobber!

THE GAMES DOMAIN ★ ★ ★ ★

URL: http://wcl~rs.bham.ac.uk/GamesDomain/

Capsule Review: One of the best sites on the Internet, the Games Domain is the ultimate repository of knowledge connected with computer and other types of games, and there are hundreds of links to shareware and freeware games that you can download.

Virtual Software Library

A project of Dr. Ziga Turk, a professor at the University of Ljubljana in Slovenia, the Virtual Software Library has grown into a collection of more than 130,000 program files and is one of the Web's most popular sites. VSL lets you find nearly any program you need, for virtually any platform from Amigas to IBM-compatible PCs running Microsoft Windows NT.

VSL is really a front-end for about a dozen software archives around the world, including the extensive SimTel archives of DOS and Windows software, the CICA software archives, and the Linux archives. There's no reason to visit these archives individually, as VSL lets you search them all from a single location.

You have several options in using VSL. Unless you have unusual searching needs, click the **quick search** button on the welcome page, which appears in Figure 22.2. You'll see the Quick Search form, shown in Figure 22.3.

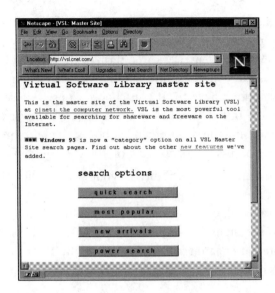

Figure 22.2 The Virtual Software Library welcome screen.

Figure 22.3 The Virtual Software Library Quick Search form.

Choose the platform for which you need software from the drop-down list box at the top of the form—you might choose UNIX, for example, or Windows 95. Then enter a search term in the left text box ("accounting," say). You can, if you wish, enter another search term in the right text box, though you don't have to. If you choose to use two search terms, select "and" or "or" to link them from the drop-down list box between the two text boxes. Using the drop-down list box at the bottom of the form, limit the number of hits to 20, 50, 100, or 200 database entries.

If you want more flexibility in your search, click the **power search** button on the welcome page. The Power Search (Figure 22.4) form lets you perform such queries as, "Show me up to 50 Amiga programs whose descriptions contain the word 'mouse' but not the word 'trackball' and were posted after January 16, 1994." Use the Power Search form if you know lots of details about the program you want, but not its name.

Figure 22.4 The Virtual Software Library Power Search form.

Don't rely on the main VSL site in San Francisco, which frequently becomes overloaded. Try one of VSL's mirror sites, called "front desks." These sites have the same archives as the main San Francisco site:

SEARCH TIP

VIRTUAL SOFTWARE LIBRARY ★ ★ ★ ★

URL: http://vsl.cnet.com/

Capsule Review: A searchable archive of more than 130,000 computer programs for every major (and not-so-major) computing platform.

Computer and Communications Companies

This searchable site provides a key-word interface to a database of computer-related companies (over 2100 of them). The search is pretty simple—it's just a UNIX grep search—so you'll need to know how to spell the company name you're looking for. Still, it's nice to get a retrieval list that contains hyperlinks that you can click, taking you directly to a software company's home page (and just maybe, its FTP site).

COMPUTER AND COMMUNICATION COMPANIES ★ ★ ★

URL: http://www.cmpcmm.com/cc/companies.html

Capsule Review: Still looking for a computer company's site, which may offer valuable information and software for a program you're using? Here's the place to look. This site offers a searchable interface to its database of 2000 software companies.

PC World's Win95 Shareware Library

PC World magazine offers this Windows 95 shareware site, which is worth a look if you haven't found what you're looking for elsewhere. Some of the programs seem out of date, though—you might search elsewhere if you're looking for the latest versions. Note that the Search link doesn't enable you to search for software, but for articles on Windows 95 themes that appeared in the magazine.

PC WORLD'S WIN95 SHAREWARE LIBRARY ★ ★ ★

URL: http://www.pcworld.com/win95/shareware/

Capsule Review: Good graphics and easy navigation make this site a pleasure to use. You'll find a good storehouse of Win95 software, but I confess that I'm more partial to the Windows 95 Page, reviewed earlier.

SOFTWARE PUBLISHERS' SITES

Though these sites typically aren't searchable archives, they're usually the only places you'll find obscure software related to a particular company's products. At the Microsoft site, for instance, you'll find the Windows 95 version of Microsoft Internet Assistant, the company's popular HTML authoring tool, and new printer drivers for Windows 95. As these sites aren't all true Web resources, I've included just a list of publishers' sites here:

- Corel: ftp://ftp.corel.ca/pub/
- Lotus: http://www.lotus.com/
- Microsoft: ftp://ftp.microsoft.com/dirmap.htm
- Netscape Communications: http://home.netscape.com/
- Novell: gopher://gopher.novell.com/11/pub/updates

CHAPTER 23

FINDING PEOPLE

Wouldn't it be nice if there was a single, easy-to-use reference source for finding people—and their e-mail addresses—on the Internet? It would, but it doesn't exist. To be sure, there are ways you can track people down, but you'll find that it's a tough job, overall, and your chances of succeeding aren't great. Still, there are a couple of services that look as though they might develop into something promising: Four11, the best of the lot, and OKRA, a new face on the scene that's great for a quick search.

CSO NAME SERVER

Remember Gopher? Before the Web, it was the Reigning Navigational Metaphor (RNM). But those days are gone—and, seemingly, so too are a number of useful Gopher protocols, such as the CSO Name Server protocol. Developed at the University of Illinois—the name "CSO" stands for that university's Computing Services Office—the CSO protocol enables Gopher users to search local white pages databases with a reasonably friendly interface—and to actually get results, sometimes. The service still exists, and you can give it a try.

To look for someone's e-mail address in a Gopher CSO Name Server, begin by selecting the country in which you want to search (see Figure 23.1); you'll see additional pages. Narrow down the choice to the organization to which the person belongs, and then try searching with the search box.

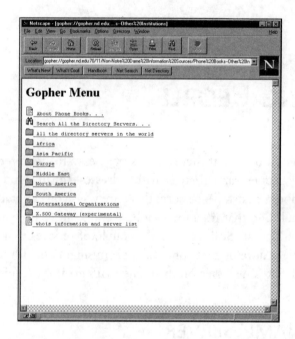

Figure 23.1 Choosing the country in a CSO Name Server.

SEARCH TIP

Looking for somebody at a college or university? Check out the CSO Name Server Gateway. CSO Name Servers are particularly well developed at North American colleges and universities.

CSO NAME SERVER ★

URL: gopher://gopher.nd.edu:70/11/Non-Notre%20Dame%20Information%20Sources/Phone%20Books—Other%20Institutions

Capsule Review: Worth a look if you're trying to locate somebody at a college or university.

FOUR11

Here's the Web's largest database of names and e-mail addresses: A product of SLED Corporation, it contains some 1.5 million names, and it's a great place to start your quest for people on the Internet. The source of the data? Voluntary registrations—some 210,000 so far—scans of Usenet newsgroups, and service provider registrations.

Four11 enables anyone to search for e-mail addresses for free. So how does the service make money? By selling Web page and encryption services.

But there is one catch. To search for someone's name, you have to add your own name and e-mail address to the database. Go ahead and do it—you don't need to worry about the Internet equivalent of junk mail, because Four11 will not sell or market the information it collects. (It's true—I've been registered for more than six months and I haven't gotten any junk electronic mail.)

To get started with Four11, access the site (http://www.four11.com/) and click the **First Time Users** link. You'll see an extensive questionnaire (Figure 23.2), which you should fill out as completely as possible. You're provided with three Group Connections—by default, Organization, Past College/University, and Interests/Hobbies/Sports—and you should take advantage of them. You can change the settings by clicking the list box's down arrow and choosing another Group Connection setting. Don't forget to list the schools you've attended—this is one way people can tell whether they've got the right person (Is this the Dave Matthews who went to Culver High?).

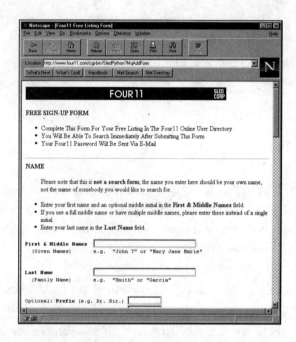

Figure 23.2 Four11 user questionnaire.

When you're finished filling out the information, click **Submit Form**. You'll receive a reply via e-mail listing your password—don't lose it! (You can change it later to something that's more easily remembered.) The password is needed so that nobody else can change your settings. Makes sense, doesn't it?

Once you've got your password, you can log on to Four11 again. After you supply your e-mail address and password, you can click the **Login** button and access the free service. After you click the **Search Directory** link, you see the search page, shown in Figure 23.3.

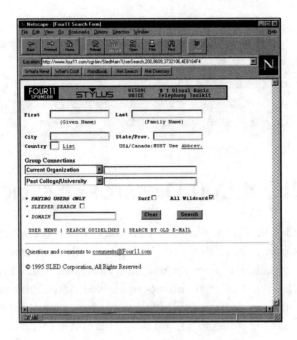

Figure 23.3 Four11 Search Page.

Try typing the first and last name of the person you're looking for—don't narrow the search unless you see too many names in the retrieval list. If you get a lengthy list of names, narrow by country first; click the **Back** button and type a country in the Country box.

Use roots of first names in case the person you're looking for typed a nickname. "Mi" will find "Mike" as well as "Michael."

SEARCH TIP

There are other ways to search Four11, too. Try blanking the name boxes and searching for people who attended your high school or college.

FOUR11 ★ ★ ★ ★

URL: http://www.four11.com/

Capsule Review: An easy-to-use search service with access to over 1.5 million names and email addresses, Four11 is steadily developing into an indispensable resource.

INTERNIC X.500 DIRECTORY SERVICES

It sounds like a great idea—up to a point. Let's create a standard—X.500 sounds jazzy, doesn't it—that will govern the creation of a worldwide database of electronic mail names and addresses. Oh, why make it so simple. Why not link it to European-backed networking standards called OSI, which are incompatible with the Internet, and make it darned difficult to use and understand, to boot! There! That will solve the problem!

If you've concluded that X.500 isn't exactly poised for a take-off, you're right. Still, lots of well-meaning people have linked their sites to X.500 indices, so they're worth searching—but don't expect to find everyone in the world.

X.500 protocols are sufficiently dense to leave UNIX mavens in disarray, but thankfully, there's a Web interface—the InterNIC X.500 Directory Service. It's organized geographically. When you access the site (http://www.internic.net/ds/dspgx500.html), you can click a link that gives you The World—and you can narrow your choices down, by country and then by region, and finally by organization. Within an organization, you can select departments, and then individuals. Limited searching capabilities are available at all levels, but bear in mind that you're searching that level only—don't expect to find a person's name at the country level, for example.

Is the X.500 gateway worth a try? Yes, particularly if you're looking for somebody in Europe, the countries of which have been sucked into the OSI bureaucracy at the behest of their politically powerful postal and telephone bureaucracies. But the number of organizations represented in any given area is inversely proportional to the strength of the Internet—there are fewer X.500-friendly organizations in California, for example, than there are in Finland. Looks like this one will eventually die on the vine, but for now it's useful for that odd international search.

> ### InterNIC X.500 Directory Services ★ ★
>
> **URL:** http://www.internic.net/ds/dspgx500.html
>
> **Capsule Review:.** A good interface to a dying service, with particularly strong and useful databases of European names and email addresses.

NETFIND

This service won't win any prizes for accessibility and ease of use, but it enables you to search for somebody's name in thousands of organizational and institutional *white pages* databases. This service is slow, clunky, and almost always fails—but hey, if it does work and you do find the person you're looking for, you'll be glad it exists.

KEY TERM

white pages
In an organization (such as a corporation or a university), a list of names and email addresses of people who have computer accounts with the organization.

To access the Netfind gateway, use http://www.nova.edu/Inter-Links/netfind.html.

To use Netfind, you have to start with a person's name and a few key words that help the system find the proper place to look. When you access a Netfind gateway, you'll see a text box. In it, type the following:

- The person's last name.
- One or more words that may help identify the correct place to look, such as a city, an organization, or a university.

Here are a couple of examples of search terms that might work with Netfind:

pfaffenberger charlottesville virginia

anderson trondheim norway

What you'll get from a Netfind search, in all likelihood, is a lengthy list of organizations that you can access in order to try your search again. But don't get your hopes up—chances are pretty good that the service will get hung up somewhere, and you'll get a timeout message. As the saying goes, try again later.

NETFIND ★ ★

URL: http://www.nova.edu/Inter-Links/netfind.html

Capsule Review: This clunky service will convince you that you're in the world of mainframes, not the Web, but it's still worth a try. Far more names and email addresses are accessible through this service than through CSO or X.500.

OKRA NET.CITIZEN DIRECTORY SERVICE

Here's the easiest-to-use Internet email database—and unlike most of its competition (Four11 excepted), it looks like it's a candidate for The Internet White Pages award. Already, OKRA contains close to one million email addresses, and it's very accessible with a fast, user-friendly search interface. OKRA's a service of the Department of Computer Science at the University of California, Riverside. Closely resembling Four11, OKRA departs from the Four11 mold in one welcome way—you don't have to subscribe in order to search.

OKRA doesn't rely on user submissions alone. On the contrary, it's based on periodic scannings of the Net, bringing back a harvest of names and email addresses. Here's how the data is gathered:

- **Usenet Newsgroups.** Articles posted to over 3,000 newsgroups are monitored, gathering author's names, email addresses, and organizations. If you've posted to Usenet, chances are you're in OKRA.

- **Finger.** About one-sixth of the data in OKRA has been collected using the Finger utility, an Internet service that enables anyone to obtain your email address if they know your domain name.

- **User Submissions.** You can send your own name and email address to OKRA.

To use OKRA, display the main OKRA search page, shown in Figure 23.4. In the Search Keywords box, type the person's last name and first name (punctuation and capitalization are ignored, and the order in which you type the words doesn't matter). Click **Query** to search the database. If a match is found, you'll see one or more names and email addresses that match your search terms. If not, you'll see a message that nothing was found.

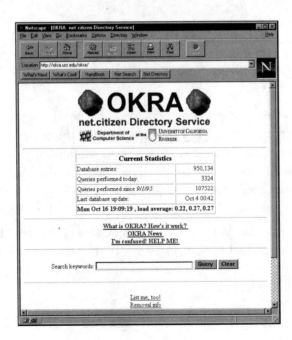

Figure 23.4 OKRA.

SEARCH TIP

Be aware that OKRA performs an exact match search—if you type **Jonatan**, that's what the system attempts to match. If you don't get good results from your search, click the **Back** button and check your spelling.

If the name you're searching for is fairly common, such as "John Lee" or "Barbara Smith," you may get so many names that it's hard to identify the correct person—if he or she is indeed present on the list. To cut down the number of items retrieved, try adding additional key words, such as the name of the organization with which the person is affiliated.

OKRA ★ ★ ★ ★

URL: http://okra.ucr.edu/okra/

Capsule Review: The best place to start if you're looking for someone's Internet email address. Close to one million names and addresses are available with a fast, easy-to-use search engine.

WWW TO FINGER GATEWAY

Finger is the name of an Internet service that enables anyone to find out your email address if they know the host name of the computer on which your email is housed. Note that some system administrators view Finger as an intrusion on security and disable it, but they're in the minority. The WWW to Finger Gateway, a service provided by Indiana University's Computer Science department, makes Finger services available to Web users.

To use the WWW to Finger Gateway, access the site (http://www.cs.indiana.edu/finger/gateway). In the text box, type the last name of the person you're looking for, an @ sign, and the host name, as in the following example:

pfaffenberger@watt.seas.virginia.edu

To initiate the search, press **Enter**.

Note that lots of things can go wrong with a Finger search, so you may get a cryptic error message—and the Gateway just passes it along without explanation. Chances are you didn't specify the domain name correctly—for example, pfaffenberger@virginia.edu doesn't work. If the search succeeds, you'll see the person's email address, name in real life, and any text that the person wished to enter in the "plan" field.

WWW TO FINGER GATEWAY ★ ★ ★

URL: http://www.cs.indiana.edu/finger/gateway

Capsule Review: Worth a try, but you need to know the full host name of the computer on which the person's email address is housed.

CHAPTER 24

FINDING JOBS

Pundits have described the Web as a "gift economy"—an economy in which goods and services cost almost nothing to provide, and are therefore given away. Whether or not this analysis of the on-line world is valid, an indisputable fact remains: real life does not feature a gift economy. Everyone needs a job, if for no other reason than to keep up with bills from Internet service providers.

The Web can assist you in your job hunt, especially if you're looking for an Internet-related or other computer job or an academic post. Web-savvy companies and institutions post job openings on the Web and will accept resumes by electronic mail. With the Web at your disposal, you can canvass many times more companies than you could if you had to actually go out, dressed respectably, and press the flesh. What is more, you can schmooze an outfit in Australia as easily as you can lobby a local company.

This section doesn't list all the employment-related sites on the Web—there are simply too many. Here, you'll find several of the best employment trailblazer sites, followed by the best *searchable* job indices. When using the Web as a job-search tool, begin with the trailblazer pages (and the Yahoo index of job-listing sites at http://www.yahoo.com/

Business_and_Economy/Employment/Jobs/), then move on to the searchable indices.

You also should use InfoSeek, Lycos, or another Web search tool to hunt for the home pages of organizations for which you'd like to work. Microsoft, for example, lists available jobs on its site, and gives instructions for applying. You may also wish to try searching for the names of municipalities in which you'd like to work, since many metropolitan area sites have listings of jobs available locally.

EMPLOYMENT TRAILBLAZER PAGES

These pages make good starting points for Web job searches. Typically, they include links to pages with resume-writing tips, predictions about growing fields, and other general information about the job market. They also include links to sites with job listings.

JobHunt

If you're looking for employment ,make JobHunt an extension of your home page. This trailblazer page, maintained by Stanford University, has links to all of the resources listed in this chapter, as well as links to human resource companies (headhunters, if you prefer). JobHunt also includes links to sites maintained by professional employment consultants who will help you write a resume for a fee, and links to the home pages of companies with recruiting pages on their sites. The JobHunt page appears in Figure 24.1.

JOBHUNT ★ ★ ★

URL: http://rescomp.stanford.edu/jobs.html

Capsule Review: A good place to start a Web job search, with links to job-search sites, other trailblazer pages, recruiting agencies, and corporate Web sites.

Figure 24.1 JobHunt.

Employment Opportunities and Job Resources on the Internet (The Riley Guide)

Long a favorite of the FTP set, Magaret F. Riley's guide to Internet employment resources now exists on the Web—and it remains a must-see for job seekers who want to use the Web and the rest of the Internet to their advantage. Riley is a librarian and Webmaster at Worcester Polytechnic Institute, and she has compiled a list not only of sites worth visiting, but of reference documents. Her reference documents have titles like "Incorporating the Internet into your job search strategy" and "How to post job listings on the Internet," and they're useful to Web novices and experts alike. Her site's welcome page appears in Figure 24.2.

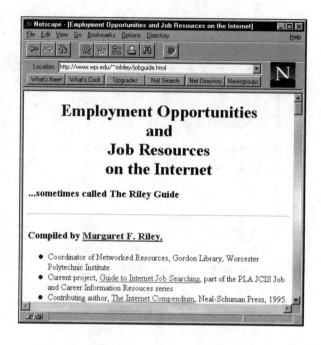

Figure 24.2 Employment Opportunities and Job Resources on the Internet (The Riley Guide).

EMPLOYMENT OPPORTUNITIES AND JOB RESOURCES ON THE INTERNET ★ ★ ★

URL: http://www.wpi.edu/~mfriley/jobguide.html

Capsule Review: Not just a trailblazer page, this site includes valuable content in the form of how-to guides for Web job seekers and employers.

SEARCHABLE DATABASES

These job-search tools will form the meat of any job search on the Web. At the sites listed in this section, you'll find archives of available jobs—and since you're on the Web and most of the world's population isn't, you'll have a head start on many of your competitors for a given job.

America's Job Bank

This site distinguishes itself with a neat hierarchical search mechanism and a jobs database of more than 100,000 listings. This site's database isn't limited to white-collar and technical jobs, either: a search for car-wash-attendant jobs turned up a dozen offerings all over the United States. Unemployment insurance taxes pay for AJB, and it gathers information from more than 1,800 employment offices across the United States.

When you arrive at the AJB site welcome page (shown in Figure 24.3), click the **Job Search** hyperlink. Then click the **Search Nationwide using America's Job Bank** hyperlink. If you know the Military Occupational Code (MOC) or job code that corresponds to your desired job, click the **Military Specialty** or **Job Code** hyperlinks, respectively. Click the **Federal Job Opportunities** hyperlink for information on government jobs. The real power of AJB lies behind the "Self Directed" hyperlink. After clicking the **Self Directed** hyperlink, you'll see a list of broad job categories, each preceded by a radio button. Click the radio button that best describes the job you want, then click the **Submit Query** button. Repeat this process with subsequent lists (the lists you see depend upon your selections). Eventually, you'll see job listings with information on how to respond to employers.

AMERICA'S JOB BANK ★ ★ ★

URL: http://www.ajb.dni.us/

Capsule Review: A large database of jobs of all kinds with a highly intuitive interface based on hierarchical menus. AJB gathers job information from 1,800 employment offices across the United States.

Figure 24.3 The America's Job Bank welcome page.

The Online Career Center

Claiming to be the oldest and most frequently accessed Web job-search site, the Online Career Center offers a wealth of job-search resources, including an up-to-date database of job listings and lots of useful information about such issues as multiculturalism in the workplace and hunting for a job while still a student. OCC combines the best features of the Riley Guide with a database almost as good as that maintained by America's Job Bank. OCC solicits subscriptions from employers who pay a one-time fee of $3,900, and $240 yearly after that, to post their ads.

To search OCC, click the **Search Jobs** portion of the red graphical menu on the welcome page (shown in Figure 24.4). You'll see several useful hyperlinks on the Search Jobs page, including links to pages that let you browse jobs available in particular cities. You'll find the search engine by clicking the **Keyword Search All Jobs** hyperlink. Enter search terms that describe the job you want in the text box. Click the **Begin Search** button, and you'll see a list of hyperlinked headings that lead to job listings. The job listings tell you how to contact employers.

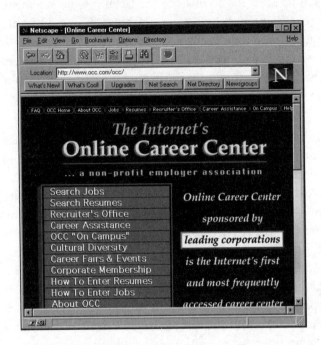

Figure 24.4 The Online Career Center welcome page.

SEARCH TIP

The OCC search engine assumes that separate words are joined with the Boolean operator AND. A search for "portfolio manager" will return entries that contain both "portfolio" and "manager." A search for "portfolio OR manager" will return listings that contain either term—a much larger list.

THE ONLINE CAREER CENTER ★ ★ ★ ★

URL: http://www.occ.com/occ/

Capsule Review: A complete job-search site, including a big current database of job listings and lots of information about workplace and job-search issues. OCC also lets you post your resume for potential employers to examine.

CareerSite

Pay special attention to this site: it's lacking some key features now, but it may represent the future of job hunting. CareerSite employs agents—computer programs tasked to complete a specific job—to match your interests and qualifications with the needs of employers. CareerSite's agents save you some time in researching potential employers, and save employers lots of time and money they would have spent on advertising and recruiting.

When you arrive at the CareerSite welcome page (shown in Figure 24.5), click the **Register now** hyperlink. You'll fill out forms in which you designate a username and password with which you'll access CareerSite in the future. You'll also fill out a form with information about your education, work history, and job requirements—an on-line resume of sorts. After entering your credentials and access information, you'll be able to use the Virtual Agent Desktop, a center for monitoring employers' responses to your posted information. Click the **Searching** hyperlink to hunt for employers who match the credentials and specifications you entered in the sign-up process (or other specifications you enter on the search form). Click the **Messages** hyperlink to view invitations from employers to submit your resume (though I left my resume up for several days and never received a single message). Click the **Credentials Maintenance** hyperlink to alter the information about yourself that you entered when you signed up. The **Search Tracking** hyperlink led to a page that did not appear to be working at this writing.

Despite its impressive potential, CareerSite needs some improvement. There's no way to specify how the Virtual Agent catalogs your resume—there's no industry list. If you enter the word "computer" anywhere in your resume, you're assigned to the computer industry group, regardless of the fact that computers may be merely tangential to your real work. Also, there's no information on the companies listed on CareerSite, even biggies like IBM and DEC.

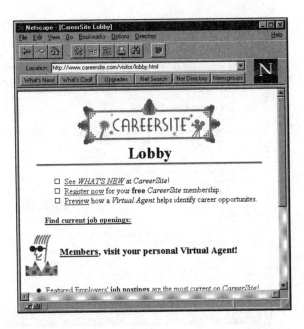

Figure 24.5 The CareerSite welcome page.

CAREERSITE ★ ★ ★

URL: http://www.careersite.com/visitor/lobby.html

Capsule Review: A virtual agent that matches your resume with employers who want people like you. CareerSite does some of the work of a human resources consultant, at no cost to you.

E-Span Job Database Search

No frills about it, but the E-Span database can return some good results in a hurry. The database—which contains mainly computer and technical jobs—comes from submissions from employers who pay to post their want ads on E-Span. The E-Span Web site is a front for a WAIS server. The E-Span page appears in Figure 24.6.

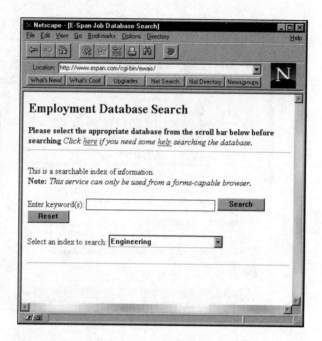

Figure 24.6 E-Span Job Database Search.

To use E-Span, enter a key word or two in the text box (separate them with the Boolean operator AND), select an industry from the drop-down list box, and click the **Search** button. You'll see a list of hyperlinks to jobs that match your description.

You can limit your search to jobs in a particular state by adding the state's postal abbreviation, preceded by QX, to your search string. To search for programming jobs in Rhode Island, for example, you'd enter "Programmer and QXRI" in the text box.

SEARCH TIP

E-SPAN JOB DATABASE SEARCH ★ ★

URL: http://www.espan.com/cgi-bin/ewais/

Capsule Review: A no-frills, up-to-date listing of (mainly technical) jobs submitted to E-Span by fee-paying employers.

CareerMosaic J.O.B.S. Database

Just one part of the great CareerMosaic site (available at http://www.careermosaic.com), the J.O.B.S. database lets you specify search terms and hunt for employment opportunities in the CareerMosaic database. Enter key words in the Description text box. (Click the **all of** radio button to accept only those job descriptions that contain all your keywords; click the **any of** button to accept job descriptions that contain one or more of your keywords). If you want to narrow your search further, enter a city, state, country, or company name in the appropriate text box, then click the **Search** key. You'll see a list of hyperlinked job summaries, which you can click to see complete help-wanted ads. The CareerMosaic J.O.B.S. Database site appears in Figure 24.7.

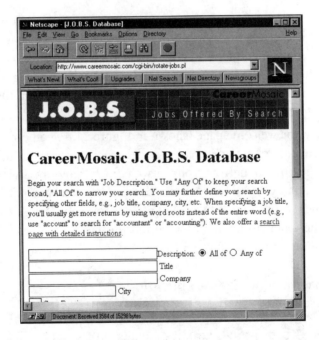

Figure 24.7 The CareerMosaic J.O.B.S. Database welcome page.

While you're at the CareerMosaic site, be sure to experiment with the company's Usenet search tool and company profiles. These tools can expand your search capability beyond the jobs included in the CareerMosaic database.

> ### CAREERMOSAIC J.O.B.S. DATABASE ★ ★ ★
>
> **URL:** http://www.careermosaic.com/cgi-bin/rotate-jobs.pl
>
> **Capsule Review:** A wonderful collection of Web reference resources, compiled by a librarian with an easy-to-follow sense of information organization.

The Chronicle of Higher Education—Job Openings in Academe

Long recognized as the premier forum for academic job hunting, the Chronicle of Higher Education was among the first job-search tools on the Web. The editors of the magazine update this site weekly, and you'll find that it's the single best place to look for jobs in colleges and universities. Though this site is a front-end for a Gopher server, the information is up-to-date and not available anywhere else.

On the welcome page (shown in Figure 24.8), you can choose to narrow your search by subject area (such as social sciences). Subsequent pages prompt you to narrow your search further by specifying disciplines. Alternately, you can search the entire Gopher database with an unadorned Gopher search engine by clicking the **entire jobs list** button, or you can use the Gopher engine to search jobs in specific regions by clicking one of the regional hyperlinks.

> ### THE CHRONICLE OF HIGHER EDUCATION— JOB OPENINGS IN ACADEME ★ ★
>
> **URL:** http://chronicle.merit.edu/.ads/.links.html
>
> **Capsule Review:** A front-end for a Gopher server containing a database of academic jobs.

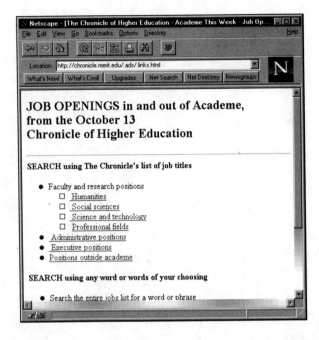

Figure 24.8 The Chronicle of Higher Education—Job Openings
in Academe welcome page.

CHAPTER 25

SEARCHING USENET, GOPHER, TELNET, AND WAIS

The Web is cool; the Web is the future. The Web is not, however, the entire story. Several holdovers from the Internet's days as a text-based communications medium remain. These throwbacks to a less-graphical time may, however, represent the best route to the information you need, and you should be familiar with them.

Usenet, Gopher, Telnet, and WAIS contain huge quantities of information—information that you shouldn't leave untapped in your Web search. This chapter explains how to search them. First, you'll learn about searching Usenet without a newsreader—and without a lot of time. Later in this chapter, you'll learn about hunting for information in Gopher, Telnet, and WAIS.

USENET

Usenet is a lot of fun, but its signal-to-noise ratio—the proportion of useful information to sludge—traditionally has rendered it more of a question-and-answer medium than a serious search tool. For years, Usenet begged for a coherent means of searching its thousands of megabytes of data. These Web resources provide those long-needed capabilities.

Searching a Usenet Archive

A new service, DejaNews boasts a big database of Usenet news articles that the site's maintainers update every two days, as well as a fast and powerful search tool for culling the articles you want from the chaff. DejaNews compliments searches of Web resources by giving you access to the knowledge of many more people, since many Internet users have access to Usenet newsgroups, but cannot use the Web. DejaNews archives news from every newsgroup—except those in the alt., soc., and talk. hierarchies, and those ending in. binaries—going back at least a month. The excluded newsgroups have a low signal-to-noise ratio, the site's maintainers claim.

You can search DejaNews in either of two ways (the site's maintainers say they're developing "power users' options" for release soon). In either case, click the **SEARCH** hyperlink on the welcome page (Figure 25.1). The simple DejaNews search involves just the options in the page you see after clicking the **SEARCH** hyperlink. Enter your search terms in the text box at the top of the page, and adjust the radio buttons to format the results of the search to your liking. Remember, making AND the default search operator will narrow your search (if you have more than one search term), while making OR the operator will broaden your search. Click the **search** button to execute your search.

Alternately, click the **create a query filter** button. The filter form allows you to limit the newsgroups or dates DejaNews searches for your key words. Also, it allows you to hunt for certain message authors. When you've created your query, click the **submit filter** button. This returns you to the main search page, but limits any searching you do there to the articles defined by your filter.

Figure 25.1 The DejaNews welcome page.

The results of a DejaNews search take the form of a list of hyperlinked article headings and a list of hyperlinked author names. The author names are especially useful, as you can click them to see statistical reports of how active a particular author is, and which newsgroups he or she posts to. This can help you disregard the work of spammers, while taking more seriously posts from people who post a lot of relevant articles to a few newsgroups.

SEARCH TIP

DejaNews uses an unusual character to concatenate search specifications on the filter form: the pipe (|). You'd specify more than one newsgroup like this: rec.music.artists.springsteen | rec.music.artists.queensryche.

Also, remember DejaNews has a wildcard: the asterisk (*). You can search for "ship*" to yield "shipment," "shipping," "ship," and "shipshape."

DEJANEWS ★ ★ ★ ★

URL: http://www.dejanews.com/

Capsule Review: A huge database of Usenet news with a flexible search engine. Use the filter form to limit your searches to a specific range of dates or to a few likely newsgroups.

Developing a Custom Clipping Service

The Stanford Information Filtering Tool (SIFT) isn't an archive, but it's a good way to keep up to date on topics of interest to you. This service—which may shed some light on the shape of newspapers to come—allows you to give a server search terms, called profiles. The server then monitors the Usenet newsgroups—all of them—for articles containing your search terms. When you log into SIFT, you see articles relevant to your profiles displayed on custom-built Web pages. In contrast to DejaNews, SIFT only lists current Usenet articles—there's no archive.

To set up your Usenet-combing profile, enter your electronic mail address and SIFT password in the text boxes on the welcome page. If you've never used SIFT before, enter any password you want—but for security, don't use the same one you use on your Internet account. Click the **Enter** button to start working with SIFT.

You can use SIFT like DejaNews by clicking the **Search** radio button on the profile-management page (Figure 25.2), or you can take advantage of SIFT's real strength by clicking the **Subscribe** radio button and creating a profile. Enter search terms in the Topic text box. Note: Don't use Boolean operators! If you enter **ice AND cream**, SIFT will treat AND like a search term, and you'll get lots of articles in return. Enter taboo topics in the Avoid text box. Click the **Submit** button to subscribe to the profile you've entered.

In the future, to read the news that fits your profiles, click the **Read** radio button and examine a list of hyperlinked headings. Click a heading to see the full text of the message it represents. Also, on the profile-management page, you can click one of the **Delete** radio buttons and the **Submit** button to discontinue a profile.

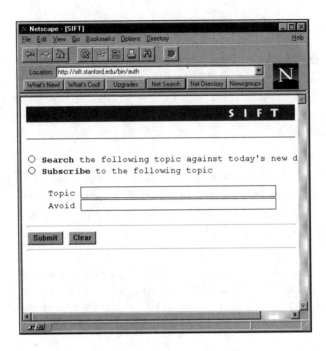

Figure 25.2 The SIFT profile-management page.

STANFORD INFORMATION FILTERING TOOL ★ ★ ★

URL: http://sift.stanford.edu/

Capsule Review: A tool for searching current Usenet news based on search terms.

GOPHER

Remember Gopher, the text-based system developed at the University of Minnesota that provided a way to find information—and waste time— long before the Web came on the scene? Gopher's on its way out now, but some useful information remains on it. Fortunately, the old standby Gopher search tools still exist.

Burrowing for Gopher Items

Veronica reigned as the Internet search tool of choice before the advent of InfoSeek, Lycos, and Yahoo. Veronica's a no-frills service in its Web incarnation: just a single box for key words. Veronica will, however, usually find the information you need if it's on any Gopher server anywhere in the world.

The site listed in the box below isn't a Veronica site; it's a Yahoo page that lists all the Veronica servers in the world. Click the hyperlink to the server closest to you, or to a server in a location where it's late at night (that may indicate less load on the server). You'll see a plain text box in which you can enter your search specifications.

SEARCH TIP

Forgotten how to use Veronica? You can use any of the three main Boolean operators: AND, OR, and NOT are all acceptable. Additionally, you can use the -t (type) switch to specify the kinds of resources you want. Follow the -t switch with a type identifier, such as:

- 0—Text File
- 1—Directory
- 2—CSO name server
- 4—Macintosh BinHex file
- 5—IBM PC-compatible binary file
- 7—Gopher menu
- 8—Telnet session
- 9—Binary File
- s—Sound
- e—Event
- I—Image (other than GIF)
- M—MIME multipart/mixed message
- T—TN3270 session
- c—Calendar

- g—GIF image
- h—HTML

For example, the search "-I leaf" would exclude everything but non-GIF images whose file names contain the word "leaf" from the search results.

VERONICA ★ ★

URL: http://www.yahoo.com/Computers_and_Internet/Internet/Veronica/

Capsule Review: This page lists links to all the Veronica servers in the world. With one of those servers, you can search Gopherspace with the standard Boolean operators and Veronica switches.

TELNET

You remember Telnet: the portion of the TCP/IP protocol suite you use to contact remote machines. It's not nearly as important as it once was now that the Web's protocols make inter-machine communication easy, but some services still use the Telnet interface. But how do you find the Telnet resources you need?

Searching Telnet

Hytelnet is another unadorned search tool, but it's the best search tool out there for hunting Telnet services. Type your search terms into the text box, press **Enter**, and Hytelnet returns a list of hyperlinked headings for relevant Telnet services. Click one of the headings, and you'll see a page describing the service in a little bit more detail, complete with login instructions. Click the hyperlink to enter the service from the description page.

SEARCH TIP

Hytelnet, by default, inserts the OR Boolean operator between any two words that don't have another operator between them. You can use any of the three major Boolean operators: AND, OR, and NOT.

HYTELNET ★ ★ ★

URL: http://www.einet.net/hytelnet/HYTELNET.html

Capsule Review: Use this service to hunt for Telnet resources. Enter your terms in the text box, press Enter, and follow the hyperlinks to the service of your choice.

WAIS

Wide Area Information Servers make it possible for information-holders to distribute their knowledge far and wide, to virtually every user of the Internet. Though perl scripts have largely replaced WAIS servers as the tool of choice for extracting information from a database and sending it off across the Net, many useful nuggets of data remain ensconced on WAIS-only servers. This section shows you how to gain access to the WAIS-server information you need.

Searching WAIS

The WAIS, Inc. WAISGATE service gives you easy access to hundreds of WAIS servers around the world, with the convenience of a common interface and simple navigation. WAISGATE not only finds the material you need, but also presents it to you in most cases. You can get the full text of biology journal articles here, for example.

To use WAISGATE, enter a topic in the text box on the Directory of Servers page (Figure 25.3). You can also specify the number of results you want by selecting a number from the drop-down list box to the right of the text box. Click the **Search** button to execute your search for the servers you need. You'll see a list of hyperlinks to WAIS server interfaces. Click the one that seems most relevant to your needs.

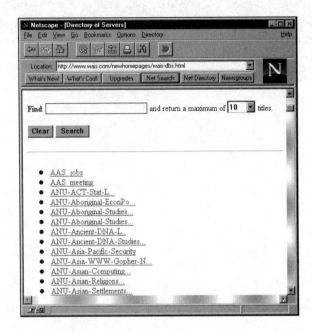

Figure 25.3 The WAISGATE Directory of Servers page.

The WAIS server interface includes a description of the server, which specifies the server's contents and gives some information on search strategies available to you. Enter your search in the text box and click the **Submit Query** button. You'll see a list of hyperlinked article headings. Click any heading to see the full text of the article.

SEARCH TIP

WAISGATE supports the three standard Boolean operators (AND, OR, and NOT) and also supports the function ADJ. Place ADJ between two search terms to find articles in which those terms appear adjacent to one another.

WAISGATE ★ ★ ★

URL: http://www.wais.com/newhomepages/wais-dbs.html

Capsule Review: WAISGATE gives you access to hundreds of WAIS servers, and puts a common interface on all of them. Search for a useful server first, then hunt for specific search terms.

CHAPTER 26

WHAT'S NEW RESOURCES

The Web is growing so rapidly that it's impossible for any manually updated service to keep up with all the new Web pages that are added each day. However, a variety of announcement services provide Web authors with the means to advertise new sites. In general, only the better sites' authors bother to do so—there's a self-selection mechanism at work. These announcements find their way into a variety of "what's new" pages, which you can scan periodically.

Is it worth your time to look at what's new pages? It's hit or miss—I've discovered some very useful pages by browsing NCSA's What's New service. Still, your best bet for keeping up with what's new is to search what's new pages and to repeat saved searches, as described in the next chapter.

NCSA WHAT'S NEW

The National Center for Supercomputing Applications (NCSA) is justly famous as the birthplace of Mosaic, the first successful graphical browser.

The action may have shifted elsewhere, but NCSA still maintains an excellent What's New service, receiving announcements from serious Webmasters everywhere. These days, NCSA's What's New service is a joint product of NCSA and Global Network Nagivator, Inc., which is in turn owned by America Online.

To access NCSA's What's New pages, use the following URL:

```
http://www.ncsa.uiuc.edu/SDG/Software/Mosaic/Docs/
whats-new.html
```

You'll see a page such as the one shown in Figure 26.1.

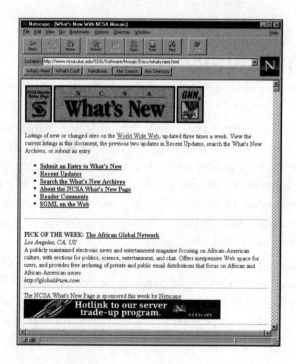

Figure 26.1 NCSA What's New page.

To view the most recent additions, click **Recent Updates** (see Figure 26.2).

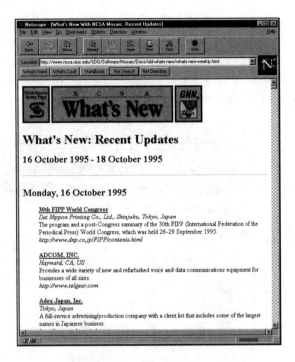

Figure 26.2 NCSA recent updates.

SEARCH TIP

NCSA's What's New database is so voluminous that you'll surely want to search it rather than browse through page after page of new offerings. You can do so in two ways: By searching the What's New database directly using NCSA's search page, or by using the CUI W3 Catalog, which includes the NCSA database and some other material. For more information on searching for what's new pages, see the following chapter.

YAHOO WHAT'S NEW

Now that Yahoo is a corporate entity with a staff of hard-working catalogers, there are as many as 1000 additions to this subject tree every day—

too many to browse manually. But Yahoo offers a what's new page that enables you to search for new offerings by category (Figure 26.3). If your search topic is nicely captured by an existing Yahoo subject heading, you can use this service to determine quickly whether there's something new in your field of interest.

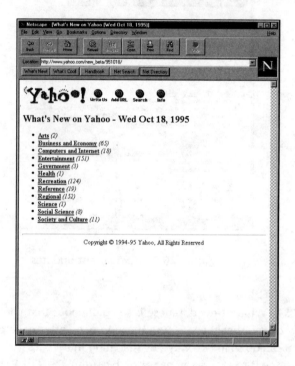

Figure 26.3 Yahoo What's New entries, classified by subject.

To access Yahoo's subject-classified what's new entries, click the **New** button at the top of Yahoo's pages. You'll see a list of dates, followed by three options; click **By Category**. If you click on one of the categories, you'll see a page in which the new additions are sorted by subject within that category (Figure 26.4).

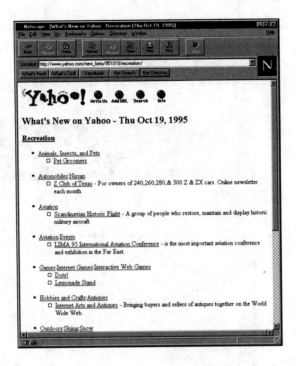

Figure 26.4 New Yahoo entries (Recreation) for October 19, 1995.

USENET ANNOUNCEMENTS

Yet another source of announcements about new Web documents is Usenet. Announcements about new Web sites can be found in the following newsgroups:

- comp.infosystems.announce
- comp.infosystems.www.announce
- comp.internet.net-happenings
- comp.infosystems.www.misc

Obviously, it's a tedious business to search these newsgroups manually—a fact that led to the Automatic News HREFs service (Figure 26.5). This service scans the above newsgroups each day, looking for articles that contain Web URLs (which contain the HTML code HREF).

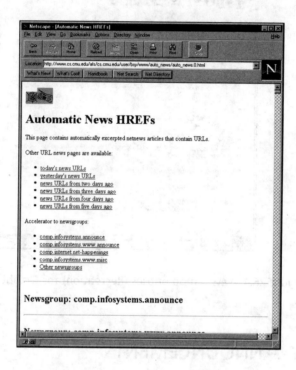

Figure 26.5 Automatic News HREFs service.

To access the Automatic News HREFs service, use the following URL:

```
http://www.cs.cmu.edu/afs/cs.cmu.edu/user/bsy/www/auto_news/
auto_news.0.html
```

SEARCH TIP

As you'll find, the Automatic News HREFs daily summaries can be quite voluminous—too lengthy to page through without feeling that you're wasting time. But bear in mind that your browser probably has a **Find** command, which you can use to perform a simple, case-insensitive exact match for a single search word. In Netscape, you can search by choosing **Find** from the Edit menu. When the Find dialog box appears, type the search word in the text box. For a case-sensitive search, click the **Match Case** option. To initiate the search, click **Find Next**. If a match is found, the Find dialog box stays on-screen, enabling you to click **Find Next** to find the next match. If you've closed the dialog box, you can still repeat the search by choosing **Find Again** from the Edit menu (or just use the **Ctrl + G** keyboard shortcut).

TradeWave Galaxy What's New

TradeWave Galaxy, one of the Web's larger subject trees, maintains a page that lists the Galaxy pages containing new items (see Figure 26.6). If you click one of the subject headings, you'll see the subject's page—and the new items are right at the top (Figure 26.7).

To access TraveWave Galaxy's What's New page, use the following URL:

```
http://galaxy.einet.net/galaxy/new-links.html
```

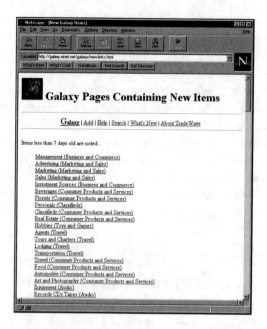

Figure 26.6 Galaxy pages containing new items.

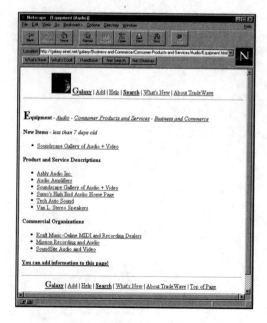

Figure 27.7 Galaxy subpage

MORE WHAT'S NEW SERVICES

Other brave souls are attempting to keep up with the deluge of new Web documents. Here's an overview of some of the better efforts:

- **Net-Happenings** (http://www.mid.net/NET/) This is a searchable Web interface to the net-happenings newsgroup on Usenet. It's a moderated newsgroup that's updated approximately four times weekly.

- **Netscape's What's New** (http://www.netscape.com/home/whats-new.html) Mozilla's own selection of the best new sites.

- **Web66 What's New** (http://web66.coled.umn.edu/new/new.html) The focus here is Web projects by and for kids!

- **What's New in Nerd World Media** (http://challenge.tiac.net/users/dstein/whatsnew.html) The hip starting points service lists its new sites.

- **What's New Too** (http://newtoo.manifest.com/WhatsNewToo/). A searchable commercial service that shows signs of lots of activity.

FROM HERE

The best way to keep up with what's new is to let the computer do the searching for you. The next chapter discusses search engines that ransack What's New databases, looking for documents that match your search interests.

CHAPTER 27

SEARCHING FOR WHAT'S NEW

The best way to keep up with what's new on the Web is to use the Web's search tools. You can search the contents of NCSA's What's New using the CUI W3 server discussed in this chapter. In addition, commercial services are appearing, such as What's New Too, that enable you to search through hundreds of new Web documents daily. Perhaps the best way to keep up with new Web offerings, though, is to use Netscape's SmartMarks utility to monitor saved searches. This chapter discusses these techniques that you can use to stay in touch with fast-breaking developments on the Web.

CUI W3 SERVER

CUI, short for Centre Universitaire d'Informatique, is a research institute at the University of Virginia. CUI houses one of the older server sites on the Web, and the organization still maintains one of the best search engines for finding new documents. It's called the CUI W3 catalog (Figure 27.1). To search the CUI catalog, use the following URL:

```
http://cuiwww.unige.ch/cgi-bin/w3catalog
```

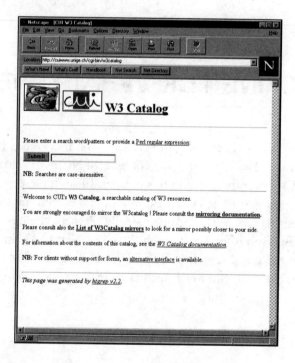

Figure 27.1 CUI W3 search page.

The CUI W3 differs from search engines such as Lycos or WebCrawler in that it doesn't employ a spider. Instead, the search software consults the following manually maintained lists. The result of a CUI search (Figure

27.2) is a list of retrieved items which are sorted according to the URL source; the sources grouped under "nwn," for example, are from NCSA's What's New pages.

- NCSA What's New (nwn)
- NCSA's NCSA Starting Points (nsp)
- CERN's W3 Virtual Library Subject Catalog and selected sublists (cvl)
- Martijn Koster's Aliweb Archie-like Indexing for the Web (ali)
- Scott Yanoff's Internet Services List (isl)
- Simon Gibbs' list of Multimedia Information Sources (mis)
- John December's list of Computer-Mediated Communication Information Sources (cmc) and Internet Tools Summary (cmc)
- Marcus Speh's User Documents physics researchers (msp)

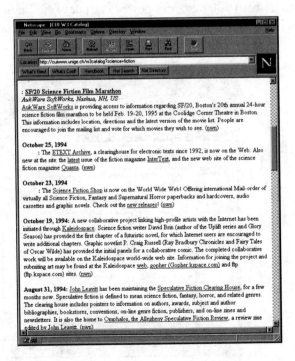

Figure 27.2 Result of a CUIW3 search.

By default, the CUI W3 search engine performs a case-insensitive exact-match search. To search the CUI W3 catalog, type one or more search words in the text box and click **Submit**.

In the retrieval list, you'll see a variety of items that are marked with a three-letter code, which tells you the source of the entry (for example, *nwn* refers to NCSA's What's New).

SEARCHING WHAT'S NEW TOO

Web authors face a real challenge nowadays in publicizing their sites. With so many new documents appearing, there's a real danger of getting lost in the flood. For this reason, commercial services are appearing that help to disseminate news about new sites. One such service is What's New Too (http://newtoo.manifest.com/today.html), which features a search interface to the more than 500 new sites posted each day (see Figure 27.3). The site, created by Manifest Information Services, is supported by advertising.

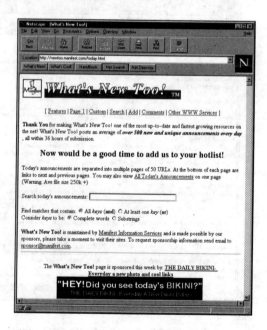

Figure 27.3 What's New Too.

What's New Too's search engine is straightforward. Here's a quick overview of the search features you can use:

- **Boolean Operators**. Choose **All Keys** (AND) or **At Least One Key** (OR).

- **Exact Match or Truncation**. To perform an exact-match search, click the **Complete Words** option. To search with truncation, click **Substrings**.

To search What's New Too, type one or more search words, choose search settings, and press **Enter**. The page that appears looks just like the one from which you searched, but scroll down—you'll see that the list of several hundred sites has been cut down to just those that match your search criteria.

REPEATING SAVED SEARCHES

One of the best features of Netscape's SmartMarks utility, introduced in Chapter 3, is the program's saved search feature. By saving your search and telling the program to monitor changes, you can see an update showing the new URLs that have appeared since you last performed the search.

To create, save, and monitor a search, follow these instructions:

1. From the SmartMarks Tools menu, choose **Find**, or just use the **Ctrl + F** keyboard shortcut. You'll see the Smart Find dialog box, shown in Figure 27.4.

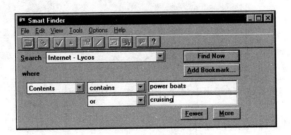

Figure 27.4 Smart Find dialog box.

2. In the Search box, choose the search service you want to use (you can choose from Yahoo, Lycos, InfoSeek, or WebCrawler).

3. In the Where boxes, make the following choices:

   In the Contents box, choose the field you want to search, if any are available (the default is **Contents**, which means that the search consults all parts of the data record).

   In the Contains box, leave the default setting (**Contains**) if you want to search with truncation; to perform an exact-match search, choose **Matches**.

   In the third box, type the first key word you want to use.

4. To add additional conditions to the search, click **More**. You'll see an additional row of boxes.

   In the first box, choose a Boolean operator.

   In the second box, type the second search word.

5. Repeat the previous step if you would like to add additional search conditions.

6. Click **Add Bookmark**. You'll see the Add SmartMark dialog box, shown in Figure 27.5.

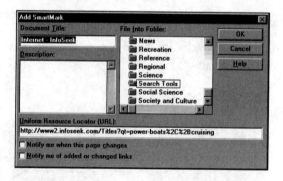

Figure 27.5 Add SmartMark dialog box.

7. In the Description area, type a description of the search.

8. Click **Notify me of added or changed links**.

9. Click **OK**.

10. In the Smart Finder dialog box, click **Find Now** to run the search.

To update the search:

1. In the SmartMarks dialog box, click **Monitored Items** to see the items you've asked SmartMarks to monitor.

2. Select the searches you've saved.

3. Click the **Update** button.

    If any of the searches you've saved contain new items, you'll see a flag next to the item informing you that a change has occurred. To view the retrieval list, double-click the saved search's button.

FROM HERE

By now, you're an expert at finding information on the World Wide Web! But there's one more step to take: Give something back. The spirit of the Internet lies in reciprocity: When you receive something of value, you should create something of value. Find out how you can contribute your search expertise to the Web in the following chapter.

CHAPTER 28

PUBLISHING YOUR HOTLIST

The final step in your quest for Web knowledge? Give something back. The Web's spirit is a community spirit—it's full of people who have learned and profited immensely from their Web involvement, and in response, are eager to contribute what they've learned so that others may share. It's far too much work for anyone, let alone a small company, to catalogue the entire Web, but thousands upon thousands of individuals are already doing so. Their trailblazer pages rank among the most useful search tools you'll find on the Web. Why not join them?

This chapter shows you how you can create a useful trailblazer page without knowing any HTML (the markup language that underlies the appearance of pages on the Web). The key lies in SmartMarks, the Netscape bookmark utility introduced in Chapter 3. If you're using SmartMarks, you can export your hotlist to a file, which Netscape automatically codes with the necessary HTML. If you'd like to learn a little HTML, you can dress up your page further, adding additional explanatory content.

Either way, you'll want to share your hotlist with others—and there are two ways you can do this. First, you can mail your hotlist to other people who have Internet email addresses. Once again, Netscape makes this easy. Second, you can make your hotlist available on a Web server so that others may access it. The following section details these procedures.

EXPORTING YOUR HOTLIST

With most browsers, you can **export** your hotlist to an HTML file, which can be loaded and used by anyone with any browser. However, you'll get the best results by using Netscape's SmartMarks utility, which enables you to select just those bookmarks that you want to include in your export file.

export
To write data to a disk file that can be read by other programs.

KEY TERM

To export your hotlist to a disk file with Netscape SmartMarks:

1. In the folder panel (the left panel in SmartMarks' window), select the folder that you want to include in the hotlist you're exporting. For example, suppose you've created a folder called Powerboats. This folder contains all the links you've found concerning powerboating. It's internally subdivided, with several subfolders. If you select the **Powerboats** folder, SmartMarks will include all of its subfolders in the hotlist.

2. From the Tools menu, choose **Export**. You'll see the Export dialog box, shown in Figure 28.1.

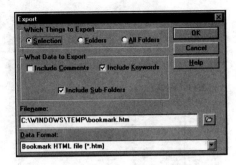

Figure 28.1 Export dialog box.

3. Under Which things to export, choose **Selection**.

4. Under What to export, choose the SmartMarks information that you want to include with your exported hotlist (activate **Comments** and **Keywords** if you'd like this information printed along with the URLs of the sites you've saved). Activate the **Subfolders** option if you'd like to include any subfolders that appear within the folder you've selected.

5. In the Filename area, type a file name that's descriptive of the hotlist's subject, such as **PWRBOAT.HTM**.

6. In the Data Format area, leave the current setting (**Bookmark File**).

7. Click **OK** to save your bookmark file.

Once you've saved your hotlist, you can open and view it using the **Open File** command of your browser (you'll find this command on the File menu of Netscape and most other browsers). As you'll see (Figure 28.2), SmartMarks saved the file so that each site you've saved appears as a hyperlink. In addition, subfolder names appear as subheadings in the hotlist. Note, in the figure, that your comments appear as explanatory text beneath each hyperlink. Pretty cool!

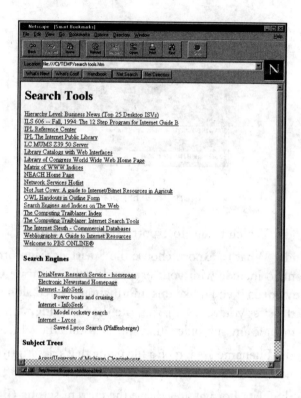

Figure 28.2 Exported hotlist loaded into Netscape.

You can load this file any time you wish to use it. As the next section explains, you can also mail it to others.

MAILING YOUR HOTLIST TO OTHERS

The hotlist you've saved is a plain ASCII text file, which you can easily email to just about anyone who's capable of receiving email on the Internet. With Netscape, you can do this from within the browser program. Netscape sends the file as an *attachment*, which most mail programs can read. The following instructions tell you how to mail your hotlist with Netscape.

KEY TERM

attachment
In electronic mail, a file that is sent along with the email message. Most mail programs can read attachments.

To mail your document with Netscape Navigator:

1. Open the document by using the **Open** command on the File menu.

2. From the File menu, choose **Mail Document**, or use the **Ctrl + M** keyboard shortcut (Windows version only). You'll see a Mail window. Type a brief message explaining what you're sending.

3. In the Send To area, type the recipient's address.

4. In the Subject Area, type the title of your hotlist.

5. Click **Attach**. You'll see the Mail/News Attachments dialog box.

6. Just click the **Attach** button to mail the file with the default attachment settings.

7. Click **Send**. Netscape mails the message, as well as the attachment, to the recipient you've indicated.

CREATING AN OUTSTANDING TRAILBLAZER PAGE

There are hotlists—and then there are *hotlists*. The best of them, the ones that truly deserve to be called trailblazer pages, have the same characteristics that lead to high ratings in the Clearinghouse for Subject-Oriented Internet Resource Guides (http://www.lib.umich.edu/chhome.html):

- **Detailed Descriptions** Each of the URLs that are cited in the page should include an informative summary of the site's content, indicating the topics covered (key words), the intended audience, a note regarding the update frequency (does the page seem out of date?), and performance characteristics (is the server slow or frequently down?).

- **Evaluation**. In addition to the description, each of the referenced sites should be evaluated. Are you trying to cover everything, or just the best sites? Add brief notes about the readability, use of graphics, quality of organization and layout, use of navigational aids, and above all, the knowledgeability/authority of the sites' authors.

- **Organization**. How is the referenced site organized? By subject? Chronology? Geography?

Don't forget to include a brief introduction that indicates the purpose of your page, your qualifications for publishing and maintaining it, and a brief description of its intended use.

Here's a sample entry in a well-developed trailblazer page:

CAROLE OAK'S REFERENCE TOOLS

This on-line reference aid contains Web resources for general reference, including government, news, weather, sports, time reports, stock reports, business information, popular areas, handbooks, dictionaries, concordances, indexes, other countries/cultures, disasters, earth and environment, health information, biosciences gateways, entry aids/bibliographic tools, and Internet in libraries. The entries are neatly organized by subject, without slow, distracting graphics, but lack explanatory text. Last updated 4 months before this review, the page is apparently intended for anyone who wishes to access reference information on the Web—but on closer inspection, one discovers that it's a demonstration of sorts. The author, a reference librarian at Boise State University (Idaho), doesn't try to list every reference work available; those proffered are described as indicating the "type of reference material available on the Web." Still, this is an extremely useful resource, one that you'll want to put right at the top of your bookmark list.

PUTTING YOUR PAGE ON THE WEB

If you would like to make your hotlist page available for others to access via the Web, you'll need two things: First, a computer that's running a Web *server*, and second, a permanent connection to the Internet. A Web server is a program that intercepts incoming requests for Web documents and dishes them out. The permanent Internet connection is needed so that your Web documents will always have the same address. That's usually not true when you're accessing the Web by means of a dial-up SLIP or PPP connection, in which a temporary Internet address is assigned every time you log on.

It's pretty easy to get hold of a freeware or shareware Web server—and they're not very difficult to set up and configure, despite what you may have heard. The tough part's getting a permanent Internet connection. If you're lucky enough to be using a computer at work that has a fast local area network connection and Internet connectivity, you can probably set up a server on your office machine—but make sure you're not violating your organization's acceptable use policies. If you're running a business or working out of the home, you'll need a dedicated line or an ISDN connection to set up a permanent Internet connection—by no means an inexpensive proposition.

But there's another way. Many service providers make disk space available for customers to create home pages (and trailblazer pages too). Shop around; you should be able to find a service provider who will provide this space for a small monthly fee.

A FINAL WORD

I've really enjoyed sharing this adventure of Web exploration with you—and I hope you've found this book useful. If you have, please spread the word to others. And if there's something that I didn't cover to your satis-faction, would you please let me know (send me email at bp@virginia.edu). I would like this book to become the premier place where people gather and share knowledge about how to pinpoint infor-mation on the World Wide Web. Many thanks for your help, and see you on the Web!

INDEX

ABOUT THE DISK PACKAGED WITH THIS BOOK

Designed for Windows systems, the disk includes the following search tools:

- **Search ME!** Keyed to this book's discussion of Web search tools, these Web pages provide links to all the search services discussed in Web Search Strategies. To access Search ME!, use your browser's File Open command to open the file named **welcome.htm** (it's located in the SEARCHME folder). You don't need to be online to open this file, but you'll need an Internet connection to access the Web hyperlinks contained in Search ME! (If you're using a Mac that's equipped to access Windows disks, you can also read these files.)

- **Internet Sleuth.** Here's a very useful compendium of more than 750 searchable databases that can be accessed via the Web—and what's more, the Sleuth pages include text boxes so that you can initiate the search right from your computer. To access the Sleuth, use your browser's File Open command to open the file named **index.htm** (it's located in the SLEUTH folder). (These files are also accessible to users of suitably equipped Macs.)

- **BookWhere!** This Windows-compatible program enables you to search for books and other resources in huge library databases, including the biggest of them all: The Library of Congress's computerized catalog. This program requires Microsoft Windows 3.1 or Microsoft Windows 95.

Also included on the disk are links to the home page of Webodex, a hotlist organizer that's highly recommended for organizing all the useful sites you're about to discover.